KU-500-006

Praise for *My History*

'*My History*, a captivating memoir of her childhood and early youth
. . . is a delight from start to finish. Antonia Fraser is warm, amusing,
intelligent, generous and original. She says that her idea of perfect
happiness is to be alone in a room with a house full of people. I can't
think of a better way to start the year than to be alone in a room
with this book'   Cressida Connolly, *Spectator*

'In the final section of this engaging autobiography come fulfilment
and resolution. There is marriage and a family of six children; there
is a new and harmonious relationship with her mother, who herself
became a historian of note . . . and with the acclaim greeting the
publication of *Mary Queen of Scots* there is the triumphant start of a
long and distinguished career'   Selina Hastings, *Mail on Sunday*

'*My History* is a hugely enjoyable squishy romp, the literary
equivalent of a big crumbling meringue at a society wedding'
                                        Roger Lewis, *The Times* 'Book of the Week'

'Fraser's previous volume of memoir, *Must You Go?*, an account of
her life with Harold Pinter, was acclaimed as a moving love story. In
this second instalment, she stands unabashed and alone – wise, self-
deprecating and always entertaining'

                                        Peter Stanford, *Daily Telegraph*

'The title of Antonia Fraser's memoir has two meanings. This is her
history, in the sense that she is describing the early part of her long,
garlanded life. But it is also an account of how she was drawn to
history, which she traces back to a Christmas present she was given
when she was four – H. E. Marshall's *Our Island Story*'

                                                            Sunday Telegraph

'Lady Antonia Fraser's memoir about her early life is sheer delight. It is the story of her childhood, adolescence and early adult life, and it is also the story of her fascination with history, which led her to her first bestseller, the biography of Mary Queen of Scots, published in 1969'   Allan Massie, *Scotsman*

'It is at its most engaging when she describes her own writing process, her deep fascination for history and the problems of its retelling'   Kate Colquhoun, *Sunday Express*

'Engaging and elegiac'   Virginia Rounding, *Financial Times*

'Above all, what comes through was her success as a historian that has been achieved by determination and hard work. You can't help admiring this very grand lady'   Vanessa Berridge, *Daily Express*

'*My History* is a travelogue of the mind through the roaming delights of youth to the full realisation of the power of the past. It is an eloquent, candid and very funny account of growing up in exalted circles, but really, and really originally, it is a glorious paean to the poetry of history'   Jessie Childs, *The Tablet*

'She writes every kind of anecdote, hard and soft, with a sustained, strong tone, inimitably her own and with always a smile behind a frown and a frown behind each smile'

Peter Stothard, *Times Literary Supplement*

'Inevitably this chronicle is at first much concerned with her parents, her mother's literary skills, her father's rumpled person, the Leftish political endeavours of both, but gradually the clever girl takes over and her very own History begins with the conviction that the medieval Matilda, Joan of Arc, Mary Queen of Scots and Marie Antoinette were much more interesting than the heroines of children's books'   Brian Sewell, *The Oldie*

Antonia Fraser is the author of many widely acclaimed historical works which have been international bestsellers. The awards she has won include the Wolfson History Prize and the Medlicott Medal of the Historical Association. She has been President of English PEN, Chairman of the Society of Authors and Chairman of the Crime Writers' Association. In 2011, she was made a DBE for services to literature. Her previous books include *Mary Queen of Scots, Cromwell: Our Chief of Men, King Charles II, The Weaker Vessel, Warrior Queens, The Six Wives of Henry VIII, The Gunpowder Plot: Terror and Faith in 1605, Marie Antoinette, Love and Louis XIV* and most recently *Perilous Question: The Drama of the Great Reform Bill. Must You Go? My Life with Harold Pinter* was published in 2010.

Also by Antonia Fraser

Non-Fiction

Dolls
A History of Toys
Mary Queen of Scots
Cromwell, Our Chief of Men
King James VI and I
King Charles II
The Weaker Vessel: Woman's Lot in Seventeenth-Century
England
The Warrior Queens: Boadicea's Chariot
The Six Wives of Henry VIII
The Gunpowder Plot: Terror and Faith in 1605
Marie Antoinette: The Journey
Love and Louis XIV: The Women in the Life of the Sun King
Must You Go? My Life with Harold Pinter
Perilous Question: The Drama of the Great Reform Bill, 1832

Fiction

King Arthur and the Knights of the Round Table
Robin Hood
Quiet as a Nun
Tartan Tragedy
A Splash of Red
Cool Repentance
Oxford Blood
Jemima Shore's First Case
Your Royal Hostage
The Cavalier Case
Jemima Shore at the Sunny Grave
Political Death

MY HISTORY

A Memoir of Growing Up

ANTONIA FRASER

WEIDENFELD & NICOLSON

A W&N PAPERBACK

First published in Great Britain in 2015
by Weidenfeld & Nicolson
This paperback edition published in 2015
by Weidenfeld & Nicolson,
an imprint of Orion Books Ltd,
Carmelite House, 50 Victoria Embankment,
London EC4Y 0DZ

An Hachette UK company

1 3 5 7 9 10 8 6 4 2

Copyright © Antonia Fraser 2015

The right of Antonia Fraser to be identified as the author of
this work has been asserted by her in accordance with the
Copyright, Designs and Patents Act 1988.

All rights reserved. No part of this publication may be
reproduced, stored in a retrieval system, or transmitted,
in any form or by any means, electronic, mechanical,
photocopying, recording or otherwise, without the prior
permission of the copyright owner.

Every effort has been made to trace the owners of copyright
material. In the event of any omissions, the publishers will be
pleased to rectify errors in future editions.

A CIP catalogue record for this book
is available from the British Library.

ISBN 978-1-7802-2794-8

Typeset by Input Data Services Ltd, Bridgwater, Somerset

Printed and bound in Great Britain by CPI Group (UK) Ltd, Croydon, CR0 4YY

The Orion Publishing Group's policy is to use papers
that are natural, renewable and recyclable products and
made from wood grown in sustainable forests. The logging
and manufacturing processes are expected to conform to
the environmental regulations of the country of origin.

www.orionbooks.co.uk

'The poetry of history lies in the quasi-miraculous fact that once, on this earth, once, on this familiar spot of ground, walked other men and women, as actual as we are today, thinking their own thoughts, swayed by their own passions, but now all gone, one generation vanishing after another, gone as utterly as we ourselves shall shortly be gone like ghosts at cockcrow.'

G. M. Trevelyan, *Autobiography of an Historian*

CONTENTS

LIST OF ILLUSTRATIONS

Pictures from The Dragon School, Oxford, are used with kind permission of the Headmaster.

THINGS I REMEMBER

❧

T HE TITLE OF THIS EARLY memoir has a double meaning. It is partly an attempt to recapture the experiences of my childhood and youth – to 'call back yesterday, bid time return'. But I have also sought to chronicle the progress of my love of History since my first discovery of it as a private pleasure when I was a child – *my* History as I believed it to be. For me, as will become apparent, the study of History has always been an essential part of the enjoyment of life. As a narrative, I hope it may evoke memories in other readers regarding their personal discovery of History.

My main source has been my own memory, aided by pocket diaries; these however were not kept continuously and mainly record whom and what I saw rather than my feelings. There are occasional fuller diaries too. I also find that I have kept all my mother's beautifully legible letters to me during the four years I was at boarding school and my father's diametrically opposed illegible ones, by the simple conservationist method of never, ever throwing anything away . . . In turn my mother preserved my own weekly letters home. For further sidelights on the past, I benefited in different ways from the reminiscences of my father's

1

sisters: Mary Clive, who took a keen, wry interest in family history, and Violet Powell, with whom I spent time in adolescence and who became a close friend once I was grown up.

Then, both my parents wrote autobiographies: my father's first memoir, *Born to Believe,* written under his original name of Frank Pakenham, was published in 1953 when he was forty-seven; my mother Elizabeth Longford followed suit thirty years later with *The Pebbled Shore* when she was eighty. My father is also the subject of a well-researched biography by Peter Stanford, an early version being published in his lifetime and *The Outcasts' Outcast,* a revised edition, after his death, in 2003.

Furthermore, my mother – in what I once described as her earliest efforts at biography – kept so-called Progress Books for all her eight children, from birth until their theoretical adulthood at twenty-one. Long before her death, Elizabeth Longford presented the individual Progress Books to her children in a move which was not perhaps entirely wise, given her instinct for candour. My own Progress Book is, from my point of view, embarrassingly frank as maternal pride struggles with irritation, and definitely loses out once I am an adolescent.

Lastly, my brother Thomas Pakenham, being eleven months younger than me – thus we are Irish twins – should remember all this too, just as I have written it down. It is for this reason, and in full confidence that he will corroborate my every word, that *My History* is dedicated to him as well as to the first teacher who seemed to understand my passion for the living past. If however there are any discrepancies in our memories, I take my stand on the great lines in Harold's play *Old Times:* 'There are things I remember that may never have happened but as I recall them so they take place.'

NOTE ON DATES

My father was born Frank Pakenham and was created Lord Pakenham of Cowley in 1945. He inherited the Earldom of Longford on his brother's death in 1961. I then received the courtesy title of 'Lady', as in 'Lady Antonia Fraser', in March 1961 when I was thirty.

My seven siblings, all younger than me, were as follows:

Thomas b. 1933; Patrick (Paddy) b. 1937 d. 2009; Judith b. 1940; Rachel b. 1942; Michael b. 1943; Catherine Rose b. 1946 d. 1969; Kevin b. 1947.

I was married to Hugh Fraser MP, later Sir Hugh Fraser, from 1956 to 1975; Harold Pinter and I were together from 1975 until his death in 2008; we married in 1980.

CHAPTER ONE

THE SOUND OF BELLS

A NY TIME, ANY PLACE, the sound of bells reminds
me of Oxford. Venice at evening: I'm transported back
to childhood. The water dissolves into the River Cherwell, St
Mark's fades into Christ Church doorway, the romantic gon-
dolas become everyday bicycles. Much later, when I discovered
for myself the poetry of Edward Thomas, his most famous poem
became transposed in my mind: all the bells of Oxfordshire, not
the birds, sang for him at Adlestrop. And for me ever since.

I was not in fact born in Oxford – although I sometimes feel I
was – but this tremendous influence began to exert itself before
I was three years old. In May 1935 I remember being lifted from
my bed at my parents' home on Rose Hill, South Oxford, in the
middle of the night and taken on an adventure. The next thing I
knew I was gazing at a lofty stone tower, all covered in lights, like
a heavenly apparition. When I asked in a mystified voice what
was going to happen now, I was told rather crossly to admire the
tower.

'It's the King and Queen,' I was informed. Which was the
King, which was the Queen? There were all kinds of possibilities
in the illuminated darkness of the summer night. For that matter

what was the King . . . Nobody enlightened me further. Soon I was taken back to bed, unaware not only that it was the Jubilee of King George V and Queen Mary, but also I had been gazing at the tower of Magdalen College, the foundation stone laid in 1492, and at 144 feet the tallest building in Oxford. Nevertheless I knew that I had been allowed to glimpse something extraordinary; I had gazed through the window into another magic world of ancient towers and stones which surely only appeared under cover of darkness.

My feeling of privilege deepened the next morning when my younger brother Thomas somehow realized that he had been excluded from a grown-up treat, and screamed with rage. This increased my feeling of possessiveness about what I had seen. Wonderland was clearly not for everyone. That memory of wonderland persisted. Asking for an unspecified recording of Oxford bells among my Desert Island Discs in 2008 – the first time such a choice had been made, I believe – I was enchanted to discover that the bells in question were those of Magdalen College. As I listened, wonderland once more returned.

I was born on 27 August 1932. The headline of *The Times* for that day was: GERMAN CRISIS; it went on to comment rather wearily: 'with the start of a new week, the stage is set for another of the periodic German crises.' (The Nazis were already the largest party in the Reichstag: six months later Hitler was made Chancellor.) An unspoken commentary on what happened when such crises bubbled over was provided by the *In Memoriam* column. It was led by the names of those who had died 'On Active Service' in the war which had ended fourteen years earlier: rather more than half the entries.

Of more obvious concern to those in London, there was a heatwave. A few days earlier, standing at the window, Virginia Woolf said to herself: 'Look at the present moment because it's not been so hot for 21 years.' As for my mother, throughout the long humid days of waiting, she spent all her time in the water happily if impatiently, often accompanied by her young sister-in-law Violet. This might incidentally explain my lifelong addiction to swimming: since my earliest memory I have always understood what John Cheever expressed so eloquently: 'To be embraced and sustained by the light green water was less a pleasure, it seemed, than the resumption of a natural condition.'

The event took place in a house in Sussex Gardens loaned by Margaret, Countess of Birkenhead, widow of my father's patron, F. E. Smith. Thus it was both a home birth, as was customary with women of my mother's class in those days, and an away-from-home birth, upped from a cottage to a grand London residence. Today I sometimes gaze at what is now Riyadh House, and contemplate the small patch of railed-in garden outside in the middle of the road round which taxis swirl on their way to Paddington. My first outing to this patch, on the fifth day, was duly noted in my mother's magisterial Progress Book (with its daunting preface by the publisher: 'If the suggested records are carefully made, they will prove of invaluable assistance to the doctor in later years'). Impossible to contemplate leaving a baby in a hugely ostentatious Thirties pram alone there now, but with the sublime confidence of the time, my mother simply noted: 'a strong wind, glimpses of sun, roar of traffic'.

She also noted that I was born at 2.45 a.m. BST, which placed me with the sun in the sign of Virgo and the sign of Cancer rising. The latter delightful information, which made me brilliantly hard-working yet oh, so sensitive and caring (no one ever seems to have a dull horoscope), I only discovered many years later when I was working with George Weidenfeld and Sonia Orwell: both of them boasted of being brilliant hard-working Virgos. It certainly meant nothing to my mother. On the other hand I was delivered by a female doctor, which obviously meant a great deal to her, with views on women which would have made her into a suffragette if the battle had not been won already by her valiant predecessors. In fact her twenty-first birthday fell in August 1927, so that she was able to vote in 1929, the first British General Election in which all women over twenty-one were able to do so.

When I was born, my parents, Frank and Elizabeth Pakenham, had been married less than ten months. My mother confided to me later that I was a honeymoon baby, conceived at Lismore Castle, in Southern Ireland, where the newly wed pair were staying with Lord Charles Cavendish and his wife Adele Astaire. When I was young, I managed to derive from this an exotic feeling of destiny – a castellated start to my life! It was in fact far more to the point that my parents' marriage was one which would last for nearly seventy years, where the deep affection never failed and nor did the lively conversation which developed from the affection, to back it up.

It must have been sometime in the 1980s that my mother reported to me with shining eyes: 'You know, Dada and I had such a wonderful time last night.' I began to speculate: Buckingham Palace, Windsor Castle (my mother was a devout monarchist in her later years) before she interrupted me: 'No, no, just us: we had a fascinating argument about the proper role of the Papacy with regard to a Protestant country. Frank thought . . . But I totally disagreed . . .' Not everyone's idea of romantic chat, perhaps, nevertheless it was clearly just as exciting for them to be arguing with each other some fifty years into their marriage as it had been at the outset. One notes, too, that in any argument they were equal partners in disagreement.

This outstandingly happy union did not in fact have a particularly auspicious beginning. Within the narrow confines of the British class system of the time, much narrower than it is today, with fewer ramifications, my parents came from completely different backgrounds. My mother, born Elizabeth Harman in 1906, was the daughter of a Harley Street doctor, Nathaniel Bishop Harman: she was in fact born and brought up at 108 Harley Street, where he had his consulting rooms as an ophthalmic surgeon. Her mother was Katherine Chamberlain, one of the seven daughters of Joseph Chamberlain's brother Arthur; this incidentally meant that my mother was a cousin of Neville Chamberlain, the future Prime Minister, although their politics would be very different.

It was an extremely affluent setting in terms of comfort and style. A tall eighteenth-century house, 108 Harley Street contained both a residence and consulting rooms. My mother revealed to me that there had been five servants and, when I expressed ingenuous surprise, said carelessly: 'Well, we needed a man to carry up the coal to the nursery on the top floor.' But of course the lavishness of domestic help, taken for granted by the middle class at that time – the Harman arrangements were nothing unusual – was a phenomenon which vanished altogether with the Second World War.

As a young woman Katie Chamberlain had herself trained as a doctor: a comparatively early example of a female in the profession. She qualified at the Royal Free Hospital; although it was said that Katie had only ever earned one fee of £3 for extracting a wisdom tooth, before marrying Nat Harman in 1905. My grandmother was then thirty-three and immediately gave up her profession to bear five children, while running the household at Harley Street. You could say that my mother was offered two possible role models if she contemplated her own mother's career. On the one hand Katherine Harman was a woman who had actually trained for a profession – out of choice, since the Chamberlain family was by most standards wealthy. This state of affairs was still unusual. On the other hand, my grandmother was a woman who had instantly abandoned her profession on marriage and thrown in her lot with her husband and family. In later years, as I began to contemplate the trajectory of my mother's life with detachment, I could discern both influences.

At the time of my parents' courtship, it was more important that the Harmans were proudly middle-class. This was a time when refinements such as 'upper middle-class' and 'lower middle-class' were not in use or, if they were, they were not in use by my mother. On the contrary, she brought me up to believe that not only were we purely and simply middle-class, but that this was the most striking, splendid, admirable thing to be. This impression is confirmed by my father's account in his autobiography *Born to Believe*: Elizabeth prided herself on being a member of the middle class, who were 'the salt of the earth'. There were other classes of course; but the upper class were the 'non-spinners' of the Bible as in 'they toil not neither do they spin' – the lilies of the field; the poor on the other hand were there to be helped. I'm not sure in her heart of hearts my mother ever really deviated from this position.

Certainly she left me with an early impression of the extravagance, fecklessness, unpunctuality and impracticality of the upper class – as epitomized by our father, in contrast to her own neat, strong virtues. My mother for example carved a joint with skill and drove a car with determination; my father did neither of these things. She also wrote in a clear, immaculate handwriting without crossings out . . . my father conveyed his thoughts in a series of parallel unbending strokes of the pen in which occasional words like TOP SECRET stood out but which were otherwise totally illegible. Nothing captured the difference between them so vividly for a child as the contrast in these two modes of parental expression.

The Harman grandparents who had produced this intelligent and attractive eldest child – Elizabeth was both these things in the opinion of her contemporaries, who elected her an Isis Idol when she was at Oxford – were formidable people. Or so I found them in the course of our frequent visits to their house, Larksfield, on the top of Crockham Hill near Edenbridge in Kent.

Grandfather was tall and terrifying as his blue eyes flashed above his white moustache. He had begun life as a Baptist, and even worked as a Baptist missionary at the Regent's Park College before turning to medicine. Reluctantly he became a Unitarian to marry Miss Chamberlain, her family being prominent Unitarians; when I listened to him in his role of lay preacher at the local Unitarian chapel, I believe something of the old Baptist must have still been lurking. His style was lofty, almost manic, inspiring: as a preacher he carried the absolute conviction and excitement that comes from knowing you are in the right, with Someone Very Powerful not to say Almighty behind you (or rather above you) in case of any trouble. Many years later, trying to recreate the speeches of Oliver Cromwell in my imagination in order to attempt his biography, I drew on my memories of Grandfather preaching – that certainty that you were on the right side.

Nathaniel Harman was born in 1869 and did not marry till he was thirty-six. I have always supposed that this feeling of God-given patriarchal authority was something he carried over with him from the Victorian era: since it was nothing that I would encounter with my own father, with time I was grateful for the experience, and not only as a clue to the oratorical style of Oliver Cromwell. All the same I could understand why even my bold, fearless mother was frightened of him.

Grannie in contrast was small, but she was also frightening if in a more intimate way. Perhaps it was the fact that the pair were addressed as Mother and Father – such coldly descriptive

words – which worried me, whose own parents were more sentimentally known as Mummy and Dada (the latter being Irish and
what my father had called his own father). But if Grannie was
small, she was also robust, with sturdy legs in brown stockings;
a black straw was perched on top of her dark hair, as it seemed
to me at all seasons. Here undoubtedly was a strong character,
as we quickly recognized. When Thomas forgot to write her a
thank-you letter for his Christmas present, she sent him nothing
the next year except a note explaining the reason for its absence.
It ended: 'You are in my thoughts nonetheless': this was more
disquieting than comforting.

Grannie also brooked no opposition when it came to domestic
rituals like washing up. On one occasion I adopted, apparently,
a slapdash approach to cleaning the breakfast china. This was
the famous blue-and-white willow ware which commemorated a
Chinese legend in which a rich mandarin's daughter elopes with
his secretary; when he pursues the couple on to a bridge, they
are turned into lovebirds, fluttering forever beyond his reach.
In vain I tried to explain that I had been busy working out the
story (which was true). I was sentenced to do the whole thing
again 'until it is clean'. 'Perhaps it will never be clean,' I replied
cheekily. 'Just like the Augean stables.' I had just learnt about
the Labours of Hercules and saw an opportunity to show off.
Grannie did not answer. Her manner indicated that this particular labour would in fact be completed and pretty soon if she had
anything to do with it.

Many years later, I acquired a copy of Grandfather's poems
from the Nonconformist Dr Williams's Library which was
downsizing its stock. I found a romantic love poem, 'True
Heart', written by Nat to Katie when their own children were
'a brood of rising youth'. He explained their courtship – that of
an established doctor to a young woman who was an aspiring

doctor herself (and then abandoned her career for a husband and family):

> I called, you came –
> Leaving your wandering thoughts
> Of men and measures great
> Installed from infancy to strength
> Of womanhood . . .

There were other references to her long dark hair and bright eyes. For the first time I pictured my awesome grandparents as they had once been, lovebirds of a sort, fluttering above a bridge.

I never knew my paternal grandparents, Thomas Pakenham, Earl of Longford and Lady Mary Julia Child Villiers, daughter of the Earl of Jersey. The latter died shortly after I was born, and my grandfather was killed leading his men at Gallipoli in 1915. This tragedy was certainly the central fact of my father's youth – he was nine years old at the time – and continued to weigh with him in countless ways; his attitudes to war, militarism, military service and pacifism could all be traced, I believe, to this moment when the little boy had to understand that his beloved father, his protector, had vanished for ever. 'On this dark battlefield of fog and flame Brigadier-General Lord Longford . . . and other paladins fell,' Winston Churchill would write in his history of the First World War. My father would intone the words to his children: the emphasis was on 'paladins'.

His grief was underlined by the fact that his mother did not like him. Frank was the second son in a family of six children, and the best defence of my grandmother's behaviour – which several of his sisters confirmed to me when I questioned them – was the siblingesque comment from one of them: 'Well, you see, Frank was a very irritating child.' The truth of it, I believe, was something different. It was not so much that my grandmother did not love annoying Frank Pakenham, as that she *did* love, and love passionately his elder brother Edward, who inherited the Longford title at the age of twelve on the death of his father. It was the kind of strong aristocratic-maternal predilection which could be felt atavistically for an eldest son.

There were many stories of her indifference – for there was no cruelty here, just a lack of interest – to her clever second son. Rumbustious, irritating, uppish my father may well have been, his uninteresting destiny to be that of an impecunious relation, possibly working in a bank, at any rate unknown to history (a remarkably false prophecy). But clearly Frank had a mind of great concentration. For one thing, from an early age he was keenly interested in politics; he was the kind of child who delights in asking the grown-ups searching questions, and perhaps we can discern some of the seeds of the irritation in that fact.

While he was still at prep school, Frank examined his mother keenly about the German Peace Proposals in a letter home: 'as I only caught a hasty glimpse of them in Mr Stubbs' paper before he took it away. From what I see,' wrote young Frank, 'it looked as if they won the war.' It was significant that Frank would cite his beloved father's 'patience and gentleness in response to my interminable questionings' as his chief personal memory of him. He recalled their countless walks – which ended of course abruptly when he was nine – and his eager enquiries: 'Is Bonar Law a good man? Could a British battlecruiser beat a German battleship?', with the odd bloodthirsty question thrown in: 'Could you shoot a man on that hill from here?'

Mary Julia exhibited a very different attitude. Frank recorded that his mother would not let him try for a scholarship at Eton, on the grounds that it would take the bread out of the mouths of the needy – although there was a tradition of Oppidan

Scholars, honoured but unfunded, which would surely have been appropriate. This indifference to her younger son's undoubted intelligence reached its most acute form in her reaction to Frank's final degree at Oxford. Travelling in a train with her best friend Olive Baring, Lady Longford started to scour *The Times* for the Oxford results. After a while, she threw down the paper in disgust: 'Oh really, it's too bad, Frank hasn't even got a degree.' She had read through the list of Seconds, Thirds and lastly Fourths. It was left to Olive Baring to take the newspaper from her hands and, after looking at it, observe gently: 'But here is Frank's name. He's got a First.'

The ancestral home, then known as Pakenham Hall, was in the South of Ireland, not far from Mullingar. Frank wrote later that Ireland was always home to him and London never was. In fact his widowed mother brought up her children mainly in a large country house in Oxfordshire, North Aston Hall. Here he played tennis for the county, as he would proudly recall when defeating his children with cunning sliced shots low over the net. He hunted as his father had before him (my grandfather was an M.F.H., which meant that hunting was a sacred subject, not to be criticized). But it was the Ireland of the holidays that captured Frank's imagination. Long before Socialism and Catholicism preoccupied him – to say nothing of his feelings for my mother – his heart went out to the Irish, the terrible desolate history of their country leading inexorably to fierce Irish nationalism. As a young don, his first book – his best book – was *Peace by Ordeal* concerning the Anglo-Irish Treaty of 1921.

It could perhaps be described as a quixotic interest in that, as an aristocratic family, the Pakenhams were Protestant Anglo-Irish Ascendancy . . . Somewhere in the past – it would be years before I learnt exactly when – a house and estate previously called Tullynally had been transformed into Pakenham Hall. It was a subsequent transformation at the end of the eighteenth century which turned Pakenham into the Regency Gothic castle that entranced my father – and would in turn entrance me. Frank wrote lyrically about the view from the top of the tower – 'all mauve and deep green' – in a rare literary reaction to landscape. It was indeed the castle's elevated position in the middle of Ireland which made it special for the young then and later: high above the bog, and near to the Lough Derravaragh, setting for the legend of the Children of Lir, who were turned into wild swans by their stepmother.

If 108 Harley Street needed five, then Pakenham Hall needed fourteen indoor servants, it seems, and twenty gardeners. My grandmother was herself brought up in aristocratic splendour as the daughter of a famous Tory hostess, Margaret Countess of Jersey, a founder of the Primrose League. The proverbial energy of her mother meant the emergence of a shy young woman in Mary Julia Villiers. As her sister Beatrice once told me: 'Our mother [Lady Jersey] had seen every play, read every book, knew every important person, we never felt any urgent need to do those things since she had done them for us.'

Nor did this splendid woman leave the scene early. Great-Grandmamma, as she was known, lived until 1945 (having been held in the arms of the famous Duke of Wellington as a baby). This enabled Frank to visit her in the course of the Second World War. She told him how surprising she found the presence of the Russians on our side: 'You see, the first war I remember was the Crimean War and we had them against us then.' I came to treasure this link with history, when such links became a private obsession of mine; she died when I was thirteen and there were frequent visits to her at Middleton Stoney near Oxford. Thus, by exaggerating only a little for dramatic effect, I could claim to know someone well who knew the Duke of Wellington.

Returning to Mary Julia, this shyness, or perhaps reserve was a fairer word, was only enhanced by the tragedy of her widow-hood. And then there were the tortures of rheumatoid arthritis of the years before her death at the age of fifty-six. (Brigadier Tom must have carried some gene of longevity since, of their six children, one died at the age of one hundred and two, two reached their mid nineties, and one was eighty-nine.)

Mary Julia became remote, so remote that her visits to the nursery were rare events indeed. Later she explained this to one of her daughters: 'You see, whenever I entered the nursery, the nanny and nursery maids all stood up. And remained standing up until I left. It seemed so tiring for them to do this, so I kept away from the nursery.' No other course of action – asking the nurses to sit down, for example – had remotely crossed her mind. This was certainly not an upbringing from which a self-reliant male, in the modern practical sense of the word, could expect to emerge. Nor did Frank confound this expectation. As he him-self admitted in his autobiography, he had never made a bed nor cleaned when he joined the army at the beginning of the war.

In short, my father not only could not boil the proverbial egg – perhaps that was not so unusual for someone of his generation and background – but he could not reliably boil a kettle. When my mother had a major operation in her eighties, considerable care was taken to instruct Frank in routine maintenance, while he lurked alone in their small Chelsea flat. There was talk of a cup of tea being successfully made and some pride on the part of the instructor. 'Yes, I have had a cup of tea. More than one,' confirmed my father with careful attention to the truth. It turned out that he had in fact paid a twice-daily visit to the workman's café up the road.

Clothes were frequently a disaster area. A handsome young man with rumpled thick brown curly hair – I can still remember the curls which gave way early to the magnificent, unmistakable, naturally tonsured head so beloved of caricaturists – he matched the rumpled curls with his rumpled clothes. Buttons escaped joyfully from buttonholes, just supposing there was a full complement of buttons there in the first place. Certainly there was always the danger of an undone button when Frank was making speeches from the platform during the General Election of 1945; we children took with sangfroid the fact that it might be necessary to admonish him: 'Flies, Dada.'

In total contrast to this charming, rumpled person was the exquisitely neat Elizabeth Harman who went up to Lady Margaret Hall, Oxford in 1926 and subsequently read Greats like Frank (having changed from English). Much loved by her parents, for all their rigid style of parenting, much encouraged, she had the self-confidence of the beloved first child. Pictures of her at Oxford, in her Isis Idol days, show a graceful figure, taller than her mother but only by a little, certainly far below my father's six foot one and a half (a height we learnt to reel off with respect, not forgetting the half).

My first memories of her, not so many years afterwards, when she was in her late twenties, were of brightness, even sharpness. Her elegant short straight nose, for example, stuck out sharply into the world, indicating that she was on the watch – in my case for wrongdoing, mainly carelessness and slapdash untidiness. (In my Progress Book, this was regularly ascribed to my Pakenham inheritance.) Her hair was black, her eyes were brilliant blue and their gaze was certainly sharp enough. I'm not sure how classically beautiful she was, but Elizabeth Harman was immensely pretty, irresistibly attractive and above all she had energy and optimism. People enjoyed the company of 'Harman', as male undergraduates rather snobbishly called the few female ones that they condescended to know.

The first meeting of this disparate pair, Frank and Elizabeth, became the stuff of legend. Or perhaps fairy story would be a better description. The story came in two episodes. In the first episode: On a summer's night a beautiful Oxford undergraduate wandered down a corridor during a ball at Magdalen College and was amazed to find a large figure, dressed in the blue-and-yellow uniform of that (now notorious) club the Bullingdon, slumped across a chair fast asleep. The face, she remembered sixty years later, was 'of monumental beauty, as if some Graeco-Roman statue – the Sleeping Student maybe – had been dressed up in modern clothes by some group of jokers'. She wondered idly what kind of girl would have left such a partner fast asleep.

The second episode took place the next night. This time our popular heroine was at a ball in New College (her current beau was the future leader of the Labour Party, Hugh Gaitskell). Shown into a room in the Garden Quad, who should be lying along the sofa 'fastly and serenely asleep' but her vision of the night before. The spirited Elizabeth did not hesitate. Bending over the vision, she planted a kiss on his forehead. 'Now kiss *me*,' she said as the vision opened his large brown eyes. 'I daren't,' he replied, before promptly falling asleep again.

One might add as a footnote to this that if my mother had found my father on a sofa for any number of balls, any number of nights, he would probably have been asleep. Little did she know at that point that there would be a myriad occasions in years to come when the happy couple would spend the evening with Frank sleeping sweetly on their own sofa, a book fallen down beside him – frequently the Bible in later years – while Elizabeth read some work of History. (The ability to fall asleep whatever the company was an endearing trait – or so I came to regard it when I found that I had inherited it myself.)

Yet after this fabled beginning, actual romance took some time to develop. The future parents did not share the same friends, nor for that matter politics at that date. My mother was starting to investigate the possibilities of Socialism, animated, I believe, by a general desire to continue the philanthropic tradition of her forebears: philanthropy was always a prominent characteristic of dissenters, such as the Chamberlains and the Kenricks (her maternal grandmother, the wife of Arthur Chamberlain, was a Kenrick). My father came of traditional Tory stock, both the Pakenhams and the Villiers being conventional Conservatives. The marriage of Julia, daughter of Sir Robert Peel, to the future Earl of Jersey in 1841 meant that Frank was actually descended from a Tory Prime Minister. As a bright young man fascinated by politics, he set his sights on working in the Conservative Central Office.

The girls my father knew were certainly not at Oxford, or if they were, it was not as undergraduates. They were in fact the young women who came from the rather narrow social class in which he grew up. They were definitely not intellectuals in the way that my mother was naturally educated to be. Typical of them was the high-spirited and eccentric Maureen Guinness with her blonde hair and huge hypnotic blue eyes (and her Guinness fortune). Frank was extremely fond of Maureen: later she would be appointed my godmother. But as a potential admirer, those timid words – 'I daren't' – summed up Frank's attitude. Inhibition, not too difficult to trace back to his awkward relationship with his mother, meant that he remained a clumsy suitor, if he was a suitor at all.

Even a story told by my mother about their first date in a restaurant – my father neither confirmed nor denied it – seemed to indicate the gap between them at that time. The meal was over. Wine remained. The lights were low over the little table. Then Frank leant forward and began to recite:

'Now sleeps the crimson petal, now the white . . .' He continued to the end of the poem:

So fold thyself, my dearest, thou, and slip
Into my bosom and be lost in me.

Elizabeth was just about to murmur: 'I love Tennyson' when Frank said shyly but with determination: 'I wrote that.' What was the proud young English scholar to say now? Laughter? Dismissal? On her answer hung the fate of eight children, twenty-seven grandchildren and goodness knows how many great-grandchildren . . . Then from Elizabeth came the simple, truthful comment: 'It's very beautiful.'

Now a dream inspired Frank to invite Elizabeth to Pakenham Hall during the summer holidays. Then matters progressed further in a direction which would be important to both their futures. They arranged to be together, working at the Workers' Educational Association in Stoke-on-Trent. It was in a hotel in Stoke, quite late at night, that Frank had the confidence to express the ardour he had long felt, and we must believe that Elizabeth shared – only to find the hotel manager irately throwing them out of the hotel on grounds of public misbehaviour: 'Look here, Pakenham, you can't stop in here.'

It was thus in the waiting room of Stoke station that my parents finally got engaged. Another legend came to be born about that too – my first husband Hugh Fraser was the local MP for neighbouring Stafford and Stone. Making an enthusiastic speech recommending me to his constituents, he surprised them by boasting: 'My dear wife Antonia was conceived in the waiting room at Stoke on Trent station.' This however, as we have seen, was very far from being the case.

Nor did the path of true love run smooth even at this apparently late stage. The next step was for Frank to approach the frightening Nathaniel Harman in his room at 108 Harley Street and formally ask for his daughter's hand in marriage. So the scene was set. Frank entered the study. Elizabeth – still known by her childhood name of Betty to her parents – waited outside. After a while both Frank and Nathaniel Harman emerged; Elizabeth knew at once that something had gone wrong. Frank looked 'pale and alarmed' – she does not record how her father looked. At any rate Frank immediately left the house and a tacit decision was taken to abandon the planned announcement of the engagement in *The Times*. Frank had lost his nerve. Nothing had happened, nothing at all.

When I became interested in my parents' previous lives, I found my mother's endurance of such a humiliation astonishing. I was quite sure that few people would have had the character or the confidence to let such a relationship survive. Yet somehow it did survive, if in an atmosphere of melancholy, even depression, on both sides. This seems to be summed up by Frank's Christmas present to Elizabeth several months later: a pearl bar brooch from Asprey's, with the note: 'Elizabeth from Frank, *Love*, kisses and tears' – pearls of course traditionally meaning tears. And my mother's reaction? As she wrote in her autobiography nearly sixty years later: 'I wore it; until one day it dropped off and was lost forever; perhaps not a bad omen, though I still keep the empty case.' When I read this, I asked her how she endured the situation, an exceptionally attractive young woman, hardly at a loss for admirers.

'Oh, I knew it would all come right in the end,' she replied with that marvellous confidence which surely drew the unhappy depressed Frank towards her in the first place. It is noticeable that my father does not refer to this incident, this false start, at all; in his account in *Born to Believe* there is simply an inevitable path towards marriage, whereas over a year passed between that episode in Harley Street and their eventual wedding on 3 November 1931. With hindsight it is easy to see that my father's emotional fear of commitment – as it would now be termed – sprang from his feeling of personal inferiority induced by his upbringing. What is much less obvious today, is the tradition of an aristocratic family in which the much less well-endowed younger son remained a bachelor for life – or until such time as his elder brother died unmarried, or without children, when his own services might be drafted in. Frank had in fact two bachelor uncles who were part of his widowed mother's support system: her own brother Arthur Villiers and his father's brother, known as Uncle Bingo. Both were and remained unmarried.

Arthur Villiers was a particular influence on Frank, in some ways standing in for the father figure who had vanished. He used to quote his own mother Lady Jersey's philosophy of life as being the right one: 'If you have to live in this wicked world, you should endeavour to make some contribution to its welfare.' Certainly Great-Uncle Arthur was as good as his mother's word. He was prominent among the Old Etonians who supported the Eton Manor Club in Hackney Wick for East London boys, devoting the whole funds of his highly successful investment trusts to philanthropy. The fact that Arthur Villiers also played cricket for Eton (modestly describing himself as the worst boy ever to get into the Eton XI) must have been partly responsible for my father's lifelong predilection for the game.

As matters progressed, Frank and Elizabeth got to the stage of working out that between them – my mother's middle-class allowance being rather larger than my father's upper-class one – they would have about one thousand pounds a year (roughly fifty thousand pounds today). Both of them felt that for two people this indicated poverty, my mother with energetic determination that my father's extravagance should be curbed, my father with a fatalistic shrug of the shoulders: for him some kind of guilt lurked around joy itself, making it certain that life could never be easy.

Stairways, their first home, was a cottage in Buckinghamshire, not far from Hartwell. I learnt later that Uncle Arthur Villiers compared Stairways to a battered HQ behind the lines in war-torn Flanders. Perhaps he had a point. My mother was fond of telling two stories about their earliest married life. In the first, the young couple wondered how they would wake up in the morning.

'But won't they bring us a cup of tea?' asked Frank in surprise.

'Darling, you don't understand,' replied Elizabeth. 'We are they.' (They soon stopped being 'they' however; I note from *Born to Believe* that subsequently a married couple got crammed into the establishment . . .)

The second story concerned the arrival of bailiffs at the cottage due to unpaid bills – that fatalistic shrug of the shoulders.

'They tried to take that pram,' my mother would declare histrionically, indicating the very pram, now filled with some subsequent arrival. 'Then I pointed out that you, Antonia, were in it.' When I first heard this story, I got a vague feeling of being unwanted – even by bailiffs, whoever they might be. Perhaps it was the presence of the many subsequent claimants for the pram. Then my mother explained that the bailiffs were actually very nice people and had ended by bringing my father that famous missing cup of tea in the morning. This left me still no clearer as to what bailiffs might be; when I developed an early obsession with the story of Robin Hood – which contained a prominent Bailiff in the first version I read – I was even more confused.

The actual wedding date had to be postponed by a week to cope with the General Election of 1931. Frank and Elizabeth were in fact working on different sides: Frank went down to support the Tory Lady Astor, one of his kindly patrons, in Plymouth, while Elizabeth was in Birmingham in support of the Labour candidate for King's Norton. The result was a massive Labour defeat and Conservative victory. This sharp split in allegiance does not seem to have caused them any problems. On the eve of the wedding Frank sent Elizabeth a short, touching note saying how much he looked forward to being married to her; years later when Elizabeth was researching the life of Queen Victoria, she was charmed to find that the young Queen had sent a similar eve-of-wedding message to Prince Albert, whom she hailed as 'my most dearly loved bridegroom'; Elizabeth routed out her own treasured note for comparison.

And so on 3 November 1931 my mother was taken down the aisle by Nathaniel Harman, while behind her trailed twelve adult bridesmaids, including Chamberlain cousins from her past (Neville's daughter Dorothy among them) and future Pak-enham sisters-in-law. There was still some social oddity about the occasion. The church chosen was St Margaret's, Westminster – a prominent and historic Anglican church next to the Abbey. Frank, if anything, was a member of the Church of England (or Ireland). Elizabeth on the other hand, raised as a Unitarian, had never even been baptized. It was left to their mutual friend, the well-informed Anglican John Betjeman, to point out that the marriage was actually invalid by the laws of the Church of England, according to which both parties had to be baptized. In view of the happy fertility of the marriage, it sometimes amused me to point out to my mother that she really needed to get married again and this time, properly . . . to legitimize us all in the eyes of the Church.

Frank left the Conservative Research Department in the summer of 1932. There followed a brief period as a journalist, first on the *Spectator*, then for the *Daily Mail*. This included – *mirabile dictu* – the writing of fashion articles, about which he later reminisced to us children, incurring a scepticism which I subsequently discovered was unjustified. Had he not once famously predicted that 'Woman this year is to be very demure, very modest and very plain Jane'? After that he found what my mother would term in her memoirs, surely correctly, 'a more appropriate job', lecturing on Politics at Christ Church, Oxford.

This was to be the setting for my earliest impressions of my father at work: the penetrating, icy cold of his rooms in Tom Quad, which made me think he must be being punished for some misdemeanour. Large, dark grey and threatening, Tom Tower forms the background to other pictures of Frank playing rugger for the college: the same cold winds seemed to prevail. But stone was of course always cold in the stories: cold, strong but also exciting. So the Oxford bells began to ring out, as my parents settled into a large house called Singletree, on Rose Hill. The road running past Singletree actually led out of Oxford in the direction of Henley; but all my memories turn the road back into the city of Oxford where the bells were sounding.

CHAPTER TWO

MY ISLAND STORY

'**N**EVER FORGET THAT THE FASCISTS have done this.' It was May 1936. I was gazing at the sight of my father's body, prone on a bed. It was covered with large blue bruises, particularly visible against the pale exposed skin of his thighs and legs. Then Elizabeth let the blanket fall again. Frank was lying in the spare room, as it was known, at Singletree, a cold room which I can never remember being used for guests: in every sense it appeared to be spare . . . In fact I felt more worried by Dada's absence from the familiar warm conjugal bedchamber than the injuries, which were beyond comprehension. Nevertheless, I did understand perfectly well that wicked people had been responsible for this reversal of the natural order. And they were called Fascists. Somehow I realized that they did not know my father personally. My bewildered sense of the grown-up world – that there were huge rights and wrongs, quite separate from the petty rights and wrongs of the nursery – began at that moment.

The injuries had indeed been inflicted by Fascists. Frank had attended a meeting addressed by Sir Oswald Mosley in Oxford Town Hall out of curiosity and had ended up by being severely beaten up by the thugs who acted as officials at the event. Like their leader they were dressed in black silk shirts, black trousers, with heavy black buckled belts and thick boots. The battle began when some protesters – mainly but not entirely Trades Unionists – started calling out 'Red Front', giving a clenched-fist salute in place of the Fascist straight arm, and went on from there. Frank plunged in on behalf of the protesters. By the time the police intervened, as well as the livid bruises, he had acquired two black eyes, received severe injuries to his kidneys from the blackjacks wielded by the thugs, and was suffering from concussion. Afterwards Frank remembered catching sight of Sir Oswald Mosley in the midst of his ordeal, still standing calmly on the platform 'like Napoleon on a hillock while the battle proceeded on the plain'.

After that, Frank joined the Oxford Labour Party. In his autobiography, he claimed that he had been considering the step for some time. After all, Elizabeth was already a keen Socialist and had worked for the Labour Party at the General Election which preceded their marriage by a week. His Conservative friends on the other hand suggested teasingly that it was the effect of being knocked on the head that turned him towards Labour – this was an alternative version of the story which had Frank falling off a horse at the Bullingdon point-to-point, losing consciousness and waking up a Socialist. Both stories were told to me by loving friends of his when I first grew up, as though I would find them as amusing as they did. To me, both stories actually illustrated the same thing: how astonishing, even laughably eccentric Frank's behaviour was considered to be by his contemporaries in wishing to join the Labour Party. So there had to be some alternative explanation to political conviction (or mere idealism).

The fact was that this radical step – as unquestionably it was for a man who had been working at the Conservative Central Office only a few years earlier – did take place in the immediate aftermath of the Oxford Town Hall meeting. As Frank wrote himself: 'after the Mosley meeting . . . I became certain that there was only one side in politics that I could ever join in the future, and that there was no time to be lost in joining it.' So politics – shared Labour politics – came to be the dominating atmosphere of my childhood. Not only did both Frank and Elizabeth stand in turn for the Oxford parliamentary seat, but Elizabeth nursed two separate parliamentary constituencies, beginning in 1937 shortly after the birth of her third child. Frank became Labour Councillor for the Iffley Ward of Oxford not long afterwards, his first 'conversion', which was from the Toryism of his youth and background to Labour.

As for Sir Oswald Mosley himself, so traumatic was this town hall incident in my childish mind, told and retold with Napoleon on his hillock very much the villain of the piece, that his name resonated with evil long before his imprisonment in the Second World War. There was however to be a postscript to the story which has always seemed to me to demonstrate perfectly my father's huge zest for the Christian doctrine of forgiveness (as well as his innocent weakness for celebrities). When I first came to London after university, I was delighted to be asked to the parties of the Crewe brothers, Colin and Quentin; these genial and generous hosts lived in Dolphin Square. All grown-up parties, as coming from Oxford I secretly perceived them to be, were tremendously welcome. Arriving for a dinner party, I found to my horror the Mosleys, Sir Oswald and his wife with her terrifyingly perfect beauty, installed on a sofa.

I wanted to do something which satisfied my own conscience while still allowing me to enjoy the delights of the dinner party. Deftly I managed to avoid shaking hands with the man responsible for that fateful meeting, those never-to-be-forgotten blue bruises. All went well. Nobody noticed. I was happy to enjoy myself as usual, while feeling just a little smug about the unstained nature of my conscience. All went well – that is, until Sir Oswald Mosley was standing to say his goodbyes.

'Ah yes, Miss Pakenham,' he said in a mellifluous voice, his bright black eyes sparkling. 'I'm so sorry we didn't talk. As your father said to me at lunch today . . . We were having lunch at the Ritz. Did you know?' Of course he had noticed my inept avoidance and elegantly demolished the reason for it. I, for my own part, had missed the post-war reconciliation of my father with the Mosleys. This led in fact to a friendship on my father's part; the pre-war victim could now envisage the Mosleys themselves as in some way sufferers, or at any rate unjustly treated and needing his Christian support. When Frank was first Chairman, then Director of Sidgwick & Jackson, he saw to it that the firm published Diana Mosley's book of portraits, *Loved Ones*, in 1985. She who as a child had been shown the bruises remained uneasy on the subject, especially as the Mosleys began to radiate social splendour in Paris.

Elizabeth was adopted to fight for the parliamentary seat of Cheltenham, her first constituency, in the summer of 1935 when Thomas and I were two and three respectively. There must have been frequent absences from home, but I don't remember registering them. To be honest, our mother was not part of our daily routine in spite of being the strongest presence in the home. Like other mothers of her sort, Elizabeth had installed a nanny immediately, a practical step from which she never deviated throughout the upbringing of her eight children, and as their numbers increased, the official nanny came to have a girl assistant.

What I do remember is the sacred nature of something called

Labour. The official colours of this sacred thing were red and yellow. Our mugs for our mid-morning milk were a variety of individual colours: there were sharp fights to secure red (best of all) followed by yellow; even more severe was the mortification of having to sip distastefully out of the despised Tory blue mug. Unfortunately the blue mugs prevailed in Cheltenham in November 1935 by two to one as they were surely always bound to do in this home of 'lost colonels' as Elizabeth described it in *The Pebbled Shore*.

In vain the children in the two Cheltenham Labour wards had chanted: 'Vote, vote, vote for Mrs Pakenham'. Sir Walter Preston, whose sporting sister wished my mother not so much good luck as good hunting, was exactly what was wanted there, while the youthful (she was twenty-nine) Socialist Mrs Pakenham was not. But there were to be further opportunities to vote, vote, vote for her. In October 1936 Elizabeth was adopted as Labour candidate for the Kings Norton division of Birmingham, the familiar city of her Chamberlain ancestors, which was of course part of the point of adopting her since it was thought this association might give her an edge over the Tory Ronald Cartland, brother of Barbara Cartland the novelist. Elizabeth was by now two months pregnant with her third child, but the political agent for the constituency, a family man himself, was not put off by this information when it was confided to him: he thought it would make her more appealing to women voters.

Kings Norton gave Thomas and myself our first experience of being a candidate's show-family. In order to demonstrate, by practical example, our mother's egalitarian views on education, we were imported to Birmingham, and sent for a week to the local state school. Unfortunately, Elizabeth, with all her enthusiasm for state education, had little actual experience of it at this level; she failed to give us any milk money. The class was enormous, forty children perhaps; as newcomers, and temporary newcomers at that, we were directed to the back of the class. No blithe scrapping for red or yellow mugs here: as I remember it, we sat rather gloomily during the break, milkless and bewildered.

Certainly I never had any luck being a show-person. My mother gave up the Kings Norton constituency and never actually fought an election there. In 1950, however, she took on the Oxford parliamentary seat which my father had fought and lost in 1945. It seems incredible to me now but admirable, to be admired but also in the Latin sense of something to be wondered at, that Elizabeth did not allow the existence of eight children, the youngest being two and a half, to deter her. As it was, her energy, the brightness of her personality and the passion of her belief in Socialism were all undimmed, although she had borne the last five children in seven years – all this in the Spartan conditions of wartime Oxford and post-war austerity Britain. At the same time I was imbued – by both my parents – with a sense that idealism was an essential part of political life, but that it was certainly not irreconcilable with political ambition, nor should it be; the two things could coexist with honour. This was a theme which always hovered at the back of my mind in considering both national and international politics, both in the present and the past. I never fully explored it, however, until I wrote *Perilous Question: The Drama of the Great Reform Bill 1832,* many years later, at which point this combination of ambition and idealism redolent of my childhood turned out to be the central theme.

At the time I did not admire these things, let alone wonder at them. I simply took them for granted, just as I took for granted my mother's decision to travel by bus wherever possible as being a fact of life, if not a specially pleasant one. I was seventeen in the February of 1950 and had already passed Oxford entrance, where I was destined to go in October. Bus travel was necessary because my mother had moved the family from Oxford to Hampstead Garden Suburb a few years earlier in order to see more of my father; he had been created Lord Pakenham in 1946 to bolster up the Labour Party in the House of Lords, and was by now a minister. I hastily agreed to go down to Oxford to help my mother in her campaign, not because I was politically sophisticated but for the very different reason that I hoped to drop in on some undergraduates along the way. Not any undergraduates, mind you, but the sort I had read about in *Brideshead Revisited*, the novel by my parents' friend Evelyn Waugh published five years earlier.

I was even delighted to sit on the platform at the end of the row because in the romantic haze in which I chose to live, the Marquis of Vidal, saturnine hero of Georgette Heyer's great novel *Devil's Cub,* might see me sitting there and . . . after that I was vague, and even vaguer about the circumstances in which the Marquis of Vidal or his like would attend a Labour Party meeting in Oxford in February.

My mother duly spoke well, clearly and cogently as she was wont to do. She wore a little red hat, chic on her black hair, conveying either a political message or a fashionable one according to taste. Then questions came.

'Lady Pakenham,' shouted one man from the floor – as Elizabeth had now become since Frank's ennoblement. '*Lady* Pakenham,' he repeated, and I did not miss the implied sneer. 'How can you put yourself forward for Parliament and neglect your eight children?'

Quick as a flash, my mother turned towards me, sitting dreaming of the Marquis of Vidal at the end of the row. 'Stand up, Antonia.'

I came out of my dreamworld and struggled to my feet; I was

wearing uncomfortable dark brown suede court shoes which had seen better days but I thought showed my legs in a flattering light. I was four or five inches taller than my mother and everything about me was round: my body, but also my round face, with my round healthy-looking pink cheeks.

'Does she look neglected?' asked Elizabeth. There was a roar of laughter . . .

Ever since that awful day when romantic dreams gave way to mortifying reality, I have felt a natural cross-party sympathy for the children of politicians who find themselves in the unwelcome limelight. It is not, after all, a situation that they have chosen and besides, who has ever really measured up to the limelight? Having said that, I have to add in all honesty that I took to the life of canvassing and delivering addresses with zest. I didn't want the palm but I did enjoy the race. There is something about canvassing that appeals to anyone who is inquisitive: a licence to poke about, ring doorbells and ask impertinent questions, all in a noble cause.

In those days, the man of the house would be mainly absent at work, since I was a daylight canvasser. There were two groups I would encounter: women, either very old or very young, clutching babies – and dogs. The latter, invariably hungry, black and enormous as it seemed to me, added the spice of danger to the occupation. Such dogs were glimpsed through letter boxes, seen ravening away in windows or, most terrifying of all, encountered close at hand in a tiny yard or garden from which they might easily escape.

'Good dog. Good *Labour* dog,' one would say nervously. Did the growls mean agreement or was this, horrifying thought, a Tory dog? The best solution was to stick the printed circular through the letter box and run for it. The wild barking which ensued once again might be endorsement or violent indignation.

The conversations with actual human beings were on the other hand invariably polite. In all my canvassing, I never encountered hostility (except from the dogs). The extreme politeness of people in face of this unwarranted intrusion by someone at least half their age, is exemplified by the following exchange:

'Good morning. I have called to ask you to support Mr Frank Pakenham, the Labour candidate' – proudly – 'I am his daughter Antonia.'

'Oh yes, a very nice gentleman. Aren't you a good girl helping him?' Said with a warm smile. 'So you're his daughter. We all support Mr Pakenham.'

'So will you be voting for him on Thursday?'

My new friend looked slightly surprised. 'No, not on Thursday, we've always voted Tory, all our lives. But we really do support Mr Pakenham. A proper gentleman, as I said to my husband.'

While our parents lapped us in the political world, my own world of dreams was absolutely set apart (and far more significant to me just because it was my own). There were various elements involved but from the age of four and a half, until the coming of teenage romance altered the balance, by far the most important element was History – *my* History. I can date the arrival of this great constellation in my life exactly according to the copy of *Our Island Story* which is inscribed Christmas 1936, a gift from my aunt and godmother Mary Pakenham.

It was not such an eccentric present for a four-year-old as it might seem, since I was a precocious reader. Perhaps my aunt's gift itself was a response to maternal boasting about my exceptional prowess; Elizabeth was certainly entitled to boast about it since she had actually taught me to read herself. In the early years of her marriage, before her formal political activities, this enterprising woman must have found herself quite bored by the conventional life of leisure she was expected to lead. Teaching her eldest child to read was evidently a task which satisfied her. But her achievement did not rest there. Somehow – we used to speculate about this – she taught me to read at a phenomenally rapid rate. Later I would win cash prizes from trusting grown-ups who didn't believe I could possibly master a chapter of, say, Sir Walter Scott at such speed. Later still, less agreeably, as a teen-ager I would incur sneers from the passenger sitting opposite me in a train: 'You don't imagine you are actually reading that book, do you?'

Neither financial gain nor public contempt mattered to me half as much as the inestimable freedom of reading what I liked, when I liked, devouring books – and all this independent of the grown-ups. To say that I would in the future read a book a day is an obvious exaggeration, often flung at me with a cer-tain subtle contempt (the implication: don't you have anything better to do?). It would be truer to say that I read something from some book daily. In the mid Seventies, when Harold and I went to Paris together for the first time, the beginning of our voyage of discovery, I noted in my diary not the thrills of romance but the following: 'There is something very odd about the time we have spent together. I haven't read a book. This is the first time probably since I learnt to read at the age of four.' To quote my favourite lines of Keats (another childhood obsession) the pursuit of reading from the start:

> Charm'd magic casements, opening on the foam
> Of perilous seas, in faery lands forlorn.

In my case the magic casements opened on to the perilous seas and faery lands of History.

In the early Eighties, when I was researching my book *Warrior*

Queens which centred on Boadicea, I discovered for the first time the interesting background to *Our Island Story*. The battered dark blue copy with its crown and royal lions on the cover assumed a whole new significance for me; I celebrated the fact by having my beloved copy, carefully preserved, rebound in handsome red leather with gold lettering. The author H. E. Marshall turned out to be a Scottish woman, Henrietta Elizabeth, and a woman writing for two children, brought up in Australia. There is an introduction (which I certainly never read in 1936) in which she explores the circumstances in which she came to write the book, in order to explain the history of that other island, 'home', to Sven and Veda. The original date of publication was 1905.

The significant words in the introduction are these: 'I hope when you grow up, you will want to read for yourselves the beautiful big histories which have helped me to write this little book for little people.' The effect on me however was not exactly what Henrietta Marshall intended with her self-styled story book: 'Remember that I was not trying to teach you, but only to tell a story.' More or less instantly, I was seized with the desire to *write* the beautiful big histories myself, never mind the fact that I was still a little person. This is because I was innocently convinced that it was easy, and what convinced me was the sheer vitality of Henrietta Marshall's storytelling, the burning interest of each particular story, the conviction I formed that Queen Matilda, Joan of Arc, Mary Queen of Scots and Flora Macdonald (note that they were all women) were a great deal more fascinating than Black Beauty and his unfortunate friend Ginger.

My original passion was for the story of Matilda, penned up in Oxford by the troops of her rival for the throne of England, Stephen. It was easy for me – so I thought – to imagine the conditions of a siege. In Marshall's words: 'The people in Oxford began to starve, for they had eaten up all the food they had, and Stephen's soldiers took good care that no more was allowed to be taken into the town.' But the real point of the story came next. 'It was the middle of winter. The river Thames was frozen over. Snow lay everywhere around. The cold was terrible, and the people had no wood for fires.' Matilda the heroine was not deterred. Dressed all in white with three similarly all-white attendants, she crept silently through the snowy streets of Oxford and out of the gates. 'Out into the snow-covered fields they crept, moving softly and swiftly, unnoticed by Stephen's soldiers.' Matilda and the three faithful knights then crossed the river undetected: there was no bridge but the frost was so deep that they were able to steal across the ice. During the frightful hard winters of the early Forties, I never failed to think about Matilda's escape: since I knew how to skate, I was confident that I would have draped myself in white and broken out of Oxford Castle.

In later years H. E. Marshall has been derided for her imperialist views. Born in 1867 and writing at the turn of the century, it would be rather surprising if she had not been coloured by such prevalent attitudes. If racist by modern standards – like most such books published for children in 1905, Africans are savages if possibly noble ones (Indians are different) – some of her incipient political judgements have stood the test of time. Her recounting of the American War of Independence is the reverse of colonialist: 'Now the people of America sent no members to the British Parliament. When King George III tried to make them pay taxes, they at once said: "No, that is not just . . . If we are to pay taxes we must have a share in making the laws and saying how the money is to be spent." This was quite reasonable, but King George was not reasonable. He said, "No".' And forward with American Independence seen as a splendid enterprise. Though there is indeed a reasonable tone throughout – Wat Tyler's rebellion is approved as 'the beginning of freedom for the lower classes in England', with King Richard II having broken his word.

The story of Guy Fawkes was another example (and one of the many subjects from *Our Island Story* I came to write about in later life). This was Henrietta Marshall's judgement: 'In the cruel manner of those days he was tortured to make him tell the names of the others who were with him in the plot. But Guy Fawkes was very brave, although he was wrong, and he would not tell.' That is surely the defence of Guy Fawkes in a nutshell.

I did move on to a subsequent volume, *The History of France*, originally published in 1911. In her Preface, Henrietta Marshall quoted a letter from an English boy responding to *Our Island Story:* 'I like that book and wish you would write one just the same, only about France, because we can't find anything nice about France.' Unfortunately my own reaction to the new book was the opposite of that intended: far from finding the French 'nice' I was filled with primitive indignation which one might almost describe as being along feminist lines. I was after all the child noted in my mother's conscientious Progress Book as demanding that Cinderella's coach be drawn by white mares, not horses, and the same child introduced to the idea of the Ugly Sisters who had cried out furiously: 'Ugly Brothers! Ugly Brothers!'

It was a question of Marie Antoinette. I had already read some children's tale about the tragic Queen, including the (fictional) girl Rosalie who had attended her devotedly in prison. Now I read of the arrogant and ill-natured Queen, 'frivolous and ignorant', who had arrived in France 'hardly able to read', showing scant sympathy for her husband's subjects. This harsh judgement was repeated at the time of her execution: 'She had been hard-hearted and proud, understanding little, and perhaps caring little about the misery of her people.' I will not pretend that full-blown into my mind at this tender age came questions like: how old was she when she came to France? (The answer, not given by H. E. Marshall, was fourteen.) And who educated her – or rather failed to educate her? But there were the stirrings of something along the lines of historical curiosity: both sources could not be right.

Nearly sixty years later, I was seized by a sudden desire to write about Marie Antoinette in a London taxi ostensibly on my way to give good advice to a god-daughter (I was looking for a new subject after *The Gunpowder Plot*). In my diary later I found that the date was 16 October, the anniversary of her execution in 1793. Even more pleasing was the discovery in the course of my researches that there had indeed been that little maid in Marie Antoinette's prison of the Conciergerie: Rosalie Lamorlière who became her devoted servant, and in old age, being virtually illiterate, dictated her memoirs. Some adapted version of this must have been what I read and put me for ever on the side of the tragic Queen against the cruel mob.

Of course I was scarcely looking for political judgements at the time. Tucked away in my nursery, undisturbed by radio (there was one set somewhere downstairs which did not feature until wartime) let alone television, I was happy in the dream world of *my* History. Oddly enough, such features of a Thirties childhood as *The Children's Encyclopaedia* and *The Children's Newspaper*, the inspiration of the journalist and educator Arthur Mee, didn't interest me at all although they hung about in the nursery. It wasn't the moral tone, the emphasis on the values of Christianity and Empire which put me off: it was the emphasis on childishness. Instinctively I wanted to discover things for myself, not have them digested for me in a condescending manner; my wartime fondness for (adult) news-papers was part of this.

Above all I was beginning to identify myself with the tragic Queen of Scots, depicted in A. S. Forrest's illustration with the caption: 'For nineteen years this poor Queen was in prison.' She is leaning gracefully on a table, one lace-cuffed hand to her sad brow, her peaked headdress surrounded by a mass of white veil-ing. This would be the peaked headdress that I chose to copy for my first wedding twenty years later. My original concentration was however on the child who became Queen at six days old, and on her girls-in-waiting, Mary Fleming, Mary Livingstone, Mary Beaton and Mary Seaton, known as the Four Maries.

This particular passion began when I found another book on the subject of Mary Queen of Scots on a friend's bookshelf and started enlarging my knowledge. The next step – not exactly a conventional step of historical research – was to find ways of in-serting myself into the story. So there were Four Maries, were there? No, there were not! There were Five Maries, and the fifth was – guess who, Antonia Pakenham, although I thought I might actually operate under my second name of Margaret (after an-other godmother, Margaret Countess of Birkenhead, in whose house I had been born) as being undoubtedly more Scottish than Antonia. I had been named for Willa Cather's novel of a Bohe-mian immigrant in the Midwest of America, *My Ántonia*, but it was many years before I appreciated the exotic beauty of my (Roman) Christian name. Margaret, or in certain moods Daisy, seemed infinitely preferable.

This insertion of the self into the story is something I have come to disapprove of intensely in modern biographers, for ex-ample that authorised biographer of an American president, much younger than his subject, who chose to insert himself (fic-titiously) into the narrative. Researching Marie Antoinette as I was at the time, I proclaimed my disapproval: I would not dream of inserting myself into the palace of Versailles, let alone the Petit Trianon, I observed sternly in a lecture on biography to the Historical Association. It is honesty which compels me to admit that this instinct, evidently deeply rooted in human nature, animated all my first encounters with History.

Two children's books I much admired carried forward this tradition. *He Went With Marco Polo* by Louise Andrews Kent was published in 1936 and *He Went With Vasco da Gama* two years later; when I was not busy attending on my little Scottish royal mistress, I spared time to join the boy hero on his dangerous, fascinating journeys with the great adventurers. Then there was *Boys and Girls of History* by Eileen and Rhoda Power, published in the Twenties; the boy actor Salathiel Pavey was an especial favourite, despite his sad fate: I could see myself acting at the Elizabethan Chapel Royal. Obviously this kind of primitive identification gives way – or should give way – to the orthodox enquiries of the biographer. Yet what starts as a child's self-centred fantasy may be a natural route leading towards the key adult question: just what did it feel like to be Mary Queen of Scots?

In my teens I was more preoccupied with Mary Queen of Scots the romantic heroine, inspired by Margaret Irwin's *The Gay Galliard*. Some of the passages describing Bothwell's rough – very rough – wooing I found excitingly erotic because they were discreetly done but you got the drift. After that, I moved on to an interest in her religion and finally to a sympathy for her sufferings as a woman in a man's world. The fact is that very early on I had been seized by an ambition: I would write the story of Mary Queen of Scots. I kept my hand in by insisting on enacting the story when staying with my cousins Henrietta and Felicia at Coombe Bissett, the house on a stream near Salisbury where their father Henry Lamb painted. Here I moved on from the childhood larks of the Four Maries to the scene of the execution. My dramatic skill frequently brought tears to my eyes:

'Pray for me, good gentlewomen . . .' I have a suspicion that the sympathetic tears of Henrietta and Felicia soon began to dissolve into giggles. I was not put off. She was *my* Mary Queen of Scots. It was *my* History. That was all that mattered.

CHAPTER THREE

BEFORE-THE-WAR

THERE WOULD COME A TIME when the bells of Oxford would fall silent, with the coming of war. This meant that the portmanteau term 'before-the-war' would take on a magic meaning. We would look back on a time of multitudinous ice creams, sunny holidays (it never rained before-the-war), grown-ups driving us freely about the country in petrol-rich cars without thinking about it. In short, those pre-war days of the many bells were very happy ones.

Life at Singletree was punctuated by visits to Bernhurst in East Sussex, not far from Battle. This was the home of an ancient American lady known as Great Aunt Caroline; she had been married to my father's great-uncle Sir Francis Pakenham, a diplomat who was born in 1832 and died in May 1905 just before my father was born. As a childless widow, Aunt Caroline looked round for an heir; when Mary Julia Longford gave birth to a second son (who would have no financial expectations) Aunt Caroline declared an interest: there would be a visit of inspection. She proceeded from Bernhurst to London, liked what she saw, and announced that she would make the baby her heir, provided that he was named after her late husband. (Sir Francis had been a seventh child out

of eight, and as such had not received either of the traditional
Pakenham names of Thomas, Edward or Michael.)

As it happened, it was not a name my father ever used: he was
Frank in every situation and on every document. Perhaps he re-
sented the exclusion from the mainstream of Pakenham names,
since he called his eldest son Thomas (like his father) and another
son Michael. Whatever inspired it, this determination to avoid
Francis meant that when the present Queen announced his en-
rolment in the Order of the Garter, in St George's Chapel in 1971,
referring to 'our well beloved *Francis*', I thought she had got the
wrong person.

At all events, little Frank, christened Francis, was destined to
inherit a pretty Queen Anne house with some useful later add-
itions, as well as seventy-five acres of farmland. From my point
of view Aunt Caroline, already not far off a hundred, was a very
tiny, very old lady, possibly left over from some fairy story, not
exactly a witch but not quite a human being either, with her wiz-
ened appearance. To me, the most fascinating thing about her
was what would now be called her lifestyle. Aunt Caroline had
a full-time companion, also American, known as Cousin Edie
(this blessed woman would later send us care parcels from America during the height of rationing). She also had a butler, forever
dressed so far as we were concerned in butler gear of white tie
and tails, whatever the weather. And of course, before-the-war as
in most childhood memories of the time, the weather was always
hot.

This meant that Tea-on-the-Lawn was an important moment
in the butler's life and indeed in ours. There was a large wooden
summer house at the edge of the wide, neatly mown lawn which
could overlook the rolling dips and hills of East Sussex down to
the River Rother. It could also gaze backwards at the house, since
a vital feature of the summer house was its huge rollers which

enabled it to revolve, in theory following the sun. This was something Thomas and I found fascinating. Once the house was ours, we would have it spun round and round to our heart's content. Probably Aunt Caroline's butler would turn it for us: we could not envisage the house without him.

No such *lèse-majesté* occurred in the reign of Aunt Caroline herself. At teatime an enormously long black flex was laid across the lawn to the summer house and a large electric kettle installed. The butler was quite portly as he bent at his task but nothing deflected him from it. The teapot was silver. There were minute sandwiches served on the most delicate china. After that, the scene became less gracious. Aunt Caroline, now in her late nineties, was confused by my appearance. With my short curly hair, cut at the insistence of my mother, she decided that I was a boy, in fact the boy who would one day inherit Bernhurst in succession to his father Francis. And she did not like what she saw. She might have approved of the baby Francis, but this restless squirming 'boy' was another matter.

'He fidgets, he fidgets,' she complained in a surprisingly strong voice, in which you could still trace an American accent. 'Why does the boy fidget so much?'

'Keep still, Antonia,' hissed my mother. 'She thinks you're Thomas.' It did not occur to me at the time that in a modern reversal of a Frances Hodgson Burnett story, I might squirm away yet more energetically until I succeeded in blighting my brother's potential inheritance. I just wished that my mother would let me have long hair to avoid misunderstanding: long thick plaits perhaps, interwoven with flowers.

Once Aunt Caroline died, memories of her were kept alive in the house by the existence of her old-fashioned clothes stowed away in a cupboard. They joined the breastplate of our dead Life Guard grandfather and his excruciatingly uncomfortable helmet, but were rather more practical. There was a tiny little cloak, for example, intricately embroidered, with lace laid over taffeta, adorned with bows. A bonnet was another favourite, and a mauve satin skirt. Her clothes fitted us children and we used them for dressing up. There was also no need to control the fidgeting, in so far as I had ever done so. Thus Thomas and I enjoyed two halcyon seasons at Bernhurst before the war. We would have instinctively understood the words of Henry James to Edith Wharton (also on a visit to Sussex): 'Summer afternoon – summer afternoon; to me these have always been the two most beautiful words in the English language.'

Cricket played by adults was an important part in these summer afternoons. Once again, the sun shines and the white-clad 'run-stealers flicker to and fro', in the immortal lines of Francis Thompson:

> For the field is full of shades as I near the shadowy coast
> And a ghostly batsman plays to the bowling of a ghost . . .
> O my Hornby and my Barlow long ago!

Our field was the Hurst Green cricket pitch, which lay behind the George, directly across the busy, dangerous main road to Hastings and the sea. Once you reached the pitch itself, roads and pub were forgotten: here was a magic enclave that might have been in a clearing in the forest.

Our father was passionately interested in cricket; as a boy, he told us, he knew Wisden by heart (a faint implication here of inadequacy on the part of his children, which was rare coming from him). His own play was enthusiastic, sometimes over-enthusiastic it seemed. Our mother was heard exclaiming: 'It's too bad! Frank was caught dancing outside his crease again and they stumped him.' Elizabeth herself was never known to take any physical exercise: she happily surrendered her unused tennis gear and even dress to me when I was eight, since that left her free for energetic gardening. She also gave the impression of disapproving of Frank's ardent addiction to sport, which he nevertheless retained throughout his life. On the other hand, her loyalty was total: if he must play cricket, he should be allowed to do so without criticism, and certainly not be confined to something called a crease, whatever that might be, and stumped – horrid word – for going outside it.

As for Thomas and me, we were left reverently puzzling: Dada *dancing*? What sort of dance was that? Nothing quite so interesting took place on our watch, although we kept a keen lookout for those twinkling toes, but I was imbued with a life-long feeling of pleasure at the idea of watching the game. Neither rainy windswept Sunday matches nor the occasional failure of family members to shine have ever quite destroyed it.

The run-stealers flickering to and fro, our Hornbys and our Barlows, were on the whole our father's friends, not famous cricketers. One match before-the-war included the writer and journalist Philip Toynbee, who as a youthful Communist had been involved with Frank in the famous Mosley incident at the town hall. His beguiling wife Anne, with her mild face and soft fair hair, enchanted us with the attention she paid to us; but for the most part the grown-ups ignored us, we were like cats watching silently in the background.

There was however one star. Aidan Crawley was then, and remained, one of Frank's favourite people. Here was a man of action with his handsome film star's looks – Rex Harrison, perhaps – and his courage: he would be shot down in the war and held as a prisoner. He returned full of idealism to be elected a Labour MP for six years, before turning Conservative and finally chairing a new television company. No wonder one obituary compared him to a John Buchan character. Above all, Aidan was a fabulous cricketer in my father's eyes.

'Aidan was Twelfth Man for England,' said Frank proudly. It took us a long time to realize that this was not necessarily the top billing. Our keen enquiry to someone else we were assured was a top-rank cricketer – 'Are you the Twelfth Man?' – must have met with some surprise.

Most exciting of all about before-the-war holiday life at Bernhurst was the possibility of a visit to Bodiam. This was a castle rising up in the green lily-strewn bed of its own moat. It had a drawbridge, towers, crenellated turrets and a well. Windows from the turrets looked directly over the water. I thought that I should like to live there, with those coveted long plaits I was not allowed to grow but which were granted to me in my fantasy life, hanging down towards the moat. Like Rapunzel in the fairy story, I would let down my hair, although I wasn't quite sure at this point whom I wanted to come clambering up it.

Bodiam Castle was about three miles away from Bernhurst, but like the cricket pitch, if more exotic, it took you into your own world: into the world of *my* History, in short. Built late on in the fourteenth century, it was intended to keep out the French during the Hundred Years War. Sir Edward Dallingridge was granted a licence to erect a castle 'for the defence of the adjacent country and the resistance to our enemies'. The French were just over the Channel, and the French, as I knew from my beloved *Our Island Story*, were out to get us. (They were of course no relation to the French, the other French, whom we would get to know and admire after the outbreak of the war, because they were Free, the Free French and thus completely different.)

Bodiam was especially important because we learnt that the sea in those distant days did not stop peacefully at Hastings and Bexhill, where we would visit it to bathe. It came rushing across

in the direction of Bodiam. I imagined as I looked out of the turrets that there were waves, possibly stormy, and boats, probably
hostile, where now there was the River Rother. However, Bodiam's satisfying life as a martial focus in the surrounding low-lying
country came to an end with the Civil War in the seventeenth
century. John Tufton, Earl of Thanet, on the King's side, led
an attack on Lewes, before being defeated at Haywards Heath
(these were all familiar local Sussex names to us). The worsted
Tufton had to sell Bodiam to a parliamentarian in order to pay
the enormous fine imposed upon him. Somehow poor Bodiam
ended up being 'slighted' – not some petty social insult, but
strong measures which put it out of action as a defensive castle.
The ruins, artistically covered in ivy, became an eighteenth-
century tourist attraction as the fashion for the medieval and the
Gothic spread.

The castle I encountered however was far from being a ruin,
otherwise I would hardly have planned to take up residence
there, plaits and all. In its next incarnation, Bodiam was carefully
adapted and rebuilt at the orders of Lord Curzon, after the First
World War; this lofty grandee politician, Viceroy of India at one
point, clearly had a taste for the majestic. What we saw therefore
was the product of many visions down the six hundred odd years
of the castle's existence. I like to think that in its turn Bodiam has
gone on to inspire further visions of History in the imagination
of its visitors, including my own. For example, I was gratified
to learn when I got interested in the whole subject of historical
biography that the great Macaulay – an early hero – had been,
according to G. M. Trevelyan, interested in 'castle building': he
once declared that 'the past is in my mind soon constructed into a
romance', something with which I could easily identify. Certainly
from Bodiam onwards, a castle, however dilapidated, aroused in
me a thrill that a Georgian masterpiece of a house could never

do: the feeling of danger perhaps . . . the possibilities of dungeons and oubliettes where there were also turrets.

Where I was concerned, an obsession with Rudyard Kipling's *Puck of Pook's Hill* made it particularly easy to insert myself into the landscape around Bodiam, much as the two children who were the centre of the story, Dan and Una, had done. The first exciting thing that I got from the book was a feeling of secrecy about Sussex. Here was not grandeur of landscape as I would later thrill to in Scotland and in a smoother more dulcet way in Dorset: instead, a series of grassy enclaves, hills which delicately revealed themselves then retreated, valleys one came upon by surprise.

As a result I began to discern secrecy in the holiday world around me. Even the hop-pickers who came annually for the summer from the East End of London to perform their task had something secret and exciting, almost clandestine about them. For one thing, we were instructed on no account to talk to these mysterious strangers, some of them children like ourselves. But apparently threatening children.

'Why shouldn't I talk to a hop-picker?' I asked, keen to make new friends, followed by 'Where is the East End?' from Thomas, who from birth wanted to know facts.

'They eat different food,' my mother said vaguely. That made the incomers even more mysterious. When pressed, she murmured something about whelks and eels, which was positively exciting. My nanny was more succinct. 'Little thieves,' she muttered. 'And big thieves too.'

All this moulded into my picture of Sussex derived from Kipling, where the magic elf named Puck instructed Dan and Una in the ways of the past. The actual book was published in 1906, at roughly the same time as *Our Island Story*, arguing for a prelapsarian period in children's literature in the decade before the First

World War. Kipling wrote it for his own son and daughter, basing the opening on a real-life performance of *A Midsummer Night's Dream* in which his daughter Elsie (ten in 1906) played Titania – and he himself played Bottom. But there was something literally timeless about the story. To me in the Thirties, it was all happening then. And years later, incidentally, I received pleasing confirmation of the enduring spell of Kipling when I learnt that the historian Simon Schama, thirteen years younger than me and living not in Sussex but in Southend-on-Sea, had found inspiration in *Puck of Pook's Hill:* 'For a small boy with his head in the past, Kipling and fantasy was potent magic,' he wrote, 'with Puck's help you could time travel by standing still.'

In the book Dan and Una, like the young Kiplings, are performing *A Midsummer Night's Dream*: unwittingly they summon up Puck by sitting in a fairy ring beneath Pook's Hill. He proceeds to entrance them with a series of stories, some of them told by Puck himself, others by Puck in disguise, others still by characters who suddenly manifest themselves in the landscape. The first one, 'Weland's Sword', is set in Burwash – the next-door village to Hurst Green – just before the Norman Conquest. In fact Kipling himself had lived at Burwash, as grown-ups frequently pointed out to us, in a house called Bateman's which was still to be revered, as grown-ups also frequently pointed out to us. But to be honest, this nodding of the head to a revered writer's house interested me far less than the fictional existence of Dan and Una.

There is a kind of pattern to the book, which begins with the forging of the sword and ends with Magna Carta. 'Weland gave the Sword,' intones Puck. 'The Sword gave the Treasure, and the Treasure gave the Law. It's as natural as an oak growing.' But there is no actual chronology. My favourite story was 'Dymchurch Flit', set in the period of the Reformation when the monasteries were dissolved and the Catholic monks forced to flee. Here it turns out to be the fairies (the 'Pharisees' in Sussex dialect) who are so troubled by the discord of the Reformation that they decide to flit.

The tale is related by Puck in disguise as a stranger called Tom – 'a grey-whiskered, brown-faced giant with clear blue eyes' – and it was Tom's simple summary of the dissolution which made a strong impression on me. I was not of course a Catholic at this time or even aware of the subject of Catholicism, my father's conversion being several years away. Religion had not yet arrived in my life in any meaningful form. I liked the drama of what Tom told old Hobden the Hedger and his simple-minded son, the Bee Boy, as well as Dan and Una: 'Queen Bess's father he used the parish churches something shameful. Just about tore the gizzards out of I dunnamany. Some folk in England they held with 'em; but some they saw it different . . . takin' sides an' burnin' each other no bounds, accordin' which side was on top, time bein'. That tarrified the Pharisees: for Goodwill among Flesh an' Blood is meat an' drink to 'em, an' ill-will is poison.'

'Same as bees,' says the Bee-Boy. 'Bees won't stay by a house where there's hating.' Tom agrees. 'This Reformatories tarrified the Pharisees same as the reaper goin' round a last stand o' wheat tarrifies rabbits. They packed into the Marsh from all parts, and they says, "Fair or foul, we must flit out o' this, for Merry England's done with, an' we're reckoned among the Images."' What impressed me most, I think, was the concept of the past as a better, happier, more colourful, *merrier* place. And somehow, in a muddled way, Catholicism was associated with that place. Along with the fairies.

I suppose there has to be some serpent in an Eden: in this case a whole nest of snakes. My parents decided to take a holiday together in Czechoslovakia in 1938: an interesting year to choose in view of subsequent events, and surely a significant element in the very strong opposition towards appeasement on both their parts. Thomas and I were to be parked in a seaside holiday home for children called Kittiwake. A certain amount of preparation must have gone on for this event, since I have memories of Elizabeth showing me an illustration of the gull called a kittiwake in a bird book. I gazed at it dubiously: I thought the bird had a sinister twist to its beak. However we listened dutifully to tales of what a wonderful time we were going to have: 'No Mummy and Dada! Just fun with other children!' Older children, she might have added. For at Kittiwake I encountered a new phenomenon: the gang of which I was nothing like the eldest member, no longer the superior, envied person.

Nevertheless all went well, or so I thought. There were games, round games, square games, a bit of acting perhaps, swimming, digging in the sand . . . And now we children were all going to have a meeting. There was an announcement, not exactly from the staff like most announcements, but a message rapidly passed from childish lip to lip. Whispered not shouted. In this way we all convened in some outdoor space where it was possible to sit in a circle. If not explicitly secret, this meeting would certainly not include the grown-ups.

I was distinctly excited, as I remember to this day: this memory of innocent anticipation haunts me almost as much as what was to follow. A keen reader of school stories – those of Angela Brazil, favourite of my father's generation, in particular – I rejoiced that I was about to take part in some kind of clandestine activity, which would undoubtedly turn out to be jolly good fun. The circle was large for there were quite a few of us staying at Kittiwake, and then an older girl whom I will call Elspeth stepped into the middle of the ring.

She made a brief, rather thrilling speech. The message was

clear. There was a traitor in our midst, a truly bad person, some-one who was at one and the same time both deeply unpopular and insufferably pleased with him or herself. What could be done about this person, this uppish yet odious person who was making our lives a misery? We all agreed that nothing was too bad for such a person. We hissed, we spluttered. No one was more elo-quent in her enthusiastic denunciations than I was. When I first read Orwell, the Two Minutes Hate in 1984, this daily routine of loyal party members expressing their contempt for the current enemy superstate aroused painful memories. For of course this pariah, this hate object, was in fact myself.

The sheer horror of the occasion lay not so much in my ex-pulsion from the gang as my total ignorance of my impending fate. And so I had betrayed . . . Exactly what had I betrayed by hissing with the rest of them? Everything, I suppose. As well as ending up a pariah, I had turned viciously on an innocent person, a victim, who just happened to be me.

On her return from Czechoslovakia, my mother lovingly painted a picture of a kittiwake for my precious autograph book. To her amazement, I burst into tears and ran from the room. Naturally I never told her why the sight of the glinting eye and cruel curving beak of the bird aroused such an extreme reaction: that was not the mode in parental relations in the Thirties – or anyway not our mode.

Besides which, she would inevitably ask: 'What did you do to deserve this?' And I had no idea. As a matter of fact, I still don't, although it could be argued that the whole experience did me a power of good, teaching me early in life that unpopularity – and thus logically popularity as well – is a mysterious quality which sometimes appears from nowhere, with nothing done to deserve it. For all that, I have never felt quite the same about gulls: un-trustworthy predatory creatures that they are. And I tore the picture of the hateful kittiwake out of my autograph book the moment my mother's back was turned.

It is curious that in all these memories, mainly good, one mysteriously bad, no images of my brother Thomas's serious illness occur. It is as though all that existed in some separate sphere. And yet photographs provide clear documentary evidence: here is Thomas, my companion, my Irish twin, my other self, in a large leather collar propping up his head and chin, and with his arm similarly held up by a stiff steel and leather 'aeroplane' sling.

Thomas somehow contracted polio at the end of 1936. Reading my mother's autobiography, published in the 1980s, I understood for the first time the frightful parental agonies she had endured: and at a time incidentally when she was pregnant with her third child. Thomas developed a temperature over Christmas and, a few days later, could not move his left arm or turn his head. Eventually he was moved to the Wingfield Hospital, not far from where we lived at Singletree, and diagnosed with polio, in those days called infantile paralysis.

This menacing disease was not unknown to us by repute. According to nursery lore, it might be lurking in certain brands of ice cream with exotic names: you went there adventurously at your own risk, whereas Wall's was dull but safe. The prospect of dangerous ice cream was in fact rather exciting, like the sort of potion a witch might devise to trap unwary children. We also knew about tuberculosis since there were several children who had had it and recovered: in this case, according to our nanny, it was evil cows who were responsible, as opposed to good cows who gave pasteurized milk – what magic pasture was that?

Where polio was concerned, I was to meet quite a few people at Oxford, and later, who had suffered from this in the Thirties. It is a phase now history in the most thankful sense of the word, ever since the discovery by Jonas Salk of the vaccine (first tested in 1952) which has led to the virtual eradication of polio, at least in the West. At that time the odd child at a party might have a leg in a splint, a sling like Thomas, or sit in a wheelchair. These were of course middle-class children, yet by repute polio was considered to be a working-class disease. My mother told me much later that Frank's political enemies, and even some of his Tory relations who deplored his Labour affiliation, had suggested that he risked contamination by living in *South* Oxford at Singletree, near the Cowley works, instead of safe donnish *North* Oxford. In short, our middle-class upbringing should have protected Thomas had it not been for his parents' persistence in living in defiance of the social order.

In her autobiography my mother actually wrote rather more discreetly if less specifically: 'It was suggested that he had picked it up on 19 December from a children's Christmas party given by the Labour supporters of Cowley [the ward for which my father was Labour Councillor].' And she added firmly that it was just as likely to have been acquired at Margaret Countess of Jersey's party for her numerous great-grandchildren about the same time.

It showed an admirable – and characteristic – loyalty to the Cowley Labour Party for Elizabeth to invoke those fabulous parties as a potential source of the disease. How many great-grandchildren did Lady Jersey have? Dozens and dozens it seemed. Most of them spoke in terrifying sophisticated voices about visits to the Park, and future London parties, which alarmed country cousins like myself and Henrietta.

'Was that your nanny you were with this morning, George?' asked a moppet called Sophy in a white frilly dress with red shoes. 'She wasn't wearing a uniform.' It was true that the nannies at Great-Grandmamma's parties – crowds of them all together like hens – wore starched uniforms, a phenomenon which did not extend to North Oxford. Somehow it illustrated our status, as in a Jane Austen novel, as being less grand than our relations. I longed to have been seen in the Park that morning, with or without my nanny in her usual dull blouse fastened by a pin brooch at the throat, and a tweedy sort of skirt. It was also symbolic of status that the fairy on the vast Christmas tree was always given to Lady Caroline Child-Villiers, daughter of Grandie (for his previous courtesy title Lord Grandison, not a social judgement on his character), the current Earl of Jersey; although, as Henrietta pointed out, Caroline was younger than us.

Had the infection *really* lurked in the famous bran tub from which each great-grandchild was allowed to extract a present? My mother showed great bravado in raising the subject. All the same I can only imagine how the original allusions to Labour and Cowley, with their nasty imputation of parental neglect, must have added to her sorrows.

All this was of course quite unknown to me then. What I saw (through the mask I had to wear for visits) was an entire set of Little Grey Rabbit toys. And Thomas didn't even like soft toys. Envy, always in attendance in family life, murmured in my ear. The next thing my unfortunate mother knew I was myself struck immobile. It was the family doctor who lured me into movement again by trailing a new doll in front of me. After a moment I could not resist; like a kitten, I pounced – and the game was up.

So Thomas eventually emerged, back into nursery life, in his steel-and-leather kit, with his neck and one side in some way withered. The true courage of his endurance, the infinitely touching speechless courage of sick children everywhere in hospital, was not apparent to me. I now see that those Nature does not manage to kill, she magnanimously makes stronger; or rather, even more importantly, she bestows the art of survival upon them. No one since has ever questioned Thomas's powers of endurance: it is as though the steel and leather entered his soul at that point. To me at the time he simply appeared to be more obstinate than before. Thomas's two favourite words, as a grown-up once wryly pointed out, were 'Wajamean' and 'Hujamean' and he was not easily satisfied by the answers he was given.

In any case, we were soon ready for the next stage in our adventure of living: evacuation. Shortly before war broke out, a taxi took us across Southern England, from Bernhurst in East Sussex to Water Eaton Manor near Oxford. Others were suffering the ordeal of being uprooted and separated from their parents. The nine-year-old Harold Pinter, for example, with the rest of his primary school in Hackney, was dispatched six hundred miles away to Cornwall, never having left home before. For me, however, the happiest year of my early life was about to begin.

CHAPTER FOUR

HIDEY HOLES

ELIZABETH PAKENHAM WAS SITTING alone in the
Great Hall of Water Eaton Manor on 3 September 1939 when
she listened to Neville Chamberlain on the wireless announcing
that war had been declared on Nazi Germany. Frank was with
his army unit at Banbury. A private crisis was developing there,
insignificant in comparison to the great international one, but
central to my parents' lives. Frank was on the edge of that nervous collapse which would result in his being invalided out of the
army in the spring of 1940.

In conversation with my mother, I once referred lightly to the
period at Water Eaton as the happiest time of my childhood. After
all, our involvement in the progress of the war at this early stage
was limited to knitting dark green woollen squares to help Gallant Little Finland win its struggle against Big Bad Russia. This
war work, as we were grandly told it was, had two effects. First
of all, it enabled us to taste for the first time the pleasantly sancti-
monious feeling that a good deed brings ('Another square done! I
must have knitted at least half a quarter of a blanket by now' i.e.
Russia is trembling). Secondly, we learnt about the fragility of international relations. That is to say, it seemed a remarkably short

time before I was casually informed that Gallant Little Finland had been subsumed into Big Bad Russia, no longer bad but led by our great ally Uncle Joe Stalin. Was I therefore now supposed to be knitting with equal zest for the Gallant Little – I mean Bold Big Russians? I retained a sneaking sympathy for my first friends the Finns throughout the war, without ever quite liking to ask exactly what had happened to them.

None of this impaired our sheer enjoyment of life at Water Eaton. Yet to my horror, when I made that casual remark about my childhood, my mother's face, normally so composed, crumpled. The beginning of the war, the deaths, imprisonments and woundings of friends, and, I suspect, worst of all the cruel memory of my father's collapse, meant that my delightful childish experience was a travesty of her adult one. Of course we children knew nothing of this. This was true to the extent that when I read in a newspaper interview with Frank in the Sixties that he could empathize with the lost and broken because he had been forced to leave the army with a breakdown, I rang my mother indignantly, thinking that this was a smear.

'But Dada had very bad 'flu, you told us. He had 'flu four times.' I even remembered that detail, which must have been added to convince us of the seriousness of the situation.

'No,' said Elizabeth sadly. 'It's all true.' Only then did I begin to realize the extent of the hurt which Frank suffered, by failing, as he saw it, where his heroic father Brigadier Tom had triumphantly succeeded, losing his life in the process. Already in the Thirties he had been divided from many fellow members of the Labour Party who opposed the idea of war and was personally distressed when the Labour Party voted against Conscription. In April 1939 he wrote a letter to the *Daily Telegraph* – giving Christ Church, Oxford as his address – protesting against the inclusion of university dons over twenty-five in the Reserved List. He argued passionately that such men, like himself, should be able to join the Territorials, or at any rate 'be given some indication of their wartime tasks'.

He continued: 'As a Socialist, I think . . . it would do University men like myself a great deal of good, and could scarcely do the Army much harm, if we were all started off at the bottom.' The *Telegraph* headed the letter EDUCATION & SERVICE. Frank went further. He sent a copy of the letter to Winston Churchill, with apologies for troubling him but adding: 'You have brought it on yourself, if I may say so, by your emergence as the one man of knowledge and purpose whom the public recognize is equal to the military necessities of the moment.'

Certainly Frank practised what he preached where starting at the bottom was concerned. He was thirty-three but prided himself on his physical fitness, his running, his playing rugger, his tennis: the semi-final of the *Oxford Mail* championships. Thus he volunteered as a private in the newly formed 5th (Territorial) Battalion of the Oxford and Bucks Light Infantry. In his auto-biography, Frank admitted to the reader that this choice of the ranks was considered strange – he knew no one there at all and had to bribe a sergeant to look after his clothes. (From the 1939 group photograph, a row of men in army trousers, braces and bare chests, I notice now that he looks better fed than his fellows.) His political enemies suspected him of electioneering; even we children found our visit to him in a summer camp distinctly odd. Dada sharing a tent furnished with a suspicious-looking bucket was somehow outside the natural order of things, and the smell from the bucket yet more disquieting. I also secretly thought that he looked ludicrous in his ill-fitting private's uniform, like a noble lion in a circus.

Eventually it was put to Frank that he should seek a commission – in whose interests was not clear – and he set off to the

Isle of Wight on an officers' training course. Once again he unintentionally managed to stand out from the conventional crowd. Settling into the railway carriage with his future fellow officers, Frank decided to break the ice in the easiest possible way.

'Well,' he said, 'what books has anyone brought?' There was complete silence. Finally one future officer, bolder than the rest, answered: 'Book? Won't there be a book when we get there?'

The trauma of all this passed us children by. It was indeed still dealt with delicately by my father himself in his first memoir, published in 1953. Here he merely referred to frequent attacks of gastric 'flu (hence the 'flu story?) which 'got to work on a nervous system already strained'. There were various Medical Boards and then he was gazetted as having resigned his commission owing to his ill-health. The effective comment followed: 'I could not disguise from myself that here was failure – complete and absolute failure', adding: 'The wound will never, I suppose, heal completely.'

This feeling of humiliation, based naturally enough on his precious memories of his own father, meant that he was much discomfited, roughly ten years later, by Thomas's failure on medical grounds to be passed fit for National Service. A rational thought might have told him that a boy who had been savaged by polio in the Thirties, with serious physical consequences and medical reports to that effect, would be unlikely to be passed fit for the army. All the same, Thomas's exultant telegram giving the results of the medical, the telegram of a gleeful schoolboy, did cause him much pain: 'Great news! Failed 100%.'

As it was, Frank fell back on becoming an enthusiastic member of the local Home Guard; here eccentricity was limited to the fact that he actually needed two forage caps to be stitched together for his uniform: a single cap could not cope with his increasingly lofty pate. 'You have a big head too,' said my mother cheerfully when I expressed my admiration for what was evidently some kind of achievement. 'When you're grown up, you will probably need two straw hats to be put together to go to garden parties.' After that I regarded the dual forage caps rather more warily.

We arrived at Water Eaton Manor, near Oxford, in the direction of Kidlington, in August 1939, just before the beginning of the war. We had been brought up to know that Water Eaton was 'Elizabethan' since we had earlier done lessons there with a governess. Naturally I already knew about the great Queen Elizabeth: the vision of a courtier's cloak being laid down sacrificially in a puddle before Her Majesty was to the forefront of my historical mind. A ruff? A mighty gilded skirt? Pointy shoes resting on a globe? These images of a magnificent woman were also associated with the word Elizabethan.

The globe was relevant because we had a picture called *The Boyhood of Raleigh* in our nursery – it was a surprise to discover that it was not actually an original painting but a reproduction. This was when Millais' famous picture of 1871 proved to be a favourite among schoolrooms of the time, with its imperialist message. 'But that's our picture!' I naïvely exclaimed, before learning to swallow my words and concentrate on what was depicted: two young boys with angelic Pre-Raphaelite complexions, Raleigh and his brother, listening to an extremely rough-looking sailor who has mislaid his shoes and is directing the boys out to sea. To something called the Spanish Main, it seemed. 'For fighting,' said our nanny, 'fighting foreigners.' 'Serving Queen Elizabeth,' said our governess. 'They did the exploring the world for her when she couldn't.' Due to the ruff, the skirt, and the pointy shoes being no good on a boat, I added mentally.

Water Eaton Manor had in fact been originally built in 1586, right in the middle of the Elizabethan period, but reduced in size later. It still seemed enormous to us, with its dovecote, its forecourt, its wide wonderful steps with huge stone globes – yes, globes again – on each side of them, and a chapel to the left. To the right lay what we came to think of as the school house. Most important of all were the big gates which faced the house at the other side of the grassy forecourt; beyond them lay fields, and beyond that the river.

There were three families sharing the house: the Carr-Saunders, who lived there, had invited the children of another Oxford don, Frank Taylor, as well as ourselves to take refuge. The effective gang therefore consisted of six children, Edmund and Flora Carr-Saunders, John and Julian Taylor, and Thomas and myself. The little ones, Nicky Carr-Saunders and our brother Paddy, hardly impinged on our consciousness at this point. Edmund, two years older than me, was an intriguing figure: dark and good-looking, he was also aloof with the tantalizing air of one who has a serious but secret project engaging his attention. Flora on the other hand, although a little younger, became my dearest friend and remained so long after the Water Eaton sojourn was at an end.

The basic reason was that we shared a taste for fantasy, historical fantasy, mixed in with the creative life of our dolls, who became historical figures. (Gilberta, my favourite doll with her halo of flaxen hair, was always up for it: Priscilla, a large innocent-looking baby doll was more difficult to fit into a historical sequence.) The grown-ups, I can see now, might have found the spectacle of seven-year-old schoolgirls obsessed by their dolls slightly odd, except the whole lot of them were far too busy with more important matters to enquire further. They would not have understood an excited entry in my pocket diary in August 1944 when I was twelve and visiting the Carr-Saunders on their farm: it was full of plans for the dramas the dolls would shortly enact.

Of course Gilberta would play Mary Queen of Scots while Priscilla would be a somewhat unconvincing Elizabeth I.

Where the fathers were concerned, Professor Alec Carr-Saunders, born in 1886, twenty years older than our parents, was a terrifying figure to us, and we tended to scuttle away into corners like rats when we encountered him. He was extremely tall and silver-haired, with the air of an ascetic monk perhaps, except that he was actually the Director of the London School of Economics and had written a famous book about population control. Teresa Carr-Saunders never seemed to our ignorant eyes to have any connection to him at all: she was much younger than her august husband and a romantic character in her own right. With a mass of beautiful thick dark hair perpetually escaping its inadequate bun, she ran about the house and farm, cooking perhaps, giving orders, actively farming (she had a degree in Agriculture at Oxford), helping other people, having imaginative ideas about farming, all done with wild but affectionate concern for one and all, animals equal with humans. I loved her.

With hindsight, however, it was more important to my future that Teresa Carr-Saunders was a passionate Catholic, and gave me what would later be described as an extremely positive image of Catholicism. (It was only recently that I discovered that her daughter, Flora, was at the same time receiving a positive image of Socialism from *my* mother, writing in her memoirs that after Elizabeth assured her the Labour Party was the party that wanted to make *everyone* happy, 'my political allegiance was set for the rest of my life'.) Born Molyneux Seel, Teresa Carr-Saunders descended from two ancient Catholic families, as she often informed us. They were, what is more, 'recusant' families, meaning literally those who refused to comply with the law by attending Protestant services. In order to have their own Catholic Masses, they needed Catholic priests who were similarly illegal and in grave danger if discovered. Not particularly interested in the theology of religion at this point – unaware of the tumult in my father's breast – I fastened on the secrecy of it all. It was emphasized that these Catholic families were loyal English, not the German spies we were beginning to read about in the newspapers. The people who sought them out and persecuted them were the baddies.

Where did the Catholics, especially the unlawful – but loyal – priests, lurk? In hidey holes, otherwise less interestingly known as priest holes. And here at Water Eaton we had, so we fervently believed, our very own hidey hole. Belief, rather than historical fact, buoyed us up in this conviction. Floorboards which lifted and gave access to a huge, dark hole under the staircase were particularly menacing. What would happen if one of us fell into the hidey hole, was left alone and undiscovered . . . All of this was both thrilling and terrifying.

At the same time the seed was sown. Religion, loyalty, secrecy, violence, persecution, the claims of the state: in the Nineties I would explore all these issues when writing about the Gunpowder Plot of 1605, and I even gave the book the subtitle 'Terror and Faith'. In the course of my researches, I specialized in visiting all the hiding places, mainly in the Midlands, connected with my plotters and their priests. Some of these hiding places associated with the Catholics would later come in handy as refuges for King Charles II, escaping after the Battle of Worcester. So in a curious reversal of chronology, I had already embarked on a round of crouching visitations when writing his life, twenty years before I studied the Gunpowder Plot.

With the latter book, it was an expedition to Baddesley Clinton in Warwickshire, about a hundred miles from London. This secluded Tudor mansion, set among woods, protected by a moat, sent my mind immediately back to Water Eaton when I visited it. At the same time the house introduced me to the work of the priest Nicholas Owen, known as Little John, who was so expert in the art of concealment that in his lifetime he devised enough hiding places to conceal twelve or more priests. Nicholas Owen was also tortured by the Elizabethan authorities until his tiny frame (so useful in his work for fitting into holes, unlike poor Charles II at six foot) was permanently twisted. One special trick of Little John was to construct one hole inside another, so that the searchers – those devilish people – would find the first hole empty and ride angrily away, leaving their prey cowering but safe in the inner hole.

The problem of the hidey holes was the necessarily sudden nature of the priests' hiding there. The cry would go up when men on horses were seen at the park gates: 'The searchers! The searchers are coming!' The owner of the house – let us say a hospitable Catholic lady like Teresa Carr-Saunders, with a large family to protect – would start bundling the incriminating priests away. There was no provision for food supplies in the hidey holes: how could there be? Nothing would have served better to enlighten the triumphant searchers that priests had been here or were coming soon. So food and drink supplies had to be hurried and improvised. On one occasion Father Garnett and a fellow priest existed for ten days on a pot of quince marmalade which his agitated hostess happened to have in her hands when the warning cries went up.

Inserting myself with some difficulty into one such hiding place, I thought: I've just had a large breakfast. And I'm about to have a good lunch. And I'm certainly not in danger of death if discovered, since I was ushered in here by a courteous host. (Huddington Court in Worcestershire, secluded and tranquil like Baddesley Clinton, is still in private hands.) How can I possibly identify myself with the real feelings of these beleaguered men?

And yet by crouching in this hole, if I cannot identify myself, I can at least empathize. I can try to think myself into the situation of a middle-aged man with bad circulation, cramped into a small hole, on the run for reasons of Faith.

At Water Eaton, some of the scaring – but also some of the excitement – undoubtedly arose out of my fear of the dark. My mother first noted this in my Progress Book in February 1939; that is to say, it antedated our arrival at Water Eaton. Apparently, Elizabeth consulted our family doctor who told her censoriously that I was reading books which were much too old for me, giving as an example Charles Kingsley's *The Heroes*. (For a while this had been my favourite book: Jason, the Argonauts – who would not want to go roistering through the ancient world with such companions?) To her credit, Elizabeth kept the doctor's verdict to herself and made no attempt to restore me to the *Tales of Little Grey Rabbit*; although even there I managed to find a picture of a small, dark, menacing weasel's snout peeking over a windowsill, the thought of which terrified me in the night hours.

This fear of mine was strictly limited to the hours of darkness, with just a little anxiety saved for dusk as the dreaded harbinger. I myself date it from a children's picture book about a village ringed with large mountains: as darkness fell, these dark rocky peaks turned into monstrous trolls and started to descend on the houses; only the dawn signalled by the crowing of the cock stopped them in their march and sent them back to being mountains again. Until the next evening came ... These tormenting images meant that I always privately thought my fear was perfectly reasonable, despite the grown-ups constantly telling me that it wasn't. Frankly, if darkness brings the trolls, isn't it only sensible to dread it?

Oddly enough, I never really got over this childhood fear of darkness, of which I was supposed to be ashamed, until I openly admitted it. A conversation with Harold helped. I took a deep breath and explained to him when we first lived together that I was frightened of the dark.

'You mean, like I can't bear flies?' he said helpfully. (Harold was a strong and often dramatically public moscophobe.)

'No, not at all like that!' I cried, outraged. I couldn't bear the idea of my heroic torment being reduced to the trivial level of insects. But after that exchange, candour on the subject somehow came more easily to me. And my new honesty, my escape from the childhood feeling of shame, disconcerted the trolls and did much to keep them in their proper environment as mountains in the future.

Sir Walter Scott, thanks to my mother, was a rather more productive, less baleful influence. For one thing, Elizabeth, a conscientious believer in reading aloud to her children, also exercised her first-class brain in cutting the books to make them palatable. In this way Lord Lytton's *The Last Days of Pompeii*, for example, positively zipped along, a rapidly moving thriller with a tumultuous ending. This is not the experience of anyone reading this noble but long-drawn-out novel from beginning to end.

In retrospect, I applaud Elizabeth's determination to involve her children in nineteenth-century classics, however long-winded. And as to reading aloud, one need only point to the modern success of audiobooks to see the wonderful power of the art. But I did get frustrated by what seemed the somewhat slow daily pace. I had to find a solution and I did. For this sly but voracious reader, it was the work of a moment to establish that my mother was absent, and then down I would creep in my nightie and read on happily, gluttonously devouring the future chapters.

Of course I was not nearly smart enough to conceal my nocturnal rovings for ever. I began to be visibly surprised at omissions, make comments on bits of the plot which hadn't yet happened.

I was finally caught out when a descriptive passage I had loved while clandestinely reading the night before was omitted. 'Oh, but I thought that she wore . . .' I began. To her credit once again, my mother never reproached me with my deceit, but merely handed me the book and said firmly, even with a certain respect: 'Antonia will now read on for herself.' Which was probably the right solution.

In this way, both in public and in private, the taste for Sir Walter Scott was inculcated. *Ivanhoe* was a particular favourite, with its rapid action, give or take the florid descriptive passages. Set in late-twelfth-century England, Nottingham and York, here was romance, lawful and unlawful, abduction, tournaments, mysterious strangers behind visors, torture, witchcraft and more, much more. The characters were as rich as the descriptions. Here were Rebecca, the beautiful Jewess who is a healer (I called my eldest daughter after her, pretending it was a tribute to Daphne du Maurier), Lady Rowena, the unexotically beautiful Saxon (I much preferred Rebecca), Isaac the Jewish money-lender, who is Rebecca's father, Wilfred of Ivanhoe, a noble Saxon, dull but good, Sir Brian de Bois Guilbert, leader of the Knights Templar, a saturnine character for whom I had a weakness, who redeems himself by his death, as well as the Black Knight who of course turns out to be Richard I in disguise, returning from the Crusades.

All of this gave me a taste for early Saxon and Norman English History which I never quite lost, despite the plodding manner in which it was taught at school. And then there was that curious sidelight on the history of the Jews, exotic, glamorous, alien, persecuted through no fault of their own: the hideous treatment of Isaac of York for money-lending chilled the blood. (Unless money-lending is a crime – but who were the money-borrowers? Christians.) Wartime would bring an influx of distinguished

Jewish refugees into Oxford, together with explanations as to their presence: but that lay ahead. Scott's *Ivanhoe* was my first impression of the Jews, as Water Eaton and Teresa Carr-Saunders constituted my first impression of Catholics.

Kenilworth was another extremely vivid experience: here we were once again in an Elizabethan manor house, although this time it was to feature lethally, not as a refuge for priests. Amy Robsart, secret wife of the Queen's favourite the Earl of Leicester, is an awkward factor in Court calculations. If Leicester were *not* married, let us say his wife died and Leicester was a free man, would perhaps the Virgin Queen in her ruff, with her pointy shoes, step off her globe and make him a happy (as well as a powerful) man?

The subsequent murder of Amy Robsart at Cumnor Place, near Oxford, is one of the great crime scenes because it is so understated. As a child I had to read it several times to be sure of what it meant; then it entered my nightmares. Leicester's servant Richard Varney decides to destroy Amy Robsart, believing this to be in the best interests of his master – and himself. A narrow wooden bridge which leads to her bedroom high up in a tower is fitted with a trap door. Now the familiar low whistle with which the Earl used to summon his bride from outside is heard, and the sound of a horse in the courtyard. Amy rushes out . . .

'Is the bird caught? – Is the deed done?' says Varney to his accomplice. 'Look down into the vault – what seest thou?'

'I see only a heap of white clothes, like a snow-drift,' he replies. This was the image which stayed with me. And here I was in an Elizabethan house not so very far from Cumnor. I could intone the old rhyme with ghoulish satisfaction:

Full many a traveller oft hath sighed,
    And pensive wept the Countess' fall

As wandering onwards they've espied
    The haunted towers of Cumnor Hall.

I could be that traveller! At any rate in my imagination.

In the real world the fields were very often flooded in that long winter, so hated by the grown-ups with their wartime anxieties, while we got on with enjoying our watery paradise. We shared it with cows, hens and above all donkeys: Flora displayed her newly acquired knowledge of Latin by calling her donkey Amat. She got the word from the book Elizabeth was using to teach us the language called *Latin with Laughter*. The tone was set by the frontispiece, which showed a cheery-looking fellow and a highly disgruntled sailor. Underneath in Latin it read: 'The poet sings; the sailor does not love (*amat*) the poet.' Emboldened by this, Flora refused to listen when it was pointed out to her that '*amat*' was a verb not a noun.

The level of our cares at this point is shown by the fact that the supreme crime was to get water over the top of your gumboots – supreme mistake too, since there was not much heat around in the stone-built house, and what existed was not dedicated to drying the soggy interior of a miscreant child's boot. There was gang life and the kind of games which a body of children about the same age evolve when the grown-ups are not paying attention. For example we re-enacted Gollums and Bellums, wafting about the forecourt in the dark (Gollums from *The Hobbit*, given to us recently by our parents' friend Tolkien, and Bellums, like Amat the donkey, came from our rather limited Latin vocabulary). The idea was to frighten each other, and we did.

Perhaps with our artificially induced terrors we were more like the children in *The Enchanted Castle*, by the adored E. Nesbit, whose every word was sacred to me. These children, feeling bored, provided an audience for their plays out of old overcoats, scarves, caps and walking sticks. They called these constructs the Ugly Wuglies: only to have the fearful creatures come alive in a scene which still makes me uneasy when I hear slow handclaps. 'And then someone else was clapping, six or seven people, and their clapping made a dull, padded sound. Nine faces instead of two were turned towards the stage, and seven out of the nine were painted, pointed, paper faces.' The cry goes up: 'Jerry, those things have come alive. Oh, whatever shall we do?' Naturally the Ugly Wuglies are as nasty, predatory and vicious as their appearance indicates: the resultant adventures test the reader's nerves to the utmost.

One author was never allowed to pollute our imaginations and that was Enid Blyton. In an excess of Thirties moralistic disapproval – the only example of such that I can remember – my mother banned her works. Unusually for me, I took no steps to get hold of the books in question later from the library. Indeed, I followed my mother when dealing with my own family, more for reasons of intellectual snobbery, I suspect, rather than anything else. My daughters, however, showed more spirit: it was not long before a stockpile of the dreaded works came tumbling out of their wardrobe. 'Jane' – a lively schoolfriend – 'gave them to us' was the explanation. 'She felt sorry for us not being able to read them. It was so exciting reading them in secret.' (A lesson, surely, in the dangers of censorship.)

We never really knew why we left Water Eaton: why not stay for ever with our sodden gumboots and our happy lives? There was of course the question of our educational future: we could not be taught by a governess all our school lives, delightful laid-back experience as that had been, including Elizabeth's lessons from *Latin with Laughter*. It is also easy to understand now why my mother decided that, with the return of my father to civilian life, we must have a proper family existence together.

It was when I read Elizabeth's entry about the fall of France in her autobiography that I finally appreciated why our happiest year had been a time of torment for her. While we frisked about carelessly, in and out of our hidey holes, real or imaginary, she had a double anguish to endure. It was not only the despair of Frank at his inability to fulfil what he perceived as his military duty and his subsequent collapse. There was the fate of many of the men who actually did go to war. Elizabeth wrote: 'his unfortunate battalion of the Oxford and Bucks Light Infantry had won glory in France at the cost of tragic casualties', adding 'Frank would almost certainly have died had he been with them.'

A house was bought in North Oxford. This was 8 Chadlington Road, running between Bardwell Road and Linton Road, very close to the River Cherwell. One day my mother announced casually: 'And there's a school next door. You're going to go to it.'

'But it's a school for boys,' I said.

'Yes.'

CHAPTER FIVE

SHE DRAGON

T HE SCHOOL NEXT DOOR TO which my mother had
so casually referred, that summer in which we left Water
Eaton, was called the Dragon. I spent the following four years of
my life there, September 1940 to July 1944.

'Next door' was not an exaggeration. Our house was actually bang next door to the headmaster's house, something that
became awkward as I could be easily spotted mooning about
in the garden making up romantic stories about myself, when
I should have been doing my prep. Luckily the headmaster,
'Hum' as A. E. Lynam was known – the Dragon specialized in
nicknames which boys used quite openly – had a head of thick
yellow-white hair which was virtually luminous. I would spy
him in his window and recite gobbledegook Latin verse loudly to
put him off the scent. Next to the headmaster's house came the
lane down to the River Cherwell and the boats; then the playing
fields stretching down to the river and the school barge; lastly the
school itself.

At the end of my first year at the Dragon, Hum gave the following verdict in my report: 'Just the start for a She Dragon.'
Apart from leaving open the question of whether he had been

fooled by my gobbledegook or heard it correctly for what it was, Hum did point to something which was generally felt but not defined. There was a species called the She Dragon. Later I heard that girls at the school were known as hags, but the term was not then in use; although it would have been curiously appropriate for me. A late developer toothwise, I was known in my family as the gap-tooth hag, with photos of me in my new uniform, beaming happily under my circular school hat, to explain why. So far as I was concerned, it was all super, if not outright wizard (the two favoured words at the Dragon) as I belted out the words 'You are my sunshine, my only sunshine, You make me happy when skies are grey' (the favoured song) on my way to school.

Altogether, with my curly hair, still kept very short by my pitiless mother, at the age of eight I looked as much like a boy as a girl. This once led to an embarrassing incident at Parson's Pleasure bathing place, where I was ushered into the wrong changing room, and had to lurk fully dressed in a corner (as a She Dragon, my chief reaction was not embarrassment but annoyance that I had missed my swim). Nevertheless, whatever I looked like, I did not feel like a boy, and nor, I believe, did any of the other so-called She Dragons.

Now officially described as co-educational, with about one third of the pupils girls, the Dragon was certainly not what is meant by co-educational in the Forties. What I did come to feel, therefore, was that I was in some way special, and this was undoubtedly based on the experience of being the member of a tiny clique. Did we girls in addition feel privileged? I don't believe so: that came afterwards, when we discovered in our different ways what an exciting and unusual education, compared to our contemporaries, we had received.

The Dragon School had been founded by a group of dons in

1877 and was originally known as the Oxford Little Boys School; eventually it became Lynam's for short, the name of the family who provided three headmasters, reigning in turn for an extraordinary span of eighty-nine years, ending in 1965. These were Skipper (C. C. Lynam), his brother Hum, and Hum's son Joc (J. H. R. Lynam) who took over from Hum halfway through my school career. It was Skipper, incidentally, who declared in a Prize Day speech that he much preferred his nickname to be used – 'I hate to be called "Sir" every half minute' – a tradition which stuck. And the first She Dragon was his daughter Kit, who arrived in 1896, to be followed by a second five years later, sister of three male Dragons; making the numbers two girls to eighty-eight boys. In my time, both these figures had substantially increased, but the gap remained proportionately enormous. In 1943, for example, there were officially forty girls and three hundred and fifty-one boys.

In the Forties, there were still older people who bafflingly referred to the school as Lynam's; but according to the record, it was the first pupils who were inspired to call themselves Dragons by the fact that one of the don-founders had the surname George. We children certainly knew what we were. 'I am a Dragon,' one would say in response to enquiries – with just a hint of polite surprise that any other answer could be expected.

Indeed, that gold Dragon, seen in profile with his long curly tail, ferocious tongue and outstretched wings, was everywhere. He was the crest on our navy blue blazers, such a familiar sight round Oxford, stamped on the memory with the motto *Arduus ad Solem*. (Striving for the Sun, which during the Battle of Britain became linked in my mind with the celebrated motto of the RAF: *Per ardua ad astra* – Through Adversity to the Stars.) The school magazine was known as the *Draconian*. The anthology of poetry, first published in 1935, which dominated our learning and our recitation aloud was called *The Dragon Book of Verse*. The metal weathervane that swung to and fro above the building which contained the boys' changing room was of course a dragon, with the school motto beneath – allowing these lines to be bellowed out meaningfully in the school song:

> And the words on that tin
> Mean go in and win . . .

Winning was extremely important at the Dragon. The lively spirit of competition extended to the parents, perhaps because so many of them (including my own) were connected to the ever-competitive academic world. Particularly, it seemed to me that the mothers were competitive; I remember them being quite as clever as their husbands and of course in many cases in wartime it was the mother who was the resident head of the household. All these mothers appeared to take an acute interest in the weekly form orders – distributed in written reports – with the corollary that certain among them were rumoured to be extraordinarily helpful with the homework. A popular master known as 'Jacko' (C. H. Jacques) used to perform light-hearted revue sketches at the end of term. When he awarded the form prize to *Mrs* Arrowsmith instead of her clever son, this was felt to be an appropriate, even admiring joke: when we applauded, we were applauding Mrs Arrowsmith as well as Jacko.

My own mother was certainly right up with the rest of them in her ambitions for me. 'Who came first?' was her only comment when I proudly announced that I had come second in Maths, a position which was frankly miraculous, given my lack of natural ability in that direction. On the other hand, constant child-bearing during the war meant that there was not much homework help to be expected. The perpetually attendant maternity nurse Elsie Violet Samways, known as Sammy, actually gave me more help listening to me practising my recitations. ('How old are you, Sammy?' This kindly woman, who seemed incredibly ancient to us, would answer any question but that: 'As old as my eyes and a little bit older than my teeth,' she would invariably reply.) It was only after I grew up that I realized how fortunate I had been, as the eldest, to have Elizabeth's keen attention at the start, teaching me that ever-swift reading, and later Latin. By the time I was eight, the spirit of the Dragon could probably be trusted to do the rest.

The dominant lessons at the Dragon School were Latin and Greek; the dominant sport rugger, as it was always called. This suited me down to the ground, often literally so in the case of rugger. All the girls at the Dragon in those days played rugger as a matter of course, there was nothing special about it – and how intoxicating the experience was! The girl described by my mother only a few years before as being absorbed 'in a dream world of tinsel and glittering beauty' was experiencing different sensations. In short, the feeling of racing up the wing, and handing off my pursuers as enthusiastically as possible, is one that remains with me as sheer pleasure. As I have come to tell the story, I was in the second XV, and prevented from playing away against the local prep school Summerfields because there was no girls' changing room. To me, this was extremely odd since I regarded playing rugger as the norm. But there is no doubt that this insouciance on the subject has merited some odd reactions over the years.

It began early. Our favourite among our parents' friends was undoubtedly John Betjeman, whom they had known since their own Oxford days. Betjeman, as they called him, would appear out of nowhere and recite cod Shakespearean verse on his knee to my mother, poetically addressed (like Queen Elizabeth I) as Eliza. I loved and envied this. So when Betjeman, as an Old Dragon, took an interest in my rugger career, I was first flattered then upset when he would not accept that I played fleet-footedly on the wing, but kept insisting that I was to be found in the hurly-burly of the scrum. It was not until I read his poem 'A Subaltern's Love Song' featuring the immortal Miss Joan Hunter Dunn that I realized that this tribute to my strength was in fact the greater compliment. In my very minor way, I was of the breed led by Betjeman's 'shock-headed victor', with her 'strongly adorable tennis-girl's hand'.

I will pass over briefly the incident while my first husband was Under-Secretary for War, when a benevolent general attempted to tell me the rules of rugger at the Army and Navy match at Twickenham. I tried to hand him off, as it were, with assurances about my expertise, which he in turn found hard to believe. But perhaps the all-round incredulity is summed up by an incident at another prep school, Colet Court, in the Seventies. I was walking down the touchline with my youngest son Orlando, watching a game of rugger, accompanied by Geoffrey Owen whose own son Tom was playing.

'Ah, Antonia,' said Geoff, 'I so well remember you haring up the wing at the Dragon' (he was two years my junior). I was smiling fondly at the memory when I suddenly noticed Orlando, aged nine, looking utterly gobsmacked.

'Orlando, what on earth is the matter?'

'But, Mummy,' he began, 'we always thought you made all that up, just to make us laugh.'

For all the competitive merriment of sport, Latin and Greek were the true dominants of the school. The chief classics master, L. A. Wilding, known of course as 'Law', who taught

Upper One for twenty years, had written a major textbook on the subject. The ability to write Latin verse was something that was expected to be instinctive and, hammered home, did indeed become so. It remains with one for a lifetime, learnt early enough.

In 1961, I received a new courtesy title when Frank became Earl of Longford on the death of his elder brother. No longer Mrs Fraser, I was henceforth to be known as Lady Antonia.

'Did you realize that your new name is the ending of a Latin hexameter?' enquired the distinguished lawyer Sir John Foster, a lofty man both physically and mentally.

'Down in a deep, dark dell sat Lady Antonia Fraser,' I replied, swiftly, adapting the old Dragon lines we learnt to guide us about the rhythm of Latin verse which began: 'Down in a deep dark dell sat an old cow chewing a beanstalk.'

'Weak ending, of course,' said Foster, attempting to claw back victory; he referred to the fact that the word Fraser consists of two syllables, the first of which gets heavier emphasis than the second, making it a trochee. A line could end strongly with the equal emphasis of a spondee: 'heartbreak' for example instead of 'happy'. I only wish I had had the guts to observe quite correctly: 'So is Foster.'

With the study of Latin and Greek went a great deal of concentration on the ancient world, as well as reading the classics. As a result, the Dragon spirit saw to it that the boys regularly took the top scholarships at Winchester and Eton. *A Dragon Century*, the school history by Jacko, reveals that Winchester was the original objective, with Eton catching up fast from the Twenties on. This history also records 1951 as The Year of the Double Top, when the first places on the Winchester Roll and the Eton Roll were both won. It seems splendidly characteristic of Dragon competitiveness that while the boys were

Later I graduated to swimming in the River Cherwell.

Paddy's christening, 1937. Front row l. to r.: Frank next to Naomi Mitchison (godmother); Thomas next to Elizabeth with Paddy; I am on the lap of the Master of Balliol, Sandie Lindsay.

2nd row 2nd from l.: David Cecil; 3rd from r.: Maurice Bowra (godfather); Julia Pakenham (Frank's sister); Ann Martelli (godmother); Michael Harman (Elizabeth's brother).

Back row far l.: John Betjeman, with Philip Toynbee in front.

Water Eaton Manor, near Oxford: the Elizabethan house where we spent an exciting year at the beginning of the war.

Above left On our bikes: Antonia and Thomas.

Below left Bodiam Castle, East Sussex: the scene of my earliest historical imaginings.

On the rocks in Cornwall where we spent our annual holiday in wartime.

Above left With Edmund Carr-Saunders doing lessons at Water Eaton: the Carr-Saunders family owned the house and were our hosts.

Below left The growing Oxford family: Antonia, Rachel, Paddy, Judith, Thomas, Christmas 1942.

A view of Magdalen College Tower, Oxford, and the bridge over the River Cherwell: the tower was my first conscious historic sight.

Above right Aged twelve, by Henry Lamb, who was married to Frank's sister, Pansy. I spent a great deal of time at their house at Coombe Bissett near Salisbury with my cousin, Henrietta Lamb.

Right Chadlington Road, North Oxford, by John Betjeman, dedicated to my mother as 'Eliza'. It shows the edge of School House on the right, and the house of the Headmaster of The Dragon School on the left (we lived next door). The Dragon playing fields are ahead.

John Betjeman portrait of self, & Charlington Rd, Oxford

THE DRACONIAN

ARDUUS AD SOLEM

The symbolic dragon was omnipresent at The Dragon School, seen here in the crest on my blazer, and on my hat, the title page of the school magazine – and the weathervane above the boys' changing room.

immediately awarded a 'no-prep', the staff celebrated with a party to which they triumphantly invited their rival masters from neighbouring schools.

It was certainly in the spirit of the Dragon School that when the time came for me to leave, I personally researched girls' schools which awarded scholarships. These seemed to be few and far between, and focused on boarding schools; although my mother had simply assumed I would be going to Oxford High School. However I had a secret ambition which was to see the name *Antonia Pakenham* inscribed on the Honours Board among the names of all the cleverest boys at the Dragon, the Bullards and the Wildings. It seemed to me later a warning against *hubris* that by the time this aim was achieved – not too difficult at that period for a girl given a boy's education – my name had to be installed at the very end of the existing Board running along the wall, an area almost invisible because it lay at the back of the stage.

Undoubtedly this competitiveness at work was acknowledged by the production of those weekly reports, giving the form order. Hum, as headmaster, read them all, commenting in red ink. There were also a prodigious number of prizes awarded. Was all this a mistake? I think my own attitude to the system was the obvious one: I liked it very much when I won, and was temporarily miffed when I didn't. And yet it is a curious fact that I have absolutely no memory of learning History, my passion in life, when I was at the Dragon. I continued to read any historical works, principally biographies, I could lay my hands on. Since my parents' books consisted of the classics and books by their friends, I took to pestering Oxford Public Library. There were no regulations against children using the adult section in those days, so I would sidle in, grab a book, get it stamped, slip out and walk home. Then I read the book. Back I would go . . . The librarian, incidentally, did not show herself in any way enchanted by my frequent appearances: she regarded them in some way as suspicious and tended to frown when she saw me arrive. It was an early instance of that rule which I had already begun to discover: speedy reading will make you happy but it will not make you popular. So for the time being all this was still part of my secret life, *my* History in fact.

When I first cast my mind back to those days, I came to the conclusion that, thanks to this possessive feeling about History, my memory must have blanked out the actual lessons. It was therefore interesting to discover from the printed forms of the school reports, faithfully preserved in my Progress Book by my mother, that there was in fact no official slot for History. In the body of the report, Classics is followed by English with a subsection for Geography, then Mathematics, lastly French. Below that, there are five tiny sections for Music and Singing, Art, Handicraft, Divinity and Science. Yet clearly we must have been taught History, and indeed my contemporary Dragons remember the lessons.

The explanation came to me from the school archivist: History was at this point included with English. After a formal inspection of the school in 1930, it was declared as follows: '"English" in the timetable is a general term, including Scripture, History and Geography as well as Literature and Composition.' Although one notes that Geography and Divinity but not History had escaped into categories of their own in the intervening ten years. Perhaps the Dragon emphasis on the Classics (on the evidence of the school report as well as my memory) was a reflection of the fact that a degree in Classics was for a long time considered the supreme degree at Oxford. My mother, for example, who had chosen to read Greats – as it was significantly known – did for a while simply assume that I would follow her, based on the advantage of being at the Dragon School. It seems relevant that I have vivid memories of learning the Classics with Law, and French with Monsieur Dodd, both listed as major subjects, but not History.

Above all my memories are of 'English'. This was not because it included History: it was due to two quite separate things. First of all, English meant reciting poems learnt by heart from *The Dragon Book of Verse* in the school hall: mainly Tennyson, according to my recollection. When I came to check the contents, Tennyson was indeed ahead of all other poets except Shakespeare, followed by Robert Browning and William Blake. I was amused to note that the last poem in this book was P. G. Wodehouse's 'Good Gnus' with its jolly, wonderfully incorrect beginning:

> When cares attack and life seems black
> How sweet it is to pot a yak . . .
> But in my Animals 'Who's Who'
> No name stands higher than the Gnu . . .

Ending:

> And one more gnu, so fair and frail
> Has handed in its dinner-pail . . .

Tennyson not Wodehouse was my man. Certainly my 'Break, break, break/On thy cold grey stones, O Sea!' was in my unprejudiced opinion particularly fine, with its tragic conclusion to which at the age of ten I gave full vent: 'But the tender grace of a day that is dead/Will never come back to me.' Thomas, a year younger, was quite good too as he rendered William Blake in a suitably high flute-like voice: 'Piping down the valleys wild/

Piping songs of pleasant glee'. Behind the reciters in the Hall was the vast mural centred round the half-naked figure of Education, surrounded by pals called Piety, Lofty Aims and Loyalty, but already one was inclined to ignore this slightly embarrassing backcloth.

The real point of 'English' for me, however, was Shakespeare and acting in the annual school play in the summer term. As it turned out, I was extremely lucky. Any girl with a good memory could hope to play a leading role under the direction of 'Bruno' (J. B. Brown); acting ability did not matter, since Bruno would do the rest. In this way I played Viola, followed by Celia in *As You Like It*. Bruno by this time had found a new favourite in the shape of Priscilla Hett, but tactfully explained to me that Celia was a better part than Rosalind. I was foolish enough to believe this during rehearsals, and still took an unconscionable time – right until the tumultuous applause for the adorable quicksilver Scilla at the end of the play, in fact – to grasp the truth.

My finest hour came in my last term when I played Lady Macbeth to the Macbeth of David 'Piggy' Pyemont: a charming flaxen-haired boy, a brilliant classicist, killed during National Service in Malaya, one of those casualties of that time after the war when peace in Europe did not necessarily mean peace in the world. In the official school photo he sports a Viking headdress with two enormous horns sprouting from it. I sit complacently at his side, with two equally enormous thick red plaits framing my youthful face. And of the various incidents during that finest hour, undoubtedly the moment when I stepped forward in front of the whole Dragon School and declaimed passionately the words of Lady M, 'Unsex me here . . .' was the highlight.

It is Bruno who epitomizes for me the best of the Dragon:

his energy, his enthusiasm for drama meant that the essential Shakespeare experience we received was the real contribution to the study of History which I got from the Dragon School. To know three Shakespeare plays virtually by heart, to love them, before the age of twelve, to realize there was a whole Shakespearean world and it was part of History – these were inestimable gifts.

Gilbert and Sullivan, also produced by Bruno, had no educational value so far as I was concerned, but was sheer pleasure. My first experience was with *Patience* when I watched Richard Wilding, future top civil servant, mincing about the stage as Bunthorne ('If you walk down Piccadilly with a poppy or a lily') while his ravishing unbroken voice soared above it all. My memories of Gilbert and Sullivan are in fact all of divine boy singers: evidently we few girls didn't have an advantage there, no doubt due to the tradition that preferred young boys in choirs to girls (or women).

Personally, I did not sing even though I took part as the third girl in *The Pirates of Penzance*. This silence was at Bruno's direct request. He had a habit of bending down and placing his ear close to one's mouth as one was rehearsing. To me he simply said: 'Don't.' Nevertheless, because he approved my acting in Shakespeare, I was allowed to go on stage and smile beguilingly in my bonnet with the others in the school photo, a happy if slightly fraudulent presence. The relief from the painful need to sing – Bruno got it absolutely right – meant that I thought of Gilbert and Sullivan then, and still do, as one of England's unequivocal national delights. Bruno's dismissal of my singing was after all only a more economical version of the art mistress's celebrated report, much quoted by my family thereafter: 'Ideas good, execution faulty.'

Seated in the front row of the *Macbeth* photo is one of my two best friends at the Dragon, both of course girls, Lalage Mais as Lady Macduff. (Felicity Wilding, whose father was Law, was the other.) Lalage was the daughter of one of our most eccentric masters: the writer S. P. B. Mais who taught us English. An expansive, loudly benevolent man of many thick waistcoats, mainly checked, he was renowned for them and even the hottest day would lead to no more than a partial unbuttoning. His teaching also flowed in a great seam of recitation, reminiscence and whatever else came into his mind at the moment. S. P. B. was then in his sixties, a veteran author and, more unusually at the time, frequent broadcaster on radio. The fact that he actually managed to be distinguished for eccentricity was a considerable achievement, because to be honest, many of our masters were in retrospect quite odd.

This was an effect of wartime, of course: adult men and women below a certain age needed to be away serving the war effort, not acting as teachers to children. As a result, many of our masters were old enough to have served in the First World War; one, Frank Cary, had lost a leg and another, 'Fuzz' Francis, had lost an eye. 'Tubby' Haines, who taught Maths, was known to be suffering from shell-shock. We girls took the effects of this shell-shock philosophically: it meant remembering to sit at the back of the class, otherwise Tubby might be moved to use your hair to scrub the blackboard in a fit of rage. This actually happened to a girl, aptly known for her pretty curly hair as 'Fuzzy' Stradling, who was seized and used as a cleaning implement. The rest of us simply thought that Fuzzy had been an idiot to sit in the front row. It was all part of the atmosphere in which the consequences of the First World War were in a strange way present with us along with the actuality of the Second; we at the Dragon still marked our First World War casualties, just as a new list was beginning.

I remember that there was one master who was a conscientious objector – my mother tried to explain to me what that was although I still didn't get it. On the one hand, his behaviour seemed to flout the known rules of the super-patriotic world in which we lived. On the other hand Mattie himself was a particularly sympathetic person, writing generous reports about my naïve would-be-Shelley attempts at composing verse. Much later, as I began to study the intricate subject of conscientious objection – Harold for example was an objector to post-war National Service in the very different atmosphere of 1948 – to say nothing of the history of First World War objectors, memories of Mattie came back and I wished vainly that I had been of an age to talk to him, instead of merely accepting his encouragement.

Then there was 'the Colonel' as J. C. Purnell was known, in charge of physical exercise and swimming (he had joined the school with his former rank of sergeant, but Curnell Purnell was the obvious Dragon nickname). Much later, Thomas, writing a history of the Boer War, discovered that the Colonel had actually fought in it, and regretted not having asked for his reminiscences. As the Colonel barked at us, intoned rhymes at us, during the daily grind on the treacherous gravel of the school playground (my knees still bear the scars of falls during play) he provided the most extreme example of the way the teachers in their experience spanned English History.

The Carpentry master, Ted Mack ('E.G.H.M.' on school notices and reports) became a family friend. About the same age as my parents, he seemed similarly old, but a great deal more benevolent when it came to treats. These ranged from a beautifully crafted wooden chest with A on it and a cradle for my doll (I have them still) to helpful little bookcases, ideal for a child so intent on creating her own space in an increasing family. Then there were the sweets: impossible to overstress the delight of sweets which were not part of one's meagre sweet ration. Ted Mack was also a keen birdwatcher, and with my mother, we all went on a holiday to Wales; Lalage Mais and her family came along for company. But of all the kindnesses Ted Mack did me, introducing me to the theatre, in the shape of Oxford's New Theatre, with regular visits, was surely the greatest.

I was fortunate in that wartime Oxford was a centre for the theatre: not only the New Theatre where famous productions from the blitzed West End could take refuge, but also the Playhouse, which was a repertory theatre of tremendous variety as well as distinction. One family outing to the latter to see a play centring on a betrayed country girl sticks in the memory, since there was no one to care for my young brother Paddy and we had to take him. 'She's going to have a what?' he shouted at one point, in the loud, commanding voice which would one day be a great asset to him as a barrister.

Other outings were at a higher level. Elizabeth conscientiously organized visits to Shakespeare at Stratford, not too far away, while petrol was available. Ted Mack on the other hand took me to absolutely everything; the essence of our theatre-going was to watch the good as well as the bad, and discuss which was which afterwards. Ted then indulged my new hobby of autograph-seeking by escorting me round to the stage door. '*Glamourflags* was not a very good play,' I wrote grandly in my pocket diary, about a revue with many different sketches; that did not prevent me from noting: 'afterwards we got their autographs'. Ivy Benson and her All Ladies Band fared better, and once again we got the autographs. I blush to think that these stars were obliged to inscribe my book: 'To the Ant of Chadlington' – the signature I always used at the time.

I have no idea what my parents thought of our theatre-going; the truth was probably that they were too frantically busy to care, and one child being occupied was one child less to tend. My mother certainly never tried to take me to the opera again after a disastrous expedition to *The Tales of Hoffmann* when I was five: as the character of the singer named Antonia duly sang herself to death, I punctuated the action with wild screams of dismay, thus bringing about a pause in my opera-going which lasted for twelve years. When it came to my friendship with Ted Mack, only the housemistress at my next school raised an eyebrow, as Ted continued to visit me, as well as performing vital offices such as sending me sweets (still) and the magazine *Punch* weekly. My mother indicated later in a roundabout way that she had received a letter on the subject. I was protected by ignorance of what the housemistress might be implying – the relationship was certainly completely innocent of anything that would now be considered 'inappropriate'.

In any case, poor Ted must have fallen ill with cancer just about this time; he died at the age of forty-one in May 1945. Before that, Thomas and I, hearing that he was in hospital in London, and not of course being told about cancer, joyfully planned an expedition to visit him. We described ourselves as Ted's nephew and niece and after an argument gained the ward where he lay. We found a wan figure, sadly shrunken from the big and burly man we remembered; but he still managed to smile at our audacity.

I note from my letters home that I tried to visit Ted again during the April holidays before he died, but wasn't allowed to do so, since as my mother wrote to me at school in May 1946, breaking the news of his death, 'poor Ted just wasted away.' I was thirteen. My anguished letter back asked why the world preferred to invent 'the most atomically fiendish instruments of death' (a reference to the dropping of the bomb on Japan the previous August) instead of finding cures for illness. How could my mother answer this unanswerable question? Wisely, she did not attempt to do so. Her next letter was full of gentle reminiscence of our happy birdwatching holiday. To this day, I remember Ted with affection, as the man who inculcated in me a lifelong love of a theatrical expedition – any time, any theatrical expedition, so long as there is excitement in the anticipation.

'Oh why oh why doesn't Dick Plummer write?' This sad expostulation comes from my pocket diary, but it is dated 1947, long after both Dick and I had left the Dragon School. We had sat opposite each other at an Old Dragon Dinner, although that night in the diary I was truthfully more interested in recording my pale blue dress and Pink Plum Beautiful lipstick than the charms of the boy opposite. The lament, days later, has an artificial sound to it as if my fourteen-year-old persona, self-reared on Georgette Heyer, thought she ought to be having those feelings. It was certainly the Marquis of Vidal, eponymous hero of *Devil's Cub*, who remained my ideal. The romances of boys and girls at the Dragon School were, in my experience, mainly epistolary: the odd note or a jovial comment written by a sister across a brother's notebook about the prettiest girl at the Dragon: 'Thomas Pakenham loves Marion Hunter.' My intimate friendships remained, as I wanted them to be, with girls.

Of course most of us knew the facts of life, or thought that we did. There would be occasional ruderies shouted out by a boy, generally from a safe distance. We girls also discussed such subjects from time to time, although in retrospect the level of accuracy was not very high and one hopes we all knew better by the time we were grown up. To give an example, when one of us brought hot news from a holiday spent near a riding stable that 'you have to do it standing up if you want to have a baby. Like the horses,' nobody contradicted her. Girls, however, were not admitted to the ritual biological instruction which I believe occurred for leavers, about which exaggerated tales were told (by boys who never failed to comment: 'But of course I knew it all anyway'). The most useful piece of information I derived from a combination of reading Trollope and an enlightened friend.

Aged eleven, I had discovered Trollope in a huge green-and-gold edition in my parents' house. (I learnt later that there was a lot of wartime Trollope reading among the grown-ups 'to get away from the war'.) Thus I was temporarily obsessed by the character of Lady Glencora Palliser in *Can You Forgive Her?* The tiny, tousle-haired heiress and her fatal love for the wastrel Burgo Fitzgerald occupied most of my waking thoughts. I was however baffled by one significant development in the plot. We all knew that Lady Glencora must dutifully provide an heir for her husband Plantaganet Palliser, himself the heir to the Duke of Omnium, because that was what the Duke requested. I turned to Felicity Wilding, slightly older than me, for help.

'When Glencora says with a blush that she's not quite sure, she thinks, maybe . . . I mean, how can she not know whether she's having a baby? Either they did it, in which case she's having a baby. Or they didn't, in which case she isn't.'

'Oh, no,' said Felicity in a world-weary voice. 'You don't understand. Grown-ups do it all the time.'

I was stunned and fell into incredulous silence. Nothing in the frequent appearance of babies in these years at 8 Chadlington Road had prepared me for such a – frankly – embarrassing revelation. I found it much more difficult to assimilate, for example, than the fate of the lovely Amabel in Harrison Ainsworth's *Old St Paul's* at the hands of the wicked but sexy Lord Rochester, in the words of the author 'seeking only in pursuit of the grocer's daughter the gratification of his lawless desires'. *Old St Paul's* was another current favourite: in fact I found Harrison Ainsworth a wonderful source of shocking enlightenment – at the level I wanted – as well as History. It was only many years later that I learnt from Robert Gittings's biography of Thomas Hardy that he himself had been obsessed by *Old St Paul's* in youth and had immersed himself so totally in the novel as a child 'that he never quite threw off its influence on his style'. I felt a retrospective sense of pride to have shared a passion with the great writer.

At the time I turned away from Felicity and went back to the safety of the written word and Trollope's political Pallisers. Instinctively I much preferred them to the then fashionable Anglican bishops, bishops' wives and deans of Barchester. I was determined to ignore any possible connection with reality and stick with the lot of them, Phineas Finn, Lady Eustace, Lady Laura Standish, Madame Max Goesler and so forth, ignoring anything unpleasant that might disturb me in my rapt contemplation of their fascinating social fortunes.

It was probably a long way away from what Hum thought a She Dragon should be thinking about. What would that be? Something to do with the Classical World, no doubt. But at this point, in my imagination, Lady Glencora was a great deal more interesting than Helen of Troy because she was my private heroine, not the character extolled in class. For the time being, it was she who accompanied me as I walked moodily on the banks of the Cherwell, flowing past the playing fields and the school barge.

Meanwhile the river itself was and remained for me as much part of the Dragon as the weathervane which told us to go in and win. I was a She Dragon, which meant that I was versed in the Classics, a dashing rugger player in my own estimation, but also a marine species, perfectly at ease in the water of the Cherwell, swimming or punting, listening to Colonel Purnell's rhythmic cries of instruction. It was a potent combination.

Then there was that other powerful element: the North Oxford world in which we lived.

CHAPTER SIX

ON OUR BIKES

W E NORTH OXFORD CHILDREN seemed to be born on our bikes, like Centaurs, with two wheels instead of horses' legs. This was the powerful image evoked by John Betjeman, Old Dragon, in his poetic autobiography:

> Take me, my Centaur bike, down Linton Road
> Gliding by newly planted almond trees . . .

As with so much else written by Betjeman on North Oxford – 'Belbroughton Road is bonny, and pinkly bursts the spray . . .' – when I read these lines in 1960 they carried me back instantly to that time, that place.

We biked everywhere: round about the network of roads that comprised North Oxford, where our friends lived, further sometimes to Marston or Headington or Shotover. Bikes were thrown down carelessly on reaching one's destination, in front gardens, even on the pavement. With renewed energy, it would be off to visit our cousins the Hopes in Rawlinson Road, and Lizzie Cairns in her magnificent house in Charlbury Road – being careful at all times to give a wide berth to the nearby house where lurked the dangerous Taylor boys. No one quite knew why the Taylor boys were dangerous, but it gave a certain pleasing spice to the journey.

There was no other traffic: seeing a rare bus nosing its way down the two main roads which kept the network together was like seeing the head of a large wild animal appearing out of the grass. Cars were virtually non-existent: my mother's old grey car spent most of the war out of commission, hunched in the gardener's shed like one of those ancient creatures in the Pitt Rivers Museum which used to scare us at dusk on a December afternoon. I can remember neither accidents nor thefts, although both must have occurred: our bikes, handed down from brother to sister and down again, had a routinely battered appearance (under the circumstances there was no serious attempt to restrict bikes with crossbars to boys or vice versa) so that I still find the sight of a brand-new shiny bicycle slightly disconcerting.

Betjeman went on to refer to 'the young dons with wives in tussore clad/Were building in the morning of their lives/Houses for future Dragons'. There was indeed a myth that North Oxford itself had its origins in the time when dons were not allowed to marry, and had to keep their unofficial womenfolk and children out of sight. The area, extending down the Woodstock and Banbury Roads as far as Summertown, with all the tributary roads, was thus the location of nineteenth-century academic harems . . . Alas, for the myth. It was not until I read Tanis Hinchcliffe's study of North Oxford published in 1992 that I realized that the origins of my childhood kingdom lay not in secret relationships but in the less exciting, more materialistic world of property development.

St John's College, which owned the North Oxford estate, sought to diversify from agricultural rents, and so leases for houses began to be sold. It was not even true that the earliest inhabitants were dons, able at last to marry and retain their positions according to an Act of 1877; this was another version of the first myth. By the time the dons were empowered, North Oxford was already in existence with 'tradesmen' and even 'spinsters' installed. In short, the dons found the houses waiting for them.

Our own house was far from being a Victorian Gothic palace, although there were some splendid examples of that venerable style nearby in Northmoor Road and the Banbury Road. Number 8 Chadlington Road was in fact built in 1911. But there was a sturdy charm to these later North Oxford houses, which were comfortable – give or take the discomforts of wartime – without being grand. For one thing all the houses were endowed with what would have been seen as large gardens and, in true villa-style, were not attached to their neighbours.

There was even a tiny circular drive outside the front door with its dolphin knocker (still in place at the time of writing) but it was on the same small scale as Vicky – for Vixen – our beloved corgi, whose delight was to race round and round it, yapping angrily and tearing at any vulnerable trousered legs that presented themselves. The arrival of Vicky was, incidentally, an early example of royalism on my mother's part. Then officially a republican, she informed us that corgis were the choice of the Princesses Elizabeth and Margaret Rose. We wondered, without ever getting an answer, whether the Palace corgis also attacked the Palace postmen, and if so, whether the Little Princesses had to sacrifice their clothing coupons to replace those ruined trousers.

This deprivation was something we took for granted, along with the deep cold of all the houses in North Oxford – any complaints were liable to be met by the unfriendly but frequently repeated enquiry: 'Don't you know there's a war on?' Then again, perhaps our house was especially cold, due first of all to Elizabeth's natural puritanism – some women were said to greet food-rationing with joy, and if true, she was one of them. Fish was a staple: we were always being told that we lived in an island surrounded by fish. Consequently it was unrationed. Unfortunately after that all the fish in our house (which would now be served at vast prices in elegant restaurants) had to be draped in a thick white tasteless sauce, making it almost indistinguishable from the perpetual semolina and rice puddings which followed. With a tiny weekly meat ration and hardly any butter, floury potatoes accounted for the rest of our diet in another phrase I came to hate, 'for the duration': the Latin *durus* for hard or harsh seemed about right. Of course, we were never hungry, unlike most people in the world; on the other hand the modern attitude to food, the thrill of cooking, the zest of it all, never remotely touched our house during my mother's long life.

After Elizabeth's puritanism came Frank's total indifference to all matters of material comfort. I have two wartime domestic images of him: one, indoors, is of a man sitting in the corner of the freezing, deserted dining room – officially abandoned in favour of the kitchen since the beginning of the war – reading a book, marking it with his vigorous pencil, as he always did (no matter whether he actually owned the book). Evidently Frank preferred peace to warmth. The outdoor picture, where the temperature might well be warmer, is exactly the same: Frank sits in a deckchair and marks his book with his strong pencil as he reads it. So characteristic and ingrained was this trait of his that, after his death, I was able to identify a copy of the New Testament left behind in the House of Lords library, without an owner's name, but full of those ritual stabbings.

To us, in his deckchair or perhaps doing his vigorous exercises on which he prided himself, our father was an essentially benign presence. In fact, when I was very young I had a shrewd suspicion that he might be Gentle Jesus, as in the hymn, because he was so Meek and Mild. Like Jesus, he did not seem particularly concerned with earthly things, that is to say, his children. The great zoologist Solly Zuckerman, another Oxford friend, liked to tell a story by which an undergraduate rang the bell at our front door, only to have my father shout: 'Come in quickly. Otherwise they'll all fall out.' This was amusing to relate but inherently unlikely: I could not imagine my father being in the slightest bit concerned about the possibility.

All the inevitable corrections of childhood were carried out with a certain zest by our mother. She was occasionally known to pursue flagrant wrongdoers with a hairbrush, although there is no record of her actually catching them – or using it. Oddly enough, the sharp, competitive mother of my childhood transposed into an exceptionally charming, mild old lady, if not exactly meek. In contrast, our benign father could be a vigorous, not to say short-tempered debater in the family circle in later years, no more pleased than anyone else at having his will crossed. In seventy years of marriage, I suppose that they had leant into each other like two trees entwining over an arch and even their temperaments had begun to intermingle. (Like Ovid's story of Baucis and Philemon, the couple who ended their lives turned into two neighbouring trees, as a reward for helping some gods in disguise.)

The public image of my parents at this time was somewhat different, as I learnt when I came across an old copy of the *Tatler and Bystander* carefully preserved by my mother, along with election addresses and other political memorabilia. Rather incongruously for the Society magazine in question, the headline, dated December 1941, featured Frank and Elizabeth as *'Both Socialists'* and

'*Both Labour Candidates*' – for Oxford City and Kings Norton. Mr Pakenham, it informed us, formerly worked in the Conservative Research Department, then Christ Church, and now was personal assistant to Sir William Beveridge. This reminded me that throughout this period my mother in theory retained her pre-war political ambitions while my father, acknowledged as candidate for Oxford whenever (and if ever) there was another election, was working hard on what became known as the Beveridge Report. Subsequently he would give two hundred and fifty lectures on the subject of Social Insurance.

'Very exciting!' I wrote in my pocket diary. 'Dada is going to abolish Want.' Rather less exciting were the formal teas we had to have with Sir William Beveridge and his stern future wife, Mrs Janet Mair at University College. All sides were uneasy; one got the strong impression that Sir William would have been far happier entertaining Want itself than facing the fairly graceless children of his assistant.

As for Frank's other activities, the philanthropy – particularly towards prisoners, for which Frank became famous in later years, or even infamous in some circles of the press – was already in evidence. One of my earliest encounters with the puzzling behaviour of grown-ups was the result of a visit by a former student of my father's at Christ Church. He came to tea. We were told we must be especially nice to him since he was now an inmate of the Littlemore Lunatic Asylum. This wasn't so far from Singletree where we then lived, and in fact our afternoon walk often took us past Littlemore where we tried to catch glimpses of the 'loonies' as being an interesting feature of the landscape. After the young man – gentle and polite throughout – departed, I asked my nanny why he was living in Littlemore. I was told that he had committed 'arson'. And what might 'arson' be? When Nanny explained, I was more baffled than ever, because surely the grown-ups would never ask someone who had done this to have tea with me. This was an advance warning of what would be a lifetime of Frank intermingling his existence – and occasionally his family's – with the unfortunate. He recorded that his first visit to a prison was in January 1936 and I would imagine his last one would have been very shortly before his death nearly seventy years later.

Number 8 Chad, as it was always known, was the first place in my life where the word 'home' began to have a solid, stable meaning. This was certainly not unconnected with the fact that I now had my own attic room, a cell in dimensions, but my own cell. (Thomas had the equivalent cell opposite; quite recently we were given a tour of our old house by the owners and, somewhat to their surprise, Thomas pointed out with freshly minted indignation that I had had – infinitesimally – the better cell.) For me, the passion I felt for this small space was mostly to do with the animal instinct for secrecy natural to members of large families. I believe this was where I first came unconsciously to define happiness as being alone in a room with a house full of people. There was in addition the slight stirring of the need for privacy by would-be creative people: what Auden called 'The Cave of Making' where 'domestic/noises and odour, the vast background of natural/life are shut off'. It was a need which would become acute once I was of those who combined the life of a professional writer with that of a mother – and all at home. I sometimes wished I could attach the tiny private cell from 8 Chad on to the sides of my Notting Hill house.

The result of St John's enterprise was described in architectural books as a suburb – but how could North Oxford be a suburb? It was the centre of the world, so far as we were concerned. There were other areas within Oxford, with exotic names such as St Ebbe's and Jericho, but their remoteness was summed up by a careless remark of my mother's about the inhabitants – 'so poor that they vote Tory' – which she later explained as something called the *lumpenproletariat*. In 1940, I had the impression that all the grown-up inhabitants of North Oxford – that is to say, all my parents' friends – were dons. Prominent among them were Lord David Cecil in Linton Road, Roy Harrod, like my father at Christ Church, with his nearby house in St Aldate's, Maurice Bowra at Wadham and Isaiah Berlin at All Souls. Similarly my mother's friends were dons' wives such as Rachel Cecil and Billa Harrod: Maurice Bowra was not married, nor at that point was Isaiah Berlin. But I was fascinated by Billa Harrod long before she became my friend when I was at Oxford. I had been her bridesmaid before the war, and at some point was told a story in which Billa had convincingly posed as a Turkish princess; given her exotic dark-eyed looks, magnolia skin and thick black hair, I found it easy to believe.

Maurice Bowra to us was a remote person, whose fabled connection to our mother – he was supposed to have proposed to her when she was at Oxford – we found difficult to equate with this short, rotund figure, so very unlike our father; his gaze, like his conversation, was way above our heads. Roy Harrod gave an impression of enormous kindness, and equally enormous vagueness; even when I came to live next door to him in London, I suspect he had no idea who I was. David Cecil, on the other hand, with his lanky figure, clever narrowly domed head and fussy aristocratic voice, was a personal favourite. He always seemed positively delighted to see me in whatever circumstances we met. It was an attitude summed up by my first dinner party on arriving in Oxford in 1950. Hugh Trevor-Roper invited me courteously, as my father's daughter; I was one of twelve people and the youngest by perhaps twenty years. There was considerable jockeying for position. David Cecil was the last to sit down and was perforce placed next to me. 'I had hoped for this,' he said with an air of satisfaction which was utterly convincing.

Then there were the friendships where the dons concerned shared something like my parents' political views: two historians were to be friendly to me in later years as 'Frank's daughter'. A. J. P. Taylor was a case in point: his vitality and charming egocentricity might have prepared one for the post-war fame he was to achieve as a broadcaster. A. L. Rowse was another whom my parents evidently regarded indulgently, with anecdotes about Leslie this and Leslie that. Years later, I was to learn that he too considered that he had exercised a certain indulgence where my father was concerned. I went to visit him in his last years in retreat near St Austell in Cornwall. He was seated in a chair at the end of his library, and owing to deafness pulled my own chair very close. We began to discuss Oxford days. 'The trouble with Frank,' he roared into my ear, 'is that he was never a Homo.' I repeated this charge to my father, thinking he would be amused. 'No, perfectly true,' he commented, scarcely looking up from the large-print New Testament that, as so often, he was reading at the time.

Obviously this is a timeless child's-eye view of my parents' circle, since Berlin for one was certainly away during the war, so that admiring anecdotes of 'Shire', as he seemed to be termed (just as David was always 'Sissil'), must belong to another era. It simply reflects the close sense of the academic community with which we were imbued. The Goodharts were there, Arthur with his awesome American wife; Herbert Hart, whose wife Jenifer, like the Ayers and Stuart Hampshire, featured in the kind of parental gossip that I picked up and somehow stored away without understanding it until much later.

The extent of these friendships can be charted in the

photographs of the christenings of my siblings. At Paddy's pre-war christening, where he was baptized Patrick Maurice, Bowra as godfather is prominent. I am pictured sitting on the lap of Sandie Lindsay, who in 1938 would feature in a famous anti-appeasement by-election at Oxford, the Vice-Chancellor of the University and Master of Balliol. Despite these distinctions, from my expression I am clearly hoping for a better lap, the choice being Betjeman, Philip Toynbee or Naomi Mitchison. When my sister Rachel was christened in 1942, David and Rachel Cecil (for whom she was named) featured, as did Maurice Bowra once more. Sometimes a golden young beauty who bewitched everybody in the academic world was present: this was Clarissa Churchill, niece of one Prime Minister who went on to marry another in the shape of Anthony Eden.

There was another aspect to it all. I now realize that despite this social life something of the old feeling of the exclusion of women in the academic world – the myth in fact – lingered at any rate into the chit-chat of my mother and her friends. 'Nothing has changed,' Elizabeth sometimes exclaimed, when conferring with Billa. Both evidently excoriated the treatment of wives in wartime Oxford, believing that all the fun (and a lot of the available food) was to be had at High Table, to which wives were apparently not invited, despite the existence of women-only colleges.

On the other hand Oxford itself, far from being a backwater, was an exciting place to be. How did we children know that it was intended to be Hitler's headquarters when he won the war, with Frank's college Christ Church as his personal dwelling? As a result of this decision, temporarily reassuring if ultimately chilling, we understood that Oxford would not be bombed. We must have picked this up from our parents' talk, over our heads as it were. It was evidently a common subject of comment. Vera

Brittain, visiting Somerville, her old college at Oxford, during this period, queried the lack of bombing in such a congested place. In a book published in 1941, she reported the Dean as saying: 'Well, they say here that Hitler's keeping Oxford for himself. He wants it to look as it always has when he comes to get his Honorary Degree!'

The fact was that Oxford, packed with refugees and evacuees of many different sorts, was not in our experience bombed. On the contrary, we heard the drone of the planes traversing the city in the night sky on their way to bomb Coventry, or perhaps Birmingham, flat. We grew accustomed to air-raid sirens and the music of the All Clear – I still can't hear any similar siren-like noise without a Proustian moment of recollection – and we had air-raid shelters (our own was in our cellar, otherwise inhabited by eggs being preserved in spirit in buckets). On one famous occasion, a siren went off when I was temporarily the only person in the house, with my baby sister Judith in her pram in the garden. Feeling heroic and at the same time very, very nervous, I hoicked her out of the pram and went gingerly down into the cellar to sit among the eggs. By the time my mother returned – it can only have been a short while later – conscious heroism had taken over from nerves and I was sitting, in her own words in my Progress Book, 'with the air of the boy who stood on the burning deck whence all but he had fled'.

We had gas masks. These had been routinely issued to us all at the beginning of the war, with a special baby's apparatus and children's gas masks in jolly colours, as if this was all some kind of asphyxiating game. After all, there had been instances of gassing in the previous war, and survivors to remind one of the fact. There were however rumours that girls slightly older than us filled their gas mask cases, which were slung over the shoulder, with make-up and mirrors. Then there was the Blackout, a new concept to us. The Blackout had a physical manifestation, large and unwieldy, which had to be sedulously applied at dusk and removed the next morning. This consisted of shutters of a thick, presumably fireproof material with wooden edges which it was among my tasks to fit to the windows. A chink of light – and well, you would bring the air-raid warden round very quickly. After that the German planes would follow and the ensuing disaster would be your responsibility.

As it happened, the only really dangerous plane which came close – very close – was one of our own. I was alone at the bottom of the garden at 8 Chad one Sunday afternoon in May 1941 when I heard the extraordinary noise made by the low-flying flaming aeroplane, and then saw the thick dark smoke go up like a pillar. My first reaction was: 'They've hit the Dragon!' On a sunny weekend, the playing fields were positively crowded with super-active Dragon boys. With the total shock and the hideous noise, I had lost my sense of direction. The plane – on some kind of training mission – had actually crashed in the next-door road (the present site of Wolfson College): three people were killed and the aeroplane was a write-off. Of course I assumed that this was a German plane: the concept of our own planes crashing, or nearly crashing on our school, was not one that I could handle. At the time I went inside the house in a state of paralysed fear, and sat down in the kitchen without mentioning what I had seen. It was only when the news was given to us the next morning that I described my experience, and then I'm not sure that I was believed.

This was not the sort of incident for which Thomas and I had prepared ourselves right at the beginning of our time in Oxford when the bells fell silent. Still very young, we understood that they would only peal out again under one of two conditions: first, if peace was declared (when we had won the war, of course);

secondly, if parachutists landed. Obviously the sound of the bells would call for some split-second decisions, as the wrong call might have serious consequences, like waving flimsy Union Jacks in the face of advancing Nazis. So Thomas and I prepared early for the possible arrival of a parachutist. First of all, we would lull him into a sense of security: '*Ich liebe dich*,' we would say. Then, when he was thoroughly disarmed, we would shout: '*Du Hund!*' and stab him to the heart. What with was still a matter of debate.

As we grew older, we began to take a passionate interest in the course of the war. With Thomas, this took the form of identifying aeroplanes, alternatively building a hot-air balloon in a poky little room by the side door which was his own war effort. The ritual did not vary. At a given moment, we would all be summoned to assemble on the lawn for the release of the great balloon. The balloon would ascend, the balloon would catch fire, at which point Thomas would rush back into the shed to build another one. My own involvement was more sedentary: it consisted of reading the *Daily Herald* and trying to work out the progress of our men, especially our sailors and their ships. I followed, for example, the fortunes of the dreaded German battlecruisers *Scharnhorst* and *Prinz Eugen*, which never seemed to be out of the *Daily Herald* headlines. (The *Daily Herald* was taken in tribute to my parents' Socialist principles, but I was generally able to have it to myself while they shared *The Times*.)

Above all, I read the paper for news of Mr Churchill, who was my hero – my first hero, I believe, who was courageous and far-sighted rather than saturnine and romantic. There would of course have been implicit parental support for this. As firm anti-appeasers, my parents had greeted Churchill's accession to leadership (and the demotion of Elizabeth's cousin Neville Chamberlain) with enthusiasm; just as my father had written to him early in 1939 on the subject of dons' military service. For my part I also admired Mrs Churchill, doing so much for the sailors on the icy convoys to Russia, and who, we firmly believed, had taken a vow never to remove the turban she always wore, just like the girls in factories, until Hitler was defeated. But Churchill himself was the real focus of my admiration. I wrote a poem for his birthday on 30 November and posted it well in advance to 10 Downing Street. On the morning after the actual birthday, my mother told me at breakfast: 'By the way, you were thanked for your poem on the wireless last night.' I was not surprised. I came to realize that there had actually been some kind of general announcement of thanks for all the greetings sent by the public; nevertheless with the true faith of the hero-worshipper I was still convinced that my poem had been in some way special to Mr Churchill.

Later, when I came to study the actual life story of my hero, I learnt a valuable lesson about the great men of history (and for that matter the great women). This was not only the statesman who won the war for us with his courage, his oratory, and as we saw it his belief in us as a nation. He was also the politician whom my grandmother Mary Julia Longford held responsible for the disaster of Gallipoli (as a result of which her husband died): to the extent that one of her daughters told me she would not enter a drawing room in the Twenties if Mrs Churchill, let alone Winston, might be there. As to subsequent decades, even reading Churchill's views about India and the Indians made this faint-hearted liberal shudder. Yet amateur study of the Second World War has only confirmed me in my admiration for Churchill the war leader. The point I derived, which came in particularly handy when I was writing about the Duke of Wellington and his fierce denunciations of Parliamentary Reform, was that a great man was not necessarily a perfect man.

I suppose our first real practical contact with the war – given that our father was living at home – was with the evacuees. I will omit the trains taking us to our holidays in B&Bs in Cornwall, so packed with troops on the move that there were even soldiers sitting on the floors of the lavatories, rather awkwardly for us children. This we simply took for granted: that's what all trains were like: very slow, eternity to get to Cornwall, with mysterious stoppages for the sake of other troop movements, and absolutely crammed with people. The evacuees were different. The evacuees were not part of the normal routine of things. They were being saved, so we were told, from the Blitz which was tearing London apart.

It is therefore odd to reflect now that it was during this period that I was sent off alone to visit a doctor in Harley Street for something to do with my back, which he manipulated. This is confirmed by my mother's entry in my Progress Book – she was evidently proud of me rather than particularly protective: 'Antonia used train, tube, bus, bicycle and feet! Did family shopping with the Points [as some ration coupons were known] at Selfridges.' In fact I travelled by bike to the station, by train to Paddington, by tube to Baker Street once a week, catching a train back which was calculated to miss the start of the bombing; all the same it was peculiar and not altogether pleasant reading the details of it the next morning in the *Daily Herald*. But my mother was confident: 'The Blitz only starts at night.' I believed her and fortunately, where I was concerned, she was right.

As it was, where Harold was evacuated from Hackney with his whole school to a Cornish castle, other East End boys had to put up with North Oxford, which may have been safe but was far less exciting. Jimmy Perkins, our evacuee at 8 Chad, wore a Churchillian boiler suit, as the Dragon boys were now wearing, and had short upstanding flaxen hair; he was a good-looking, good-natured little boy with, unsurprisingly, a strong Cockney accent. I have a feeling that he must have been bewildered by 8 Chad if only because the food in his allegedly dangerous home would have been a great deal better (and the house a great deal warmer). He did not last very long with us; perhaps, like Harold who insisted on returning to war-torn Hackney from the safety of Cornwall, he was homesick and preferred to face the bombs.

In quite a different category were the boys at the Dragon School who had themselves been evacuated to Canada or the United States at the beginning of the war by anxious parents, and began to return from 1943 onwards. They struck us as an arrogant bunch. Immensely tall, altogether much bigger than us, immensely strong, with flashing white teeth, they nevertheless appeared to us to have fallen way behind in their work. Or perhaps this was the spirit of the Dragon speaking: for how could anyone possibly be better educated than at the Dragon itself?

Our dealings with the real American servicemen who, later in the war, came to flood Oxford from nearby air bases were on the other hand entirely delightful. This generous race of men, in their odd uniforms with the jackets sawn off at the waist, made me Americanophile from the outset. There were a number of reasons for this. First, they presented us with sweets, and nylons for those who wanted them. I was too young to be interested in the stockings but sixteen-year-old Eileen, who helped our nanny, had one ambition which was to go out with a Yank and acquire a pair of proper American nylons. Secondly, the kindly Yanks escorted us blithely into cinemas, past the box office (also paying for us) where the Adult rating meant that you needed a grown-up to get in. Frankly, Thomas and I didn't have many ambitions as all-consuming as the need to go to A-rated films at, let us say, the Super or the Ritz.

'Please could you tell them that I'm your little girl,' went the dialogue. 'And I'm your little boy,' Thomas would add. Thanks to the good nature of the Americans, this approach was surprisingly successful, although I can't help feeling that we owed something also to the wartime spirit of the women in the box offices concerned. Some of the so-called family parties must have looked astonishingly disparate.

All in all, it is easy to understand why the awful warning that Elizabeth gave me on the subject of American soldiers fell on stony ground. She had heard that I had been seen wandering alone about the paths of Marston, just outside the town itself. Actually I was composing my new novel in my head about Lucy and Rollo in the English Civil War (owing a great deal to *Children of the New Forest*). Elizabeth told me solemnly that in future I must beware of Marston: 'You might meet an American soldier.' It was with difficulty that I restrained myself from asking eagerly: 'Oh, whereabouts exactly?'

At the same time, of course, in terms of practical contact with the realities of war, Oxford was full of Jewish exiles who had been arriving from universities and elsewhere since the Thirties. There were academics, musicians – masses of musicians – and many others. Gina, for example, was a sweet, rather silent Czech girl who helped my mother in our house in some way. I realize now that she must have been Jewish, but the point was never made to us exactly why she was in Oxford in the first place; we just knew that Gina and people like her needed help and kindness, and that was extremely important in our parents' eyes and thus in ours. The true horrific details of the Holocaust were first broken to me by reading the *Daily Herald* at the time of the opening-up of the concentration camps in 1944. I shall never forget that moment.

But I also still recall the childish disbelief in which I first took refuge – this is too awful to be true. It was easier, far easier, to fling down the paper, do the washing-up (my turn) as hastily as possible, and bike off into the paradise of friendly roads and crescents in which we were lucky enough to live.

CHAPTER SEVEN

GIRLHOOD ENCOUNTERED

'**M**Y HEART ACHES AND A drowsy numbness pains/My sense, as though of hemlock I had drunk' . . . actually it's my head that aches and I only wish a beastly drowsy numbness would steal me altogether until the end of term. Is hemlock on Points?? Quoting from my beloved Keats in a letter home was not enough to solace me for my deep visceral unhappiness at my first boarding school.

I was well aware that it was all my own fault. When Mary Queen of Scots decided to escape from rebellious Scotland and seek refuge in neighbouring Protestant England instead of Catholic France, her advisers argued strongly against it. As she told a confidant during the long years of her captivity, 'but my best friends permitted me to have my own way'. This was certainly true of my parents, who would have much preferred Oxford High School on grounds of finance alone (the family was growing all the time and, let's face it, the three existing boys would need to be sent to boarding schools without the option that girls were considered to have). As I've described, the choice of Godolphin School, Salisbury was dictated by vanity or, to put it more charitably, competitiveness: I wanted to get a scholarship.

Then I arrived at the school with my trunk, after two or three changes of train, and found myself in St Margaret's House, Fowlers Road, under the tutelage of the housemistress, Miss Darroch. The trouble is that I was not really a girl at this point. Having always felt strongly that I was a girl during the four happy years that I was at the Dragon, I now encountered Girlhood as such and discovered that I did not fit in at all. I was like Kipling's Mowgli in *The Jungle Book,* the feral child who had been brought up by wolves and had difficutly adjusting to existence among human beings, despite awesome powers of hunting and tracking. I had been educated completely wrongly for the place in which I now found myself, my Latin and Greek, my hunting and tracking, being far in advance of girls who were my contemporaries, but in other ways I was far behind. As I would observe to a meeting of Old Dragon Women in 2008, ranging in age from early twenties to early eighties, the Dragon School equips you for life, but not for a girls' school in the mid Forties. Afterwards I found that there was a high proportion of agreement from the older members of my audience.

At the time, at just twelve years old, I was still comparatively small (I grew nearly three inches between the ages of thirteen and fourteen, according to my Progress Book). More importantly, I was emotionally quite unable to fit in with these girls in my house who were well on their way to being women. Godolphin compounded the problem by attempting to treat me as my real age within the house, while classing me in a form at school with much older people. The result, not surprisingly, was that I had no friends.

The humiliation of the weekly journey down the hill from St Margaret's to Salisbury Cathedral for a church service remains with me. We walked in a crocodile, two by two, and invitations to form part of a pair were subject to intricate social negotiation;

except that I never got any. I walked solemnly week after week with Matron, a sweet woman who was clearly embarrassed by this state of affairs. At least the Cathedral itself constituted a haven where I would pray for a partner the week following, in between eyeing the tombs and more fruitfully conjecturing about the history of the inhabitants. I suppose I was suffering from a form of depression which muttering poetry did something to alleviate: not only Keats and his hemlock, but those lines of Marvell haunted me:

> But at my back I always hear
> Time's wingèd chariot hurrying near;
> And yonder all before us lie
> Deserts of vast eternity.

(Although, given that Marvell was actually addressing his 'Coy Mistress' and urging on an immediate passionate coupling, they were singularly inappropriate.)

Of course there were other elements here, which it is much easier to appreciate with the perspective of distance than it was at the time. Part of the unhappiness was due to the inevitable break between junior and senior schools: I had been a queen bee at the Dragon, at least in my own estimation, and here I was a lowly worker bee. Part of it also sprang from my parents' inability to visit me. It is true that parental visiting (let alone children going home during term time) was on a completely different scale to modern practice; the difficulties of wartime travel, lack of petrol, absence of parents abroad, or in my case the domestic cares of a rapidly growing family, all contributed to this. Most parents probably lived closer to Salisbury than we did and found visiting a great deal more practical. The fact was that the wistful entries for future dates in my pocket diary – 'Mummy may come' – never seemed to be cancelled out with: 'Mummy did come.'

My relations who lived nearer were kind and supportive. There was a particularly happy episode when Julia and Robin Mount, my father's youngest sister and her handsome, raffish husband who had been an amateur jockey, came to take me out. Aunt Julia was lavish in her beauty, with a figure that Renoir would have painted; she had long, unconfined blonde hair, a miraculous pink-and-white complexion, and huge blue eyes, one with a slight cast in it which only added to the fascination. Both were very intelligent, but that appeared to be a source of pleasure to them, not a spur to ambition, as in North Oxford. It was, I realized later, typical of their exciting bohemian-Wiltshire lifestyle that the Mounts bought me a copy of *Middlemarch* at Beech's Bookshop in Salisbury (I'd never even heard of it) and they also pressed sherry upon me at lunch. Although North Oxford dons were legendarily supposed to offer twenty-four-hour sherry, this certainly did not apply to us at 8 Chad. I had never tasted the delicious sweet liquid. (I loved it.)

As the first of my parents' children to go to boarding school – in 1944 there were six of us – I now began to think of 8 Chad as some kind of Eden from which I had been expelled; and like Adam and Eve, I had contributed to my expulsion. It was ironic because I had never properly appreciated the hustle and bustle of family life when I was actually in the middle of it, tending to regard my younger brothers and sisters (other than Thomas who was A Fact of Life) as rumbustious nuisances who might interfere with the meaningful kitchen colloquies of me and my Dragon friends. One day, as I have said, I would define happiness as being alone in a room in a house full of people. I had already tasted the pleasure of being alone in my 8 Chad 'cell'; now I began to understand that the real paradise was being able to combine that personal solitude with lively surrounding activities (non-intrusive ones, perhaps).

So my letters pulsated with affectionate references to 'the Monstrous Regiment' – once I had come across John Knox's de-nunciatory phrase concerning female monarchs and was able to apply it to four-year-old Judith and three-year-old Rachel. I worried that Thomas, eleven months my junior and similarly with that awkward August birthday, would suffer the same problems of age vs learning as myself when he transferred school: 'I hope for Thomas' sake that he hasn't got a scholarship, it would be terrible for him to get one before he was thirteen.' And I asked tenderly after the latest exploit of Patrick, whose bright brown eyes were often alert with some kind of defiance of authority.

Boisterous – with a merry gleam in those brown eyes which went with the defiance – Paddy always represented a separate force. He was three and a half years younger than Thomas, and exactly the same distance from Judith, born in 1940. Our father adored him, a protective love as we understood later (but not then, as children don't) which may have sprung from a fellow feeling for a less-favoured second son – except that Paddy was actually as a result *more* favoured than Thomas, the eldest. Paddy was extremely handsome, the best-looking in the family, and a good athlete, which appealed to his father. I realize now that Frank had an honourable wish to protect this brilliant, ever popular young man from his own demons – Paddy was what would now be called bipolar, which in the end cut short a successful career at the Bar – but once again we did not understand, just as the traumas of Frank's own childhood were quite unknown to us.

Catherine Rose, my youngest sister, was born in February 1946: my pocket diary is ecstatic on the subject: 'BABY BORN

– Girl. Thank you dear darling God. I am one of seven!' This was a far cry from my previous naughty private jokes with Thomas after we read *Jude the Obscure*. We particularly liked the episode in which a strange child called Little Father Time decides that his family's woes are due to its size, eliminates two of his siblings and hangs himself, leaving behind the message: 'Done because we are too menny.' We enjoyed wailing those words to each other – in private. Now it was all anticipation of ecstasy: 'HOME! Breakfast at half past 8! *No row* if you are *late* (we HOPE) NO frowns from *women in gowns* (Poof!) No slimy girls with corkscrew curls (Oof) But HOME.' And so on and so on.

The fact was that life back home was beginning to be exciting in a new way, a political way. My mother had taken the heroic decision not to stand for Parliament in the next election, given that she would probably win Kings Norton, whereas the fate of Oxford, my father's putative constituency, was much more open to question. The consequence was that 8 Chad became a hotbed of political talk, while walking anywhere with Frank meant, in our opinion, that he greeted every single person he met with a friendly 'Good morning' and then the explanatory phrase we grew to dread: 'I'm Frank Pakenham, your Labour candidate . . .'

'Dada,' we cried in vain, 'everyone *knows* who you are!'

Still worse was the moment when one of us tried to explain: 'You see, Dada, you look *different* from everyone else.' Elizabeth was extremely cross at this, while for her part frequently rushing at her husband in an attempt to remedy his general eccentricity of dress. What we children said was true. With his height, his noble head with the dome increasingly visible through the decreasing rows of curls, his spectacles and, yes, his untidiness, Frank Pakenham must have been a conspicuous figure in North Oxford, long before his election posters went up. The best of the posters was headed: 'A Non-Stop Drive for Housing' and it showed Frank apparently driving a pony trap which contained as passengers the younger children and Elizabeth. It was admitted later that the pony had adopted a different attitude to the subject, and had in fact come to a firm stop at the traffic lights, refusing to proceed. But then fun with posters was part of the philosophy of an election.

Frank's opponent – the sitting MP – was his contemporary and old friend Quintin Hogg, who had won the seat in 1938 during that famous by-election in which the issue of appeasement was prominent, with Hogg backing Chamberlain and Sandie Lindsay standing against him. Then Quintin's posters were defaced as follows: 'A Vote for Hogg is a vote for Hitler.' In 1945, huge posters of Mr Churchill dominated the Conservative campaign throughout the country, the war leader being conceived to be the greatest Tory asset. In Oxford, wags occupied themselves scrawling across these posters: 'Love me, love my Hogg.'

For myself, aged twelve, it was quite possible to gaze at these vast portraits of their benevolent subject with affection and admiration, while passionately wanting Labour to win – like the majority of the electors, as it turned out. But there was a gentlemanly relationship between Quintin and Frank, emphasized by the fact that my parents asked him to tea at 8 Chad during the election period. After that, things did not go quite so well, since Paddy aged eight blithely refused to fetch a teacup for Quintin on the grounds that he was the enemy; general embarrassment prevailed until Quintin gallantly pretended that he would have done the same as a boy. Compared to this storm over a teacup, the rumour spread in Oxford that some of us six children had been adopted was rather more thrilling. Naturally I was privately inclined to toy with the idea of secret royal ancestry . . .

The actual timing of this General Election was peculiar. The war in Europe had ended in May 1945, but the war in the Far East continued. Labour nevertheless decided to end that wartime policy of coalition as a result of which there had not been an election for ten years. The Beveridge Report for example, that exciting War on Want on which my father had worked, had been published in 1942; yet its provisions had never been tested with the electorate. Under the circumstances everyone of all opinions was agreed on the importance of this particular election. At the same time, many of the armed forces, a vital part of the electorate, were serving abroad. A Labour poster of three servicemen actually bore the legend: *Help them finish their Job!* And the line underneath ran: *Give them houses and work! Vote Labour.* Yet it was by no means clear – how could it be? – how these three courageous war-weary figures would actually vote. The solution was found: Polling Day was to be on 5 July but the declaration of the poll would be held back until 26 July so that the votes of all the serving men and women abroad could be counted.

This three-week delay lent a kind of mystery to the whole process. For me at school, it was like following an exciting story in a newspaper serial, and having to wait on tenterhooks for the next episode. Not that I was in any doubt about the key result. Frank Pakenham would win the seat at Oxford – I knew that for sure. It was the shape of the results countrywide which were unknowable. In the case of Oxford, my joyful expectation sprang from the confidence of the party workers who in all our chats were certain, quite certain that their man would beat Quintin Hogg. This was the first instance I came across of the optimism which enables party workers to carry out their fairly thankless task with energy and humour. Nor do I exaggerate their point of view. An illuminated address had already been prepared and even framed, congratulating Frank on his electoral success, ready to be presented immediately after the announcement of the poll.

Frank always said that he enjoyed the campaign, although he admitted to being taken back when Sir William Beveridge, the man for whom he had worked, made a speech for the Liberals in Oxford. It was not personal: simply a mismanagement of the Liberal Beveridge's schedule by party bosses. They had always had a very friendly relationship and he was my brother Michael's godfather. But Frank was evidently not able to show the same insouciance as my first husband. Elizabeth, victim of a party schedule for a West Midlands tour which included Hugh's constituency of Stafford and Stone, found herself speaking out against him at the General Election in 1964. I was appalled. Hugh was mischievous: 'Don't you see the jokes I am now able to make? My mother-in-law has spoken out against me! Every married man will vote for me.'

Finally 26 July dawned. A landslide being unexpected, the total victory of Labour over the Conservatives was dazzling. In statistical terms, there was an eleven per cent swing to Labour, who won nearly four hundred seats to the Conservatives' just below two hundred. The Liberals hardly seemed to feature at all, with twelve seats where they had previously held twenty-one. The Communists had only two seats (which was satisfying to the type of Labour Party to which my parents belonged). The waiting period had only added to the deliciousness of the triumph, the first significant indication of the way Britain was to go after the war.

As for myself, I was actually spending the day in the various trains needed to convey me from Salisbury to Oxford. When I reached Oxford station, for once I did not deposit my school trunk there, leaving a carrier service to take it to 8 Chad days later, as was the standing instruction; I would then proceed on to my home by bus and on foot. No! Or as Eliza Doolittle put it so succinctly: 'Not bloody likely!' I would take a taxi, swirl round by the town hall, salute my father's victory which I knew would be signalled by a banner with details of the respective figures; then I would swirl on to 8 Chad, trusting to the atmosphere of rejoicing to gloss over this unparalleled extravagance. We reached the town hall. I bounced out of the taxi in order to get a better view of the result which would be hanging outside.

I can still remember the disbelief with which I looked at the figures:

HOGG 14,314

PAKENHAM 11,451

After that came the Liberal with just over five thousand votes.

My first thought, to be honest, was about the taxi. How on earth would I explain to my mother? Of course when I arrived, a taxi, unlawful or not, was the last thing on anybody's mind. The illuminated address from the local Labour Party, already prepared, seemed to sum it all up. The elaborate phrases of congratulatory enthusiasm over my father's performance – all these remained. Inserted after the event was this sad caveat: *'although success was elusive'*. It was to become a family catchphrase for any splendid effort which deserved to succeed – but didn't.

I can only imagine the very human disappointment my father must have felt at his failure at a time of general triumph and rejoicing all around him. I learnt from his autobiography that Frank did not actually know a single other candidate who lost. Hugh Gaitskell, Evan Durbin, that great cricketer Aidan Crawley – these his friends were to go forward in the splendid government which was to bring about a new and more perfect world. Frank was not. Soon afterwards, however, there came a suggestion as to a way he could after all partake in the experiment.

The arcane rules of the United Kingdom hereditary peerage – in an age before life peerages existed – came to his assistance. My father's elder brother Edward Longford and his wife Christine, now in their forties, had no children; as we shall see, this was no great sorrow to them, in their engrossing Irish lives. It did mean that when Edward died, Frank would succeed to the hereditary Irish English Longford title, as well as a lesser barony bringing with it a seat in the House of Lords. It was now suggested to Frank that he should accept a peerage of his own, in advance, so to speak, of the one inevitably coming his way which would scupper his House of Commons ambitions sooner or later. This was the theoretical situation which fifteen years later actually happened when Anthony Wedgwood Benn inherited his father's Stansgate title against his wishes – and succeeded by righteous energy in changing the law so that eventually he regained the Commons.

Labour was pitifully weak in the House of Lords – under the hereditary system how could it not be? Hereditary peers of Socialist inclination were always liable to be thin on the ground. Nevertheless a Labour government had to have its efficient representatives in the Upper House. When it came to creating new peers, newly elected Labour MPs were understandably reluctant to blight their political careers by going to the Upper House. But here was Frank Pakenham, young and active (he was forty in December 1945), one who had been a Labour Councillor and confirmed his credentials by fighting a seat at the General Election; as an heir to a peerage, he was destined for the Upper House sooner or later, so why not sooner, and direct his political career via a different route? Vitally, Frank would now be able to play an active part in the great Labour experiment which was about to begin.

In spite of these cogent arguments, I believe it must have been a struggle for my father to abandon his ambition to enter the superior arena which was the Lower House. In his autobiography, Frank shrugged it off, on the grounds that he was not the sort of sociable person who would have got on well in the Commons; but one must remember that he was writing in the early Fifties, at a time when he was establishing himself among the peers and would hardly have admitted publicly to a preference for the Commons. He made an amusing story out of his brief encounter with Mr Attlee, who merely asked him: 'Would you care to help us in the Lords?', to which Frank replied: 'Oh yes, yes, I'd help you anywhere.' The result was an appointment as a spokesman for government policy in the Lords, with the technical title of Lord-in-Waiting, the first of a sequence of positions in this Labour administration.

My mother, in her memoirs thirty years later, gives a different picture. She admits that she was sad to see Frank, her *alter ego* as she puts it, surrender the supreme ambition only achievable in the Commons. (It was Frank's friend Evan Durbin who pointed out that as a Roman Catholic he was in any case forbidden by law from becoming Prime Minister.) During the discussions, Elizabeth laughingly spiked the Bible with her finger, asking for divine guidance on the subject – a habit of hers which gently teased my father's predilection for Bible-reading. On this occasion, the Bible was in its most helpful form. My mother had hit on the opening verse of Psalm 122. She read out: 'I was glad when they said unto me, Let us go into the house of the Lord.' In view of the fact that Frank would subsequently enjoy over fifty-five years of active service in the house of the Lord, including four years as Leader, we must believe that the Bible got it absolutely right.

Back at Godolphin, my own anxiety focused on the first letter which would be addressed to: The Hon. Antonia Pakenham, this being the so-called courtesy title given by convention to a baron's daughter. I wanted my mother to write it out very large so that the exciting envelope would not be missed, as it lay on the chest in the hall of St Margaret's with the other house letters. The envelope with the weekly letter inside duly arrived. 'The Hon.' was writ large. Nobody commented. The letter continued to lie there, I continued to hope. I did not remove the letter until a girl asked me with genuine goodwill: 'Did you know that there's a letter for you on the hall chest which has been sitting there for ages?' She had nothing more to say. Then at last I slunk away with my letter in my hand. All the same, in the privacy of my cubicle in my dorm, I thought 'The Hon. Antonia Pakenham' looked pretty wonderful: a touch of Jane Austen there perhaps, the sort of person whose arrival in Bath might be keenly awaited.

My presence at Frank's official introduction to the Lords as Lord Pakenham of Cowley was rather more successful (I wanted him to be called Lord Bernhurst, which was so much prettier, but Labour Cowley had to be there). I wore my Godolphin school uniform, the most respectable form of dress that I could muster. This included a white shirt and an extremely bright red tie. As I sat in the gallery allowed to peers' unmarried daughters, casing the joint for a single man in possession of a good fortune who must be in need of – well, at least a dancing partner – an aged peer made slow progress into the House. When he saw me, he stopped. Then he leant in my direction. 'That is a very suitable tie for your father's daughter,' he pronounced. Given my father's strongly anti-Communist feelings, this was not precisely accurate. Nevertheless, thereafter I felt much more warmly towards the Godolphin uniform which had received favourable attention in the Upper House.

I was now thirteen and a half. I was unaware that there was another impending change in my home situation which would have repercussions on my school career. At Godolphin I was working towards my School Certificate in the summer and the deep unhappiness of the previous year had passed. My results in the exam were no more than adequate: the joy of working had temporarily deserted me, due perhaps to my melancholy.

For the future, it would prove important that I did have a passionate interest in genealogy which took me into historical byways without seeming to have much connection to the History I was learning. I tried making up imaginary family trees – the Lord of the North Wind married to the Princess of the Sunset with their twelve children etc. etc. – but actually found this much less exciting than tracking the Pakenham family tree, including our descent from King Charles II via a favourite mistress, Barbara Villiers, Duchess of Cleveland, and one of her sons, Henry FitzRoy, created Duke of Grafton. A Pakenham cousin had been a herald, as a result of which a large illuminated family tree hung up in our North Oxford house which I was inclined to study; it began with a certain Saxon Walter de Pakenham, found in Suffolk before the Norman Conquest. Walter did not really engage my interest quite as much as the words next to his name on the tree: 'Married to Lady Unknown'. I was definitely descended from Lady Unknown. Subsequently I brought home a book from the Godolphin school library on how to make genealogical tables, and quickly moved on from the Pakenhams to all the royal houses in Europe.

Privately I was industrious, but publicly not noticeably so. The results of my School Certificate might indeed have been better if I had not cut papers short in order to get back to reading *Gone with the Wind*, Scarlett O'Hara's troubles seeming more important at the time than Geography – or even school History. In terms of History, it was more important that a crush on Prince Rupert of the Rhine in Margaret Irwin's *The Stranger Prince* impelled me to commit a crime. I stole the frontispiece of the book, which I remember as a romantic portrait by Van Dyck, from the school library. I recall the incident with shame, but not exactly regret. Harold stole a copy of Beckett's novel *Murphy* from Hackney Public Library at about the same age. Apart from illustrating the difference in our mental development, he too felt no regret; as to shame, he pointed out that no one else had ever taken the book out . . .

At the same time, the childhood lure of historical fiction was gradually beginning to diminish in favour of the real thing – so much more interesting in the long run. After *The Stranger Prince* I never enjoyed another Margaret Irwin quite so much and soon abandoned reading historical fiction altogether. It is a taste which has never returned: somehow my attention wanders fatally in the first few pages as I begin to allow myself tiresome speculations about the actual facts which entirely miss the point of the whole colourful enterprise.

In contrast to Margaret Irwin who marvellously transmitted romance, a great deal of proper education continued to take place when I read 'real' History for myself during the holidays. Staying with Henrietta Lamb at our aunt Mary Clive's wartime cottage in Herefordshire was a particular pleasure because we enjoyed unfettered access to every kind of book that had ever caught her fancy – which was many; Mary, like her sister Pansy, Henrietta's mother, gave the impression of having done nothing all her life but read books. Thus I discovered for myself Marjorie Villiers' recently published *The Grand Whiggery* and conceived a lifelong passion for the Whigs, those racy aristocrats obsessed in equal measure with sex and politics. Finally, I managed to satisfy it sixty years later, with my book about the Great Reform Bill of 1832. Affectionately I traced the lineaments of Charles Grey, once the young lover of Georgiana, Duchess of Devonshire, in those of his older self, the heroic liberal reformer Lord Grey, who emerged as the hero of my book.

My parents' library was, generally speaking, more serious and less up to date. It was in this way that in a fit of teenage lethargy in the Oxford drawing room, too lazy to cross the room, I picked up the nearest book at hand, and it happened to be Gibbon's *Decline and Fall of the Roman Empire*. It was leather-bound and gold-tooled, a wedding present to my parents, but given the wartime restrictions on paper and printing, I read all the classics in this sort of unfriendly form. After a moment, the starchiness of the edition was quite forgotten. I was hooked.

At first it was the language: I struggled briefly with the magnificence of the style, and then allowed myself to be swept forward. As Winston Churchill, the most distinguished apostle of Gibbon's style, put it in *My Early Life*: 'I devoured Gibbon. I rode triumphantly through it from end to end and enjoyed it all.' My admiration for Gibbon's precepts for historians came later. 'Diligence and accuracy are the only merits which an historical writer may ascribe to himself,' he wrote, followed by the waspish reflection: 'If any merit, indeed, can be assumed from the performance of an indispensable duty.'

As a teenager, after the language, I was interested in Gibbon's attitude to hereditary monarchy, since royalties (and lords and ladies) were what currently took my fancy. He begins by dismissing it, in terms that would appeal to any modern republican, as something which it is impossible to describe 'without an indignant smile'. 'Of the various forms of government which have prevailed in the world, an hereditary monarchy seems to present the fairest scope for ridicule.' But he then proceeds to demolish to his own satisfaction all other possible sources of power, including the army, and above all: 'we shall cheerfully acquiesce in any expedient which deprives the multitude of the dangerous, and indeed the ideal, power of giving themselves a master.' So Gibbon triumphantly concludes: 'The superior prerogative of birth, when it has obtained the sanction of time and popular opinion, is the plainest and least invidious of all distinctions among mankind.'

This was all good stuff to one who was too young to take in the implications of the Abdication. I had spent the war conventionally admiring the exhausted-looking King George VI – no wonder, when he was never out of his naval uniform. Then there was the sweetly smiling, rather more flourishing Queen Elizabeth. What splendid people to refuse to evacuate the Little Princesses away from danger! In addition we were told that the Royal Family observed the rules of rationing with the greatest strictness. And who could resist the charm of the Queen, boasting of bomb damage to Buckingham Palace with the words: 'Now we can look the East End in the face.' Photographs of her daintily picking her way through the ruins left by the Blitz, her pastel dresses forever pristine amid the encompassing rubble, completed the picture.

By the end of the war attachment to the monarchy seemed wound round the concept of patriotism like ivy round an arch; pull it away and the stones might come loose. In August 1945 Thomas and I spent the night in London before catching the boat train to Holyhead. In this way we found ourselves in the crowds outside Buckingham Palace on VJ Night, whooping and cheering among soldiers and sailors of all nationalities, and that seemed a very good place to be.

Above *As You Like It* school play at
The Dragon, summer 1943. Front
row 5th from l.: Priscilla Hett, the
star who played Rosalind, myself
as Celia, which I was surprised
to discover was the lesser part,
Tim Raison as Oliver.

Right Myself aged nearly twelve
as Lady Macbeth, the peak of my
acting career; the thick auburn
plaits of my wig were all I had
ever wanted.

Frank as a don at Christ Church: he prided himself on his athleticism and is seen leading the pack round Christ Church Meadows.

Above Family holiday in the west of Ireland, 1947: Paddy, Thomas, Antonia and Judith on a Skellig Island, with another one visible in the distance.

Right On the beach near Bude, Cornwall, in characteristic pose.

Aged fifteen: the bookworm.

My 'nice, Catholic friends' at St Mary's Convent, Ascot, in 1948: l. to r.: Lucy Pollen, Jennifer Seward, Buffy Rowell, Cynthia Hume, Antonia.

My sixteenth birthday, 27 August 1948, which I spent as an 'exchange' with a French family near Bordeaux. Ungratefully, I wrote in my album that the grapes in this picture were the only nice thing about the visit.

Left My parents' active political life: Frank among German civilians after he was made Minister in charge of Germany in late 1946.

Below left and right The two portraits of my parents were those that I took to boarding school.

Right My mother on the hustings, wearing a red hat to show her Socialist allegiance; Frank looks rather abstracted behind her.

Pakenham Hall, Westmeath (now known as Tullynally, its original Irish name), photographed by Thomas.

A few years later the Royal Wedding of Princess Elizabeth to Philip Mountbatten provoked a similar reaction. (The Little Princess had grown up, and had in fact impressed us all by passing through a phase driving an army lorry in uniform.) My parents, due to Frank's government post, were actually given seats in the Abbey; they had already gone to St James's Palace to view the wedding presents. Here, among other gifts, tea cosies crocheted by members of the Women's Institute jostling with precious jewels, Elizabeth admired what she described as 'the costly present we sent: a fifty-shilling volume of seventeenth-century poetry, selected by Peter Quennell, with a preface by Edith Sitwell'. She added: 'we feel it will help to fill up one of the middle-brow guest rooms – until the new royal home is burnt down by Communists.' Elizabeth's original republicanism was definitely on the wane: 'I must say I begin to feel quite sloppy about Philip, with his film star face and fair hair,' she confided to me in her letter.

Meanwhile, on the wedding day itself, I positioned myself once again as on VJ Night among the crowds outside the palace and got myself ready for action. The moment came. The fairy-story carriage containing the bridal couple, on its way back from the Abbey, swept inside the great gates. We cheered – no, we roared. And then, instead of remaining passively in our places, we all rushed the gates themselves, so that they opened and some of the crowd – including me – got inside. It was a short-lived triumph; we were soon ejected. But we had been inside the sacred territory. When I told my mother about it later, I could see that she did not altogether believe me; indeed, I would not altogether believe myself, if I had not subsequently tracked down a report of the 1947 incident in the press at the time of another Royal Wedding in 2012. The thrilling, slightly dangerous emotion of being part of a crowd remains with me. That shout: 'Show us the dress!

We want to see the dress!' Was that me, or my companion Lucy, in our dowdy navy blue mackintoshes, or the powerful woman beside us with a strong Yorkshire accent in what looked like a decommissioned army greatcoat?

To such inchoate feelings, Gibbon gave an intellectual backing, even if it was rooted in the prejudices of the eighteenth century: his remarks about army rule remind us that when he was born in 1737, the Cromwellian era had ended less than eighty years previously. It was not that I hankered after a more absolutist monarchy; as the daughter of a Labour minister I was hardly likely to do that. But for the first time I found the whole concept of monarchy extremely interesting, quite apart from my addiction to reading about the lives of the more romantic members of the caste.

My parents, I noted, always attended with alacrity those events at Buckingham Palace that came the way of a government minister. This seemed to be true for the Labour government as a whole, anxious to declare their patriotism, including respect for the monarch, and rebut any possible connection to that rabid Communist Party further to the left. The mid 1940s were a time of acute austerity in England. The lack of pleasant food was not really made any better for us ungrateful children by the frequent admonition to eat up what was actually on our plates and 'Remember the starving children of Europe'. (Rebels were heard muttering: 'the starving children are welcome to this', and that didn't make it any better either.)

Restaurants were forbidden to serve more than a certain number of courses, bread on a side plate counting as one course. This restriction led to embarrassing incidents, as when Frank, who never noticed what he ate, innocently devoured a piece of bread on top of his meal. The waiter at the George, when taxed about this law-breaking, made things worse by saying airily: 'Oh, I thought Lord Pakenham would like preferential treatment.'

Buckingham Palace was perhaps the only place in the country where traditional grandeur was still maintained in the broad principles of the entertainment, even if the details were not yet fully restored. Where else would you need a long dress for a reception? Certainly not in North Oxford. Thus I accompanied my mother to that great Oxford emporium Elliston & Cavell to acquire a suitably sober yet elegant dress for the six months' pregnant wife of a government minister. A black crêpe number, with a glittering miasma of jet beads around it to distract attention from the lack of waist, was thought to strike the right note.

On her return, Elizabeth remarked crossly: 'Everyone else was wearing long white gloves.' But she cheered up with stories of how Edwina Mountbatten, wife of Lord Louis, had been among the Royals, and how Gerry, Duke of Wellington, had snorted: 'Curtseying to Edwina! Curtseying to Edwina!' The best story of course concerned Frank. Keen to demonstrate his loyalty, he became unconsciously affected by all the women curtseying to the Royal party as it entered. Instead of bowing respectfully like the men, this convert-Catholic enthusiast went much further. He genuflected very low and crossed himself. It is to be hoped that the Duke of Wellington didn't notice.

My mother, telling me the story, talked with that mixture of affection and exasperation with which she often used to describe Frank's exploits. Then there was not only her true love for him but also her basic powerful respect for his character, including his religious convictions. The time had come when she had to confront all this in terms of their marriage, the most important thing in her life. The decision she would reach led to a profound change in my own life. Already Frank's conversion to Catholicism in 1940 had reconciled certain aspects of his Anglo-Irish family history with his Faith. I was now experiencing, with Thomas, the complexities – and the pleasures – of Anglo-Irish life for myself.

CHAPTER EIGHT

ARE WE REALLY IRISH?

'ARE WE REALLY IRISH?' I asked the question of both my parents, determined to sort out the subject of British, Irish and English once and for all. Frank said 'Yes'. Elizabeth said 'No'. And there the subject rested in a nest of nebulous patriotic feelings, held towards both countries. Edmund Spenser once described Ireland at the end of the sixteenth century as being like an egg, aloof in the ocean, an image which haunted me when I worked on the life of Oliver Cromwell. The Ireland we knew however was in no way aloof. But just how was the egg joined to England? A further complication was to ensue after my marriage to Hugh, a Scotsman: we taught our children to describe themselves innocently as 'half English, half Scottish and half Irish' which, whatever the laws of mathematics, seemed to cover the situation perfectly.

In my childhood, the correct description was probably 'Anglo-Irish', a term which captured a particular society then. Certainly Ireland, the idea of it, permeated our Oxford lives long before I remember visiting it. We would for example receive shabby little boxes containing shamrocks sent from Dublin in time for St Patrick's Day; the plants, of which I was told I must be proud, drooped on my school blazer and I have a feeling they may have fallen off somewhere between 8 Chad and the Dragon. At the same time my father was aiming firmly at the British Parliament.

The duality continued: Frank supported Ireland at International Rugby the whole of his life including the period when he was a (British) government minister. It existed in a variety of different ways. As a child, I had always imagined that the Pakenham family, who originated in Suffolk, somehow wafted over the sea into Ireland – by popular request might be going a bit far, but along those lines. Later there was talk of an Elizabethan Pakenham who had gone over to Ireland with the Lord Deputy. It was not until I came to research my Cromwell biography seriously in 1970 that I encountered the truth. Prendergast's *The Cromwellian Settlement of Ireland* is invaluable because the actual documents concerned were destroyed during the Troubles. Major Henry Pakenham of Colonel Daniel Abbott's Dragoons acquired his property, then known as Tullynally, as a soldier in Cromwell's army. It was an uncomfortable moment.

Frank cast an interesting light on this tentative discomfort in conversations we held during the precious last year of his life. Although in his mid nineties, he was in full possession of all his faculties, except his sight, which had never been good since childhood; like many people with bad sight, he had an exceptionally acute memory. After writing a biography of Marie Antoinette, I had that sensation familiar to me from the moment when, against all advice, I followed the tragic heroine Mary Queen of Scots with Cromwell himself: now for something completely different. In this case, I fixed on the Battle of the Boyne, which I thought would enable me to explore the subject of Ireland with more detachment than had been possible with Cromwell. The project languished after a year, basically due to my lack of sympathy with both leading characters, William III and James II.

The Irish lessons on which I had optimistically embarked, hoping to have the promised conversations in that language with my friend Edna O'Brien, vanished without trace. What remained was the fascinating residue of my father's reminiscences when I questioned him about growing up as a member of the Protestant Ascendancy in Catholic Ireland.

'We always felt it was their country,' he told me. Frank then revealed with shame – or rather, after sixty years, with admirable humility – an incident from the period of his conversion to the Catholic Church. In London at the Jesuit Church in Farm Street, in Oxford at St Aloysius, Greyfriars in the Cowley Road or St Benet's in St Giles, the Mass was glorious. But the first time the practice of his religion necessitated going to the local Catholic church in Castlepollard on a Sunday, he felt a real pang of reluctance.

'You see, we had been brought up to think of it as the dirty church . . .'

At the same time, my father, whether as Frank Pakenham, a little boy, or Frank, Earl of Longford, a Labour minister, felt invincibly Irish. He was also absolutely clear on his views about the partition of Ireland into North and South. A passage in his autobiography published in 1953 sums it up: 'Irish Partition remains to be tackled: it is contrary to nature and totally wrong.' He went on to suggest that Partition would not be ended overnight – correctly enough – but pronounced it 'essentially one of the most soluble of the unsolved problems of the world'. Why then did Frank never show any sign of wishing to live in Ireland? It transpired later – I never knew about it at the time – that the childless Edward Longford did once raise the possibility of his younger brother, with his large family, taking over Pakenham Hall in Westmeath; nothing further happened and the project languished. Since Frank's love of Ireland extended to brief, flurried visits – two nights maximum

– before he rushed back to that British political world which he ardently enjoyed, it is difficult to believe he could have settled happily in a stately home on the edge of a lake in the middle of nowhere (by his standards).

By default, it became understood that if anyone succeeded it would be Thomas, as the eldest son, although he was not of course the eldest child – which happened to be me. The laws of primogeniture (actually male primogeniture) by which Thomas the male succeeded before Antonia the female were never explained to me. I simply grew up knowing them. Thomas used to tell a wicked story in which the butler at Pakenham Hall took us to a pub in Castlepollard, and then commanded: 'Step forward, the next Earl of Longford.' According to him, I then attempted to step forward, only to be elbowed aside in favour of the boy Thomas. Alas, no such pub visits ever took place. Because I grew up with the knowledge that I would not inherit, it was never a problem. (The winner-takes-all rule was probably more difficult to accept for the younger brothers of the heir who were in the line of succession, unlike us girls.)

The study of History makes it easy to understand why male primogeniture was a practical solution: in feudal times and earlier it was a fighter who was needed to lead the tribe in action. Goddesses did go into battle, but that was in the world of myth; although by and by I was fascinated to discover the reverence with which real-life warrior queens were treated, when out of curiosity I came to write a book on the subject from Boadicea to Mrs Thatcher. Nowadays the law is inevitably changing as the world changes; a man may be needed to wield a lance in battle but anyone can, as it were, wield a computer, regardless of sex. But it would be wrong not to observe, as a last word on the subject, that in the case of the Pakenham family, the antiquated law got it absolutely right. My brother Thomas, now known throughout the world as the Man of the Trees for his exciting celebrations of the leafy world, was well fitted – certainly much better fitted than I – for his role as a feudal lord, if his weapon was the camera, not the lance.

In fact I never expected to inherit anything: this was not in my romantic personal view of how life was to be lived. While of course life at the Dragon School, coming together with my mother's innately feminist feelings, meant that I never had any sense of female inferiority. I expected rather to be the beggar girl who caught the eye of the prince, rather than the princess; I had some sense that life that way would be more fun. Or perhaps the beggar girl (intensely beautiful) who, armed with a first-class degree, wrote bestselling books: there was never any limit to the ambitions of my imagination. As it was, nothing formal on the subject of Thomas's future was, as far as I know, ever communicated to us. Thomas and I were merely told that we would be going on visits to Ireland. We would be staying with Lord and Lady Dunsany (our late grandmother's sister) at Dunsany Castle in Meath, with sorties to Pakenham Hall to visit Edward and Christine Longford.

Anglo-Ireland is celebrated in literature as a nostalgic, slightly decrepit society, with the decrepitude of the characters echoed in their beautiful falling-down houses and ruined estates. This was the world of Aidan Higgins's wonderful novel, *Langrishe, Go Down* set in the Thirties (for which by coincidence Harold had written the screenplay before we met), or one of my favourite books, J. G. Farrell's *Troubles*, which takes place ten years earlier. Such picturesque melancholy was not at all our experience. Thomas and I on the contrary found our Ireland to be a paradise, a land flowing literally with milk and honey – or rather beef, butter and chocolates.

This was because we went regularly from severely rationed

Oxford to a country where there was not only no rationing but a natural lush fertility specially created to nourish the young and greedy. On arriving in Dublin by boat, with hours to spend before we took the bus to Dunshaughlin in Co. Meath (where we would be met by a pony cart), our first move was to head for the sweet shops and do all we could to empty them. At Dunsany there were four large meals a day, the tea alone encompassing more food than breakfast and lunch together at 8 Chad. At Pakenham Hall, it is enough to say that our uncle Edward was known, not without reason, as the Fattest Man in Ireland.

In another less materialistic way, Ireland in the Forties was also Paradise for us. Our hosts, the Dunsanys, embodied the two qualities most appreciated by the young. And they were complementary. Great-Uncle Eddie was deeply, gloriously, heroically eccentric. Great-Aunt Beatrice was the incarnation of kindness. Perhaps the young Beatrice Villiers had never been a beauty, but children are not interested in formal beauty. It was the charm of her soft face, still-black hair swept up into a small bun, and her high round cheekbones, like little apples, which beguiled us. She also had imaginative generosity of spirit – allowing me to investigate the contents of her large case of jewellery, for example, telling me the story of each item, why she had received this pearl necklace, that diamond brooch (although I do not remember her actually wearing any of them on her discreet printed summer dresses).

Beatrice presided in an unostentatious way over Dunsany Castle. This was a stalwart building, dating from the twelfth century, with four towers which implied armed defence in past years. The walls were massive and, as I remember it, covered in voracious ivy. At the time of our first visits, there was no electricity: only paraffin lamps, with the occasional small torch-light for reading in the drawing room. (Electricity was not installed there until 1946.) Getting up to bed through the shadows of the vast staircase aroused considerable apprehension, as may be imagined, in one still anxious to conceal her shameful fear of the dark; but of course it was exciting at the same time. There were many maids, by our standards, as well as a butler. My favourite was the lady's maid Bridget: in her sober uniform with a white cap, and her sad Irish beauty, black hair, white skin, she was like a character out of *Upstairs, Downstairs* before it was written. Gentle, quietly helpful Bridget – what did she make of my frightful wartime schoolgirl's wardrobe?

But really it would be right to take Great-Uncle Eddie first. He was the flamboyant one who caught the eye. For one thing, his towering height made him the natural centre of attention. He seemed to us to be seven foot tall, and was actually about six foot five. Now in his sixties, he was still handsome, with a finely shaped silver beard and regular features. Then he exuded energy, and with the energy came surprise – whatever would Dunsany do next? A plethora of stories were told about him within the family circle: one might call them tales of the unexpected. Walking round a lake with Eddie when they were a courting couple, did Beatrice really ask: 'I wonder how deep that lake is?' And did he really reply: 'Go in and see', suiting the push to the words? I found this one difficult to believe because his public behaviour to his wife was always so chivalrous; although it is true that her nickname for him of 'Pony' might have been profitably altered to 'Wild Horse'.

It was easier to credit the story of his behaviour during a game of Dumb Crambo, because it focused on surprise. Dunsany was asked by one side to enact the word 'shirt' for the other side to guess. This was his response. Going behind a screen, Dunsany proceeded to throw not only his shirt, but all his clothes over the top into the drawing room, one by one. Aunt Beatrice became visibly agitated. Finally, the last garment, one imagines of the most intimate sort, having been deposited publicly, Dunsany said in a sepulchral voice: 'And now I'm coming out.' There was general consternation followed by genteel panic.

'Pony, Pony, there are ladies present!' Beatrice began to squeak in real distress. 'No, Pony, no . . .' Before her husband stepped from behind the screen – fully dressed in a completely different set of clothes.

At the time when Thomas and I knew Great-Uncle Eddie, he was in his late sixties. His physical stamina seemed undiminished: he would be up at dawn to go duck-shooting and liked to tell the story of comparing notes with his gamekeeper Toomey. The latter, according to Dunsany, was an ardent Sinn Feiner. They would meet later in the morning and – once more according to Dunsany – the dialogue would go like this:

'I got two duck this morning, Toomey.'

'And I, my lord, got two trains.'

It is pleasant to record that in spite of this, or perhaps because of it, Toomey worked for Great-Uncle Eddie for forty years. Shooting was certainly a passion, sometimes a disconcerting one, as when a shot would ring out. Dunsany had seized a gun kept handy and potted a rabbit on the lawn from the first-floor window.

Not all Dunsany's pursuits were sporting in the outdoor sense. He was also celebrated as a chess player. The Cuban José Raúl Capablanca, world champion for six years in the Twenties, once played him. We were brought up on the fabled sentence which occurred at the end of the game: 'Capablanca resigns' (I believe it was actually a draw). The trouble was that, where chess was concerned, I just about knew the rules, although Thomas had a certain skill which I definitely didn't. It might have been better in both cases if we had been able to say that we were totally ignorant. For Dunsany, his mighty energies ever seeking diversion, would prowl about the enormous drawing room, looking for what would undoubtedly turn out to be a victim.

'Have a game?' These were the words we dreaded, not so much a question as a command. Then Dunsany would continue his prowling, while one of us sat down obediently at the board. After the first few moves, with his enormous hands dominating the board, he played blind, looking out of the window, possibly for vagabond rabbits (although I do not remember him actually shooting at them during a chess game: he always took chess seriously, even with us). We told him about our moves, at which point he would dictate his own, his fine head held aloft and distant. Of course he always won. All this meant that Thomas and I crept about the drawing room during the day for fear of 'Have a game?', as though it was a dragon's lair, with a chess-playing dragon inside it.

Great-Uncle Eddie had his other passions – and his phobias. Some of them were curiously modern. He felt strongly for example on the subject of white flour, and salt, which should be rock salt and not commercially processed. He did not hesitate to say so wherever he was. This made entertaining him at Bernhurst something of a trial for Elizabeth who, being uninterested in the topic, never remembered the passion from one visit to the next. Advertisements altogether aroused his ire. For that matter so did T. S. Eliot. Then there were dogs' tails, which should never be docked: Great-Uncle Eddie's dogs had magnificent feathery tails.

Dunsany violently disapproved of the Duchess of Windsor, going back to the days when she was married to her second husband, Ernest Simpson. This disapproval extended to the former Edward VIII. Of the Duke of Windsor he was fond of saying with a kind of grim pleasure: 'He used to be the Admiral of the King's Navy, and he gave it all up to be the third mate of an American destroyer.' Was there some anti-American feeling here? Or was it merely generational: Great-Uncle Eddie and Great-Aunt Beatrice being affected by the influx of American heiresses into English Society in general and the English peerage in particular. Beatrice, a most charitable woman, was in her turn fond of a story about an American, keen to emphasize her newly won place in the ranks of the aristocracy, who caught the tail-end of a conversation about *The Prince* by Machiavelli.

'Gee, that dear Prince!' the newcomer was supposed to have cried. (Beatrice's American accent was lamentable even to my ears.) 'Didn't I see him just yesterday at the races?'

Great-Uncle Eddie, apart from being a sportsman, had been a soldier, fighting in the South African War as a young man. No one could fault his courage: the comparatively elderly couple had only recently escaped from Greece, where they were caught, with Dunsany lecturing, at the beginning of the war. But his profession, if that is the right word, was actually that of a writer: he was a poet, a novelist and a playwright. He wrote in fact all the time, with a magnificent quill pen, and the sight of his huge splendid scrolling writing still moves me. There was for example a *jeu d'esprit*, 'Lines to Antonia', written to invite me to Dunsany:

Come when the hay has grown
And visit us, Antonia
When all the lilac's flown
But there is still begonia
Come when the midgets drone
(Better bring some ammonia)
And our new gramophone
Will play you a sinfonia.

This was actually printed in *Punch*, to my immense pride. As a tangible record of his affection, Great-Uncle Eddie gave me a paperweight of ruby-red glass; it still stands on my writing desk. 'See, how the sun makes it light up when you roll it down the bank of a river,' he said, suiting the action to the word so that I had to scramble to save the pyramid-shaped object from disappearing. (Perhaps that story about Aunt Beatrice and the lake was true after all.)

More seriously, a back staircase was plastered with the framed playbills of his many performed plays. Then there were the Jorkens stories; Jorkens, a retired big-game hunter, spends his time in the Billiards Club (billiards are not played) where he trades stories for whisky. My favourite, with its mad mixture of logic and fantasy, was when Jorkens saved the Gulf Stream for Britain by buying it from a man in a pub who happened to have it for sale. Dunsany's love of his spaniels was commemorated by *My Talks with Dean Spanley,* a marvellous novel in which an alcoholic clergyman is convinced he is the reincarnation of a dog called Wag. The Dean goes into reminiscent mood when he is supplied with sufficient Tokay at the Club: how his name was really Moon-chaser not the pathetic Wag, and how he carried out his elected task of keeping the earth safe from the moon by vigorous nightly barking. 'Ah, the moon,' says the Dean. 'Yes, he never came any nearer. But there's no saying what he'd have done if I hadn't been there.'

For me, however, Dunsany's greatest work was his novel about the political troubles of the fight for Irish independence, *The Curse of the Wise Woman.* The old woman concerned uses her magic powers to save the bog, the sacred bog which epitomizes Ireland, which is about to be ruined by outsiders with machinery for the sake of industrial production. But the action takes place within the carapace of another story which is not magic at all. It begins with a boy in a big Irish house, who is mysteriously instructed to keep his eyes fixed on a Dutch picture in the corner of the room if his father ever gives the order. The order comes. His father somehow vanishes through the bookcases of the library, while the boy gazes fixedly at the Dutch picture. And then four men arrive with the sinister greeting: 'There is no one we have a greater respect for than your father but it is a pity he mixed himself up with politics the way he did.' The boy gets the point immediately: 'Then I knew they had come to shoot my father.' The boy has seen the face of the leader of the assassins – but he chooses not to identify him and one day the potential killer will be leader of the country. He will also be grateful to the boy who stayed silent as he knew his father would have wished.

Not only the bog is there, the geese – the cry goes up 'the grey lags are coming' – and the flash of the snipe, but in a brilliant manner the intricate politics of the country: what F. E. Smith, my father's hero, called 'this island of incomparable beauty . . . so individual in its genius, so tenacious in love and hate, so captivating in its nobler moods.'

Every now and then, Thomas and I would be piled into a taxi to make the cross-country journey to Pakenham Hall in Westmeath. Here we found a very different couple as well as a very different castle. Taking the castle first, Pakenham gave no impression at all of armed defence, unlike Dunsany. It had been transformed in the age of Regency Gothic and now sprawled graciously across the head of a green valley, with views of mighty trees and peaceful cows in the distance. In the foreground just below the castle lay a kind of grassy platform, useful for what I came to think of as Irish tennis (interrupted only by real rain storms, not softly falling drizzle). The most remarkable room in the house was the library, an eighteenth-century gentleman's library, plus the Irish books that interested Edward and Christine.

Then there was the Great Hall, high and dark with a threatening family tree somewhere at the top of it that one could barely read, unlike that friendly herald's tree at home.

Edward Longford, when we first were aware of him, must have been in his early forties. But his extraordinary physical appearance made it difficult to attach any particular age to him. To my eyes, he always looked the same age during the fifteen-odd years I visited him: that is to say, immensely large, weighing something like thirty stone. At the same time, he was made of the most wonderful material, with rosy cheeks and a glowing air of wellbeing which made nonsense of the modern rules of health.

Nor did his enormous bulk appear to incapacitate him from anything he really wanted to do: Uncle Edward always had his own way. The footman once put the mountainous plate intended for the lord in front of me by mistake. As I sat, somewhat stunned, I saw Uncle Edward banging his empty mat in furious agitation like a huge child in a high chair deprived of his lawful bottle. For undoubtedly one answer to the question, why was Edward Longford so fat, was that he ate a vast amount of food lavishly provided by his loving wife. The adult bottle (of wine) was not actually of any importance, although one glorious episode demonstrated that he could drink with the best of them, if he was so minded.

In the Fifties, the known lack of drink at Pakenham once prompted my brother Thomas to take action on behalf of us Frasers who were planning to visit. Aware that Hugh liked his due ration of whisky and his wine at dinner, he helpfully prepared the way by saying (inaccurately): 'My brother-in-law is an alcoholic.' What no one at Pakenham knew was that our generous host in the South of Ireland, Andrew Devonshire, with equal consideration, had dispatched us on the train with a case of bottles for secret consumption in our bedroom. Drink flowed downstairs in a way I had never seen before. Drink also flowed upstairs. My main memory of the ensuing stay is of the zest Uncle Edward himself brought to consuming alcohol, draining whole bottles – 'It doesn't last, you know,' he said with authority – but unlike us, without any apparent ill effects.

Another example of Uncle Edward's surprising ability was his skill at billiards. Playing with us, he would deftly carry out a particular shot, with the billiard cue held behind his back in his plump, pink hands, and his enormous round stomach extending over the green baize of the table in a way that seemed to defy physical reality. Another passion was driving his car very fast, like Mr Toad, down the middle of the Irish roads: mercifully there were very few other cars on the road at the time. Edward was, like his siblings, a clever man who had learnt the Irish language, part of his support for the new independent Irish state, and translated poems from the language. (Eamon Longphort was his adopted Irish name.) He once took us to Fore Abbey, originally a Benedictine monastery near Lough Lene, and from a commanding position in the ruins, like some great abbot from the past, harangued his congregation of two in both Irish and Latin.

Christine Longford was a couple of years older than her husband; they had met as undergraduates at Oxford. Christine's mother Mrs Trew still lived in Oxford (occasionally tended to by my father in her later years), but Christine, like Edward, had made her life entirely Irish. Her appearance was in itself fascinating, apart from being in complete contrast to that of Edward. Her thick dark hair was cut rigidly across, straight without hint of a curl; she wore no make-up. All this was quite austere. But her smile, over the cigarette perpetually held in her hand, was somehow complicit in any pleasure. She once hissed at me, seeing that I had picked up *Memoirs of Hecate County,* a collection of novellas by Edmund Wilson, which happened to be lying in the drawing room: 'the sex one is on page . . .' I was embarrassed at the time, but not too embarrassed to remember the page number and race to it as soon as I was alone. (And yes, she was absolutely right, 'The Princess with the Golden Hair' was sex indeed: it was subsequently banned in the US.)

There was something of a brilliant monkey about Christine: a Chinese monkey perhaps, which a propensity for Chinese jackets, and Chinese artefacts to furnish Pakenham, encouraged one to perceive. The brilliance showed itself early when she wrote a novel, *Making Conversation,* while still at Oxford, and she continued to write plays and novels. She certainly encouraged the free, almost anarchic side of Edward, who appeared to prefer Chinese art to his ancestral belongings. In consequence, he disposed of various possessions, and in one legendary incident at least, Frank was the beneficiary. Uncle Bingo, bachelor younger brother of the late Lord Longford, was dining at his club. He gazed for a long time at a large piece of silver in the centre of the polished table. Then he said in a fond, reminiscent voice:'There used to be a piece just like that at Pakenham when I was a boy.'

'That *is* the piece that was at Pakenham when you were a boy,' replied the Club Secretary briskly. 'Your nephew Edward sold it to us.' Uncle Bingo was said to have been so put out that he proceeded to leave everything to the innocent Frank. (That part at least was true; it was a matter of regret that the bequest arrived in time for the collapse of the Stock Exchange and vanished almost as quickly as it had come.)

Edward and Christine, despite the Chinese imports, never struck me as particularly interested in their Westmeath surroundings. What excited them both was the Gate Theatre in Dublin, into which they poured their energies and a great deal of Edward's fortune; he became Chairman of the theatre in 1930. Years later, it always seemed to me wonderfully fitting that the

Pinter Festivals which Harold appreciated most in his long career took place at that very same Gate Theatre, under the management of Michael Colgan. Older members of the audience would tell me: 'Oh, I remember your uncle Lord Longford, holding out his begging bowl outside the steps of the theatre.' I loved the image: Uncle Edward shaking with laughter, all of him, which he did quite regularly, making some excellent jokes – and accosting playgoers to contribute in that accent which had become a sort of Irish all his own. At this point I was tempted to reply: 'And now it's my husband who's holding out his begging bowl – metaphorically speaking.'

Harold had toured Ireland as a young man with the celebrated actor-manager Anew McMaster, a formative experience described in his affectionate memoir *Mac*. Our earlier Irish experiences having taken place at roughly the same time but in very different circumstances, we united happily in enjoying the Gate Festivals. I even got to stay at the Shelbourne Hotel. In the Forties, had I not dreamt in vain of that entry in the social column of the *Irish Times*: 'Miss Antonia Pakenham has arrived at the Shelbourne'? Now I was there.

The whole family, not just the Irish twins, Thomas and myself, did have one holiday together in Ireland in the summer of 1947 around the time of my fifteenth birthday. Elizabeth was expecting her eighth child in November, which did not deter her from booking us into a hotel at Derrynane, near Waterville, in Co. Kerry on the coast in south-west Ireland. There the green grass went down to the sea, in a wide bay, with black-and-white cows munching right to the edge of the waves.

This was an exciting glimpse of another Ireland from the lakes, bogs and lush pastures of Meath and Westmeath, and the stately jolly lives we had led there, wandering idly down the paths, swimming in the lakes, when not stuffing ourselves with unrationed food handed over by butlers. For in the corner of the bay lay the house of Daniel O'Connell, the Irish politician known as the Liberator. For me, there is no more attractive character in Irish History than O'Connell. I only came to study him properly at the time when I was working on the Great Reform Bill of 1832, in which, newly enabled to sit in the British Parliament by the Act of Catholic Emancipation, he exerted vital influence. Nevertheless, the sense I acquired in 1947 of his personality, against the background of the Irish landscape, remained with me. (O'Connell was born at Carhen, about nine miles from the house at Derrynane.)

Reading his biography by Patrick Geoghegan, I found that O'Connell in his time had been fascinated by the juxtaposition of sea and land in Kerry: 'the mountain waves coming in from the illimitable ocean in majestic succession, expanding their gigantic force, and throwing up stupendous masses of foam, against the more gigantic and more stupendous mountain cliffs that fence . . . this my native spot'. It was while daydreaming of bygone Irish heroes to the sound of the sea that he was seized with what he called a 'high resolve': this was to 'leave my native land better after my death than I found her at my birth'. Perhaps it was the spirit of O'Connell brooding over the bay which influenced me, while at Derrynane, to feel really Irish. Even my mother altered her perspective, I noticed. A fellow guest at the hotel looked at our surname in the visitors' books and asked curiously: 'Are you the Irish ones?'

'Yes,' replied Elizabeth curtly.

It was however our visit to the Skelligs, two wild rocky islands off the coast of Kerry, which clinched the matter. These islands were famous for their seabirds: gannets and puffins abounded; in the waters around them were to be found seals, dolphins, whales and even basking sharks. Sitting looking out to sea on the Great Skellig (known as Skellig Michael) – next land mass America, we were told – I felt more Irish than I would ever feel again, with the solitary opportunistic exception of my visit to Paris to promote *Marie Antoinette: The Journey*. There I was enduring a certain amount of haughty criticism of a xenophobic nature: what is an English lady doing, writing a biography of our queen? Even though we greatly dislike her and regularly describe her as *la reine méchante*. Then I had an inspiration. What was all this about an English lady? Enough!

'*Moi, je suis Irlandaise,*' I pronounced firmly, in that accent my daughter Natasha described as just like the Queen's but not so good. '*Les* Wild Geese,' I added helpfully, referring to the Catholic Jacobite Irishmen who had been exiled and fought for France in the seventeenth century and later. The word *Irlandaise*, if not the somewhat extravagant comparison, did its work; henceforward I was a respected Irish lady, benefiting from France's warm feelings for historic Ireland. The duality had come to my rescue.

George Bernard Shaw visited Skellig Michael in 1910 and described the adventure afterwards to a friend: 'I tell you the thing does not belong to any world that you and I have lived and worked in: it is part of our dream world . . . I hardly feel real again yet!' This, I found, was an impression shared by Robert Macfarlane in a book about wildness written a hundred years later: 'It was a place for deep dreaming.' Certainly in 1947 I was happy at the Skelligs, including in my own dreams a handsome young lighthouse keeper. I did not have the courage to speak to him: there was a theory that the people of the Skelligs still spoke the original Irish and I was frightened of not understanding his reply, whether favourable or dismissive. Nevertheless he could not dismiss himself from the daydreaming I shared with Shaw and Robert Macfarlane, sitting there on the rocks and looking out towards the New World, from my own Old Irish World. Or was it really not my world at all but 'their country' as my father was to describe it to me later?

It was not a question to which I ever found the final answer. It is quite certain that writing a biography of Oliver Cromwell didn't help to solve the problem; perhaps it could hardly have been expected to do so. On the one hand, there was Cromwell's admirable admission of the Jews on his Protectoral nod, which King Charles II made legal. On the other hand there was Cromwell's notorious military campaign in Ireland in 1650 . . . Following his footsteps during the latter expedition, I went at the beginning of the Seventies with Hugh to Drogheda, site of the siege after which some of the worst of the legendary atrocities took place. To have the real experience, I wanted to find the reputed Cromwell's Mound. Despite diligent searching, we got more and more lost until I spotted a priest standing with two nuns beside a small black car. These were surely my friends. They would help me.

'Excuse me, Father,' I began, 'I am looking for Oliver Cromwell's Mound . . .' Before I could get any further, the priest crossed himself and pushed the nuns into the back of the car. Hugh came to my rescue.

'You really are an idiot,' he said. 'This is Ireland.' It is true that I had come hotfoot from Huntingdon where Cromwell had been born and East Anglia where he was the local hero. 'I know what to do.' And he took command of the situation.

'Good afternoon, Father,' he said unctuously. 'This is my wife, the daughter of the holy Lord Longford. You know Lord Longford: wonderful Catholic, Lord Longford. And my wife – another good Catholic – for reasons I can't quite explain, is going to write a biography of the wicked, tyrannous usurper, scourge of the Irish, Oliver Cromwell. So the direction of his Mound . . . ?'

'Thataway,' said the priest, pointing happily. So Frank Longford, the descendant of Major Henry Pakenham, but a 'good

Catholic', by his conversion validated another descendant who chose to research Oliver Cromwell.

I will end all this ambivalence suitably enough on the only anecdote about Cromwell I could discover in the Irish Folklore Society, which I had imagined wrongly would be a rich source of tales. Here it is. Question: Which is worse, Cromwell or the Drink? Answer: the Drink is worse than Cromwell, because everyone that Cromwell killed went to Heaven, and you can't say the same for those killed by the Drink. This I would describe admiringly as a thoroughly logical Irish story, a story from the country to which I hope at least half of me belongs.

CHAPTER NINE

NICE CATHOLIC FRIENDS

❧

'YOU SEE, ANTONIA, WE THOUGHT that you should have some nice Catholic friends.' It was with these words that my mother explained to me what she chose to describe as 'the sad news'. I was to leave Godolphin School in July 1946, and go to St Mary's Convent, Ascot, in the autumn.

I burst into tears. Elizabeth tried to comfort me. Whereupon I broke it to her that they were tears of delight, whereupon she was extremely surprised. With hindsight, I suppose her mistake was symptomatic of the distance which could then arise between parent and child at boarding school, before frequent visiting on both sides became the norm. At the time I was simply amazed that she did not know that I had always wanted to be a Catholic.

Of course going to a Catholic school did not necessarily mean I would convert to Catholicism. My mother explained to me carefully that I was to be allowed a choice. After all, I would be fourteen in August. Thomas at thirteen would also be allowed a choice. The other five would simply be transformed into Catholics from the theoretical Anglicans they had become at their splendid Oxford christenings. The event which was to bring all

155

this about had occurred in April: Elizabeth, six years after Frank's conversion, was received into the Catholic Church.

It will always remain a matter of puzzlement to me that this, the famously – and genuinely – happy marriage included such a long period of what one might describe as spiritual estrangement. Elizabeth, the Unitarian girl, had described the priests she saw in Grenoble, where she was sent to learn French, as 'black beetles' and joked that she had been terrified when a black beetle got on to a tram with her. Elizabeth, the Socialist woman who had abandoned Unitarianism and had no religion, was antagonized by the behaviour of the Catholic Church during the Spanish Civil War. Her idea of religion, she once told me, was singing 'Jerusalem' 'with linked hands and wearing rolled-up shirtsleeves'. (In my whole life I don't think I ever saw my mother with rolled-up shirtsleeves.) On the other hand, from 1940 onwards Frank regularly attended early morning Mass while we were at 8 Chad. He would return into the family kitchen to hear on at least one occasion a jovial cry from Elizabeth: 'Beat the Orange drum, children!' I was intrigued by the notion of this Orange drum, which I imagined to be singularly bright and beautiful like a huge fiery sun. It seemed a pity it was not actually provided for us to play on at the breakfast table.

At some point – my intermittent pocket diaries do not record the start of it all – I started to accompany my father from time to time to St Aloysius. This cannot have been without my mother's permission and was perhaps part of the thaw which reached its dramatic ending in 1946. At all events I loved it. I loved the Mass for all the obvious outward reasons which attract the impressionable to the Catholic Church: the incense, the bells, the sound of Latin, and above all the feeling of mystery. This was a mystery from which I was for the time being excluded. My diaries record: 'Dada went to Communion. I did not. I am not a Catholic.' When my Catholic friend Flora Carr-Saunders visited, I recorded again that she went up to Communion with my father but I did not. I became increasingly aware of this exclusion, and upset by it, so that I foolishly boasted to David, a boy at the Dragon who *was* a Catholic, that I had actually taken Communion with my father at St Aloysius. David told his mother: clearly the divided religion of the Pakenham family was of interest to fellow Catholics and this Communion was exciting news. In the small world of Oxford, the report of my behaviour came back to my mother. I assured her it wasn't true, full of shame at being caught out in the lie. I am sure she understood that the childish lie was the product of wishful thinking.

As a family in these pre-Catholic days, we did sometimes go to a service for the young at St Andrew's Anglican Church, in Linton Road. Here Thomas and I experienced what would now be called 'Happy Clappy'. The hyper-energetic vicar stirred up us children to sing lustily in chorus: 'I'm H-A-P-P-Y, I'm H-A-P-P-Y, I know I am, I'm sure I am, I'm H-A-P-P-Y.' What made us so jolly and so happy? Jesus of course. But this was more of a fun experience than a religious one. My first religious feelings were encouraged by Jean, the nanny. Except the word 'nanny' does nothing to convey the charm of Jean Birch, with her sweet face, soft pale skin, and the brown hair which all too soon would be swept up into a WRNS cap when she left to join the Senior Service. Her charm was felt by others: there was a choice of boyfriends for such an attractive girl in wartime Oxford, including undergraduates.

One in particular, a polite fellow called Roden, aroused the disapproval of our cook for being a gentleman, that is a class above Jean; Mrs Pope, beloved Popie of many years' service, announced: 'He should know better.'

'But, Popie, what about Jean? Shouldn't she know better?'

'Jean is trying to do well for herself. That's different.' Actually, even I could see that Jean, and no doubt Roden too, were simply trying to have a nice time in the fraught atmosphere of war.

No one for me could be above Jean. The day she left for the WRNS to do her duty for her country (as she explained) was the saddest day of my young life; we went immediately to Cornwall on holiday to bridge the gap. I was ten. All I did was gaze out to sea, muttering: 'Jean is gone', and write melancholy poems. Nevertheless Jean had already given me the inestimable gift of treating religious conviction as something joyous: not in the happy-clappy mode, but in the true mystical sense. The St Aloysius experience built upon this foundation and convinced me that I wanted, needed to be a Catholic.

Jean herself was more of an Anglo-Catholic, that is, a High Church Anglican, sharing many of the Catholic rituals and practices, but not a Roman Catholic who acknowledged the authority of the Pope. By coincidence, several years later my mother, Thomas and I had an Anglo-Catholic period; I believe this step was suggested to Elizabeth by the sympathetic Anglican Bishop Kenneth Kirk of Oxford, as a kind of testing-ground for future developments. What the Bishop, Regius Professor of Moral and Pastoral Theology, correctly understood about Elizabeth was that her marriage to Frank was the centre of her existence. She had to find a way to reconcile herself to his deeply held Faith.

In 1969, after the tragic death of my youngest sister Catherine in a motor accident at the age of twenty-three, I spent some of the first period of mourning alone with my mother; she talked intimately about the circumstances which led to her conversion, her unbearable feeling of separation from Frank, and how until this moment her Faith had all been in terms of her relationship to my father. But now: 'I'm glad I'm a Catholic.' I felt a tremendous sense of relief: that in circumstances that were so terrible, so utterly senseless to the outward eye, she could find any comfort.

Clearly Anglo-Catholicism aided Elizabeth to take the final step in 1946. Her actual instruction was performed by the Dominican priest Father Gervase Mathew at Blackfriars in St Giles, playing the role that the Jesuit Father Martin d'Arcy had played with my father. Gervase became a great family friend, together with his more worldly brother, Archbishop David Mathew. When he agreed to talk to me informally about the Catholic Church, out of kindness, I was both daunted and enchanted by his style: he would hiss out some abstract word connected to the Faith – as it were, 'Immaculate Conception'. Then Gervase would fall into complete silence for several minutes. I would venture to break the silence with an inane social remark, feeling the occasion demanded it – 'Elizabeth sends her love' – just as Gervase launched into a long, fast, sibilant disquisition on the Immaculate Conception and how it should never, ever be confused with the Virgin Birth . . . It became a test of my nerve. How long would he remain silent? How long would I manage to remain silent myself? For all this, I was devoted to Gervase, and curiously enough once we moved on to Byzantine History, his speciality, he was all instruction and no silence.

Priests, fascinating intellectual priests, played their part in my parents' lives. There remained the problem of the Catholic friends. No wonder my parents felt grateful for getting to know Harry and Catherine Walston: the latter was a Catholic and Harry became a minister in the first Wilson government, which in their circle was a comparatively rare combination. The mesmerizing Catherine Walston had wild brown curly hair, milky skin and blue eyes, together with a figure which was at the same time boyish, feminine and seductive. Like Frank and Elizabeth, the Walstons had a large family, but unlike my parents, a large country house. Here Catherine dazzled the eye (as she was already known to have dazzled the eye of Graham Greene), especially wearing jeans at the Mass celebrated in the drawing room. This was Catherine's speciality: to charm and outrage – just a little. For what was wrong with wearing jeans? One would not think twice about it now; it was simply that none of us had ever seen a pair before, except on some kind of American lumberjack (Catherine was actually American), and here was Catherine with her extremely shapely figure . . . What did the priest think, for example?

This general lack of Catholic friends reached its climax with the birth of Kevin in November 1947. We were accustomed to having numerous godparents, such was the custom, and poor Kevin, as the eighth child, could hardly be denied the same potential source of material gain. In the end my fifteen-year-old self had to be drafted in. My mother wrote to me frankly on the subject: 'I feel that in about five years time Dada and I will have hundreds of charming Catholic friends, all suitable to be godparents, but at present the numbers of the elect are limited.' It would just have to be me. The *Catholic Herald* actually featured me on the front page, wearing the obligatory hat loaned by Elizabeth and holding the protesting baby; underneath the photograph it read: LITTLE GODMOTHER. In my tweed suit I did not look particularly little. In spite of that, I was immensely proud.

Elizabeth's efforts at being a good Catholic mother had all her characteristic energy and resource. She encountered, for example, a particular problem with Guy Fawkes Day on the fifth of November. How could we, a nice Catholic family, burn the effigy of a Catholic conspirator with his pipe, in his black slouch hat and his ancient fit-for-the-bonfire trousers? Yet we must not be deprived of the national celebration. The solution: we burnt the effigy of the Communist Foreign Minister of Romania, one Ana

Pauker, a Cold War hate figure ... who oddly enough wore a black slouch hat and ancient trousers and smoked a pipe. Perhaps this episode is responsible for the fact that in later years I began a crusade to call November Fifth 'Bonfire Night'; we should celebrate Samhain, the Celtic feast when the autumn leaves were burnt and the dark of the year began, which stretches back into our history, instead of the original 1605 Anti-Catholic concept of Guy Fawkes Day.

The choice of St Mary's, Ascot was inspired by a friend from Frank's youth, Daphne Baring. A painter herself, she was now married to the sculptor Arthur Pollen with six children; as a couple they were delightful new friends for both my parents, Catholic, artistic and extremely cultured. Perhaps Antonia and Lucy Pollen, who were the same age, would bond together if Antonia went to St Mary's? Oddly enough, this did actually happen, unlike most such parental plans for their young; Lucy became my closest friend. But before that, before I could have this really nice (and clever and humorous) Catholic friend who looked like an angel in a Flemish picture, someone with whom one could discuss the finer points of Gary Cooper as well as Shakespeare, I had to encounter the whole mysterious world of Catholicism itself at close quarters.

As a matter of fact, I was secretly prepared for it. This was because Miss Lemarchand, a mistress at Godolphin, on hearing of my future fate, had pressed a novel into my hands, *Frost in May* by Antonia White, which had been published in the early Thirties, in order, as she put it, to warn me. As a warning it had exactly the opposite effect. I was tremendously excited. The plot concerned a Protestant girl, Fernanda, known as Nanda, who like me was sent to a Catholic school. (In her case, it was her intelligent, dominating father who was a recent convert.) The ending of the book is extremely painful, as Nanda is ejected from this mysterious, wonderful Paradise, and above all from her new friends, headed by the careless aristocrat Leonie, for reasons she barely understands.

In 1946 I put the ending from me – I still find it painful today on revisiting the book – but devoured the descriptions of the Catholic world of which I was hopefully to be a part; above all I would meet latter-day Leonies. What would they be like, these girls with their ancient names? What had their ancestors been up to? How had the ancient families managed to remain Catholic during the years of persecution? Many hadn't, as I learnt later, but had returned to the Faith in more settled times. Nevertheless there was a kind of delightful arrogance about these so-called old Catholics, epitomized for me by an incident in the House of Lords. My father, walking along a corridor with the Duke of Norfolk, the premier Catholic peer, fell to his knees and attempted to kiss the ring of the Cardinal Archbishop of Westminster who happened to be passing. Miles Norfolk made no such move.

'Bloody convert!' he exclaimed with great geniality.

When I first started to write crime novels in the late Seventies, I tried to recreate the experience of that first autumn at Ascot. In *Quiet as a Nun* I proposed that the woman who would go on to be the heroine of my series, Jemima Shore Investigator (actually a TV journalist, not a real detective) had been sent as a little Protestant day-girl to the next-door Convent of Blessed Eleanor for reasons of wartime convenience. She is called back to the convent to solve the mystery of the death of one of her schoolfriends, once Rosabelle Powerstock, for many years a nun known as Sister Miriam, who has died alone in a ruined tower in the convent grounds. There were no ruined towers at Ascot amid the well-kept rhododendrons and no mysterious deaths. Still less did a ghoulish figure known as the Black Nun go prowling round the convent at night (my nuns would have made short work of him, running after him with the shiny wooden rosaries pinned at their sides jangling, as they did when supervising hockey).

Jemima was glamorous, much admired, single by choice, no children, herself an only child, red-haired and willowy enough to wear a white trouser suit as her preferred costume. There were no parallels there. But I drew happily on my intense feelings en-countering Catholicism, Catholic nuns and Catholic girls – the ones who were to be my nice new friends. I also drew on the fact that both Jemima and I experienced all this in the autumn with the trees beginning to shed their leaves in the school drive with the onset of winter. But of course no leaf was allowed to sully the drive. 'The nuns must catch the leaves before they fall,' says Jemima's mother, as she delivers her nervous daughter for her first term; it was true enough of Ascot in the Forties, the immaculate condition of everything there presenting a strik-ing contrast to the hurly-burly of post-war living conditions in North Oxford.

The feast of All Saints on 1 November was my first experience of full-throated female celebration with its robust hymn:

For all the saints who from their labours rest
Who thee by faith before the world confessed
Thy name, O Jesus, be forever blessed . . .

It was in direct contrast to my other favourite musical moment: the singing of *Panis Angelicus* at Benediction when the women's voices were tender and exquisite.

I was enchanted by the two moments every day at twelve noon and six p.m. when the bell tolled for the Angelus: we all stopped whatever we were doing and prayed. I got used to the sight of a nun who had been busily strafing the corridor with a broom suddenly coming to a dead halt and bowing her head. I even liked the ritual of being called by a nun at 7.15 (for Mass) with the words *Benedicamus Domino* and having to reply *Deo Gratias*. It seemed a very civilized way of being woken up, if one had to be woken up. After that it was black veils with our uniforms for Low Mass, and white for Benediction and Feast Days. In fact I loved all the rituals, most of all perhaps the developing ritual of the year itself in the daily Mass, the Saints' Days and the great feasts (I am still inclined to date my letters that way – Feast of St Catherine for 25 November, St Lucy for 13 December, John Baptist for 24 June).

I gave a lyrical description in my letter home of the Feast of Corpus Christi in the summer term, marked by an elaborate procession of priests, crucifixes and banners. The school carried smaller 'bannerets': red for the Sacred Heart, blue for Our Lady, lilac for St Joseph and yellow for the Pope. They came in two shapes, known irreverently as 'nighties' or 'pyjamas' according to whether they were square or forked at the end; I noted that I carried a lilac nightie. This was an English summer. When the rain came pelting down, we girls were not deterred but simply continued 'with measured step and (mostly) solemn face' in the direction of the chapel. The priest, however, took a short cut out of the rain.

Unlike Jemima Shore, who remained an agnostic Protestant, I received instruction towards my conversion from the awe-inspiring headmistress 'Ig', actually Mother Ignatius IBVM (Institute of the Blessed Virgin Mary). For a time these letters got confused in my mind with other ever-present initials: AMDG for Ad Majorem Dei Gloriam, to the Greater Glory of God, which we were supposed to write at the top of our essays. The confusion was dealt with in teasing fashion by Mother Bridget, who received the essay in question – 'So you're actually already a nun?' But she also gave me the impression, however kindly, that this sort of thing was only to be expected from a Protestant.

Actually I was fast moving away from being a Protestant, in so far as I had ever been one, in practice as well as principle. I retained – and retain – a deep affection for the Church of England which finds expression in my love of Anglican (and Nonconformist) hymns, although many of those have since sneaked into the Catholic services. From my point of view, the instruction with Mother Ig went well and I enjoyed being presented with the intellectual arguments as a backing for my emotional determination to become a Catholic. Already doctrine interested me: I wrote back from Godolphin in my last term to report to my mother that the Infallibility of the Pope had been raised in the Divinity class; it was discussed 'in a rather supercilious Protestant tone – rather as if a person safely behind bars was wondering how a lion masticated his food. I kept my own mouth shut.' Now I was encouraged by Mother Ig to open my mouth and argue, even if Mother Ig, with great zest, always had the last word. She was particularly fond of the prophet Jeremiah, who seemed to her not the hectoring killjoy of popular imagination, but a lovable man in need of understanding (hers).

I also enjoyed the special attention, marking me out from anyone else in the school; this was responsible for my decision to be received in full grown-up fashion in front of all the girls in the chapel and furthermore to vanish before their eyes into the sacristy to make my first (Catholic) confession to the priest within. A less public alternative was offered for this confession but I rejected it. As it is, I cannot remember the sins I confessed; I do remember being determined that this would not be a speedy process; my sins in the eyes of the school must be long-drawn-out and worthy of the event.

This took place on a Saturday. The next day, Sunday 1

December, my longed-for First Communion took place. It was the Feast of the Forty English Martyrs, as I would discover later, foremost among them Blessed Edmund Campion (later canonized), the Elizabethan Jesuit who had been executed on this very day in 1581. This was a most appropriate date for one who would now become increasingly obsessed by English Catholic History.

The actual founder of the Order of the Institute of the Blessed Virgin Mary, an English Catholic woman called Mary Ward, had been a fanatic for female education, which had sadly dipped with the disappearance of the convents at the Reformation. Born in Yorkshire in 1585, Mary Ward came of a prominent recusant family: two of her uncles were involved in the Gunpowder Plot. Mary Ward first went abroad to join the Poor Clares at St Omer, where she later founded a boarding school for English girls. She also came back secretly to England with her female associates to support the recusants: together they became known as the *Apostolicae Viragines* or more light-heartedly the Galloping Girls. Mary Ward's real contribution at this date was her conviction (which has a very modern sound) that women, just like men, could do 'great things': in this respect there was no difference between them. As for the Catholic religion: 'It is not *veritas hominis*, verity of men, nor the verity of women, but *veritas Domini*' – the truth of God. She added, after citing the example of the female saints: 'And I hope in God it will be seen that women in time will do much.'

Studying the life of this remarkable woman for my book on woman's lot in seventeenth-century England, in the 1980s, I was gloomily unsurprised by the fact that Mary Ward and her new order ran into trouble with the Papacy. It was not until 1703, long after her own death, that the congregation received papal approval. Finally in 1951 Pope Pius XII described Mary Ward as the outstanding pioneer of the lay apostolate of women and beat-ified her. In any case, the tradition which she founded remained and I benefited from it: the Institute of the Blessed Virgin Mary put education first in a way that not all Catholic girls' schools appeared to do at the time. At Ascot in the Forties, nuns be-lieved that it was not only for the Greater Glory of God that we should go to Mass every morning, but also concentrate on our lessons, work hard for exams and see to it that our essays came in on time.

There was an explosion in my study of Catholic literature, or rather literature written by Catholics. G. K. Chesterton had been known to me in Oxford, more for the Father Brown detective stories than anything else. Now I explored it all, the paradoxes, the pleasures, with enthusiasm. Hilaire Belloc's *Cautionary Verses* had formed part of our nursery lore but not his histories. The rhymes were always a delight. There was Lord Lundy for example:

'But as it is! . . . My language fails!
Go out and govern New South Wales!'

We learnt with some pleasure that our father's generation had not been permitted to recite this one aloud, since their grandfather, Lord Jersey, actually *had* been sent out to govern New South Wales. Later the histories came to trouble me as a would-be historian when I studied Belloc's *James II* as back-ground to my biography of his brother Charles II; the Catholic partisanship was so blatant and yet so vigorous that I feared to be seduced even as I muttered with Whiggish disapproval. At the time I found Belloc's historical work in the convent library and gorged on it.

I also discovered a new favourite poet to replace Keats: this was Gerard Manley Hopkins. Learning the onomatopoeic lines became a spare-time hobby, although my favourite, suitably enough under my new circumstances, was 'Heaven-Haven: A nun takes the veil':

I have desired to go
Where springs not fail,
To fields where flies no sharp and sided hail
And a few lilies blow.

And I have asked to be
Where no storms come,
Where the green swell is in the havens dumb,
And out of the swing of the sea.

It still remains a refuge in times of stress. I even inserted a small picture of Gerard Manley Hopkins as a young man in my Missal, along with the other holy pictures. The collection of miniature holy pictures for this purpose was a practice which I much enjoyed; even if, as a Protestant convert, I was a late starter and it was a long time before I could emulate the Missals of my friends, stuffed with the memorial cards of their grandparents as well as pious portraits of the saints.

Not everything about Catholicism was quite so easily assimilated. My first Catholic Easter was spent at school. There was a retreat: three days of silence, four sermons and holy reading. I boasted to my parents in a letter of getting through eight lives of the Saints and Martyrs to one read by everyone else: St Antony of Padua (my patron saint), St Margaret of Scotland, St Frances of Rome and so on. But for all this, it was a matter of more concern among us girls whether Franz Werfel's *The Song of Bernadette*, which was such a great read, counted as being holy enough: I have an awful feeling that I put another book's ostentatiously holy cover over the original one, just to make sure.

All of this was exciting as well as exacting. It was when we came to the Good Friday litany, a long list of people we prayed for, that I was temporarily disconcerted. We prayed, we knelt, we rose. Then came the moment when we were asked to pray for 'the perfidious Jews'. We did pray, but we remained standing. I was deeply shocked, as much by the fact that we stayed on our feet as by the use of the word 'perfidious'.

'But I thought we were the perfidious ones?' I said in bewilderment. In a confused manner, I was alluding to everything I had recently learnt about the war, the camps and the Holocaust. Technically, of course, the Latin word *perfidus* can also mean without faith – the Jews being obviously without Faith in the Catholic sense. But the first meaning to English ears is undoubtedly 'treacherous': a message underlined by the ostentatious refusal to kneel. It is also significant that Pope John XXIII, that valiant man now rightly a saint, removed the word from the litany in 1959, four years after the gratuitous omission of kneeling was ended.

At the time, coming from Oxford, where there were so many Jewish refugees, as has been noted, all treated with sympathy and respect for the sufferings which had caused them to flee their native country, I simply did not understand this extraordinary apparent gap in the thinking of the wonderful Catholic Church. Nowadays I am aware that my heart still lights up whenever I read about the Catholic priests and nuns who chose to hide away the Jews in the countries where they were being tormented.

The winter of 1947 was famously hard, as though the weather was determined to underline the perilous economic situation of the country. It also lasted an extremely long time. My mother's letters in early March are full of accounts of taking two and a half hours to dig out the car from the snow one day, and then having to do it all over again the day following. There had been five hours of electricity switch-off, as she put it. Everything was frozen inside and out: not a drop of running water in 8 Chad. For a whole week heavy buckets had to be carried back and forth from next door. Then a slight thaw meant that an unwelcome torrent flowed down from the cloakroom ceiling and the cracked nursery radiator belched out a lake of stinking black liquid. The plumber only came two days later.

I prayed earnestly in the Ascot Chapel for St Jude, patron of Lost Causes, to come to the aid of the beleaguered household. But I rather preferred my mother in this vigorous, disaster-coping mode to the mother who wrote me impatient letters about my failings, as in the following: 'I found in your bedroom a perfectly good stocking without a single hole or darn in it but a ghastly rent right across the ankle behind the heel . . . not the first. Your dragging it on to your leg without the slightest care and simply tearing it in half must stop at once, otherwise . . .' She did not specify the reprisal but did sign herself 'Mummy Ogress', the nickname I had once given her. I continued to receive these letters and others like them without, so far as I can recollect, al-tering my conduct in any way.

Fortunately Elizabeth had the great distraction from both freeze and family of Frank's burgeoning political career. He was made Minister in Charge of Germany, under Ernest Bevin as Foreign Secretary, and paid his first visit in this same icy spring of 1947; in the next two years he would make twenty-five more visits. Conditions for the civilians there were appalling. But conditions had been of course appalling for millions of others, innocent people, throughout the war, to say nothing of the atrocities committed. It was a war which had ended less than two years earlier. Nevertheless I was deeply shocked when my father was execrated in the Beaverbrook press for announcing: 'I shall pray for the Germans night and morning.' (Didn't Dada pray for everyone night and morning, including Vicky the corgi, if he remembered?) From Frank Pakenham, it was an utterly natural comment, just as it was natural for him to learn enough German to read the New Testament. And as a matter of fact, the other feature of his arrival in Germany – his rash jump from the aeroplane, unaware that steps were on their way, leading to a heavily bleeding forehead in all the photographs – was equally in character.

What followed, his attempt to do something to help the German civilian population, was probably the most important episode of his life, before he dedicated himself to penal reform. I was reminded of it fifty years later: after my father's death I received out of the blue a letter from a German who had been a sixteen-year-old girl at the time; she wrote of her gratitude to the one man who had made her feel that Germans were not all, as she put it, lower than beasts.

Frank did not confine his interest in Germany to the interior of the country. He gave an order – one of the very few he personally gave concerning our education – that his elder children were to learn German. From my encounters with a German nun at Ascot, I now received something more than lessons on the importance of Heine and Goethe. For Mother Hilda, or *Mutter Hilde* as she had once been, burst into tears on my arrival in the tiny tucked-away room designated for our special lessons.

'I haf thought I vill nefer teach German again,' she sobbed. Mother Hilda was quite small and of a certain age (it was difficult to tell the age of the nuns with their black wimples covering their hair and bands across the tell-tale forehead). Although she had wisps of white hair showing delicately on her upper lip in an incipient moustache, there was no question of her looking any-thing but female, and a respectable female at that. Nevertheless instantly into my mind came the stories of parachutists mas-querading as nuns, which of course the credulous (like me and Thomas) were delighted to believe, which coupled with Mother Hilda's strong German accent might well have led to some un-pleasant experiences. I began to have a dim understanding of what it must have been like to be an alien in our country in the past war, even one manifestly dedicated to the service of God. As my correspondent expressed it to me fifty years later, not all Germans were lower than beasts; or to put it another way, not all Germans were Nazis. I had to step back from my conventional total condemnation, based on newspapers and films.

I was extremely happy during my two years at St Mary's, a fact borne out by my letters home, and not unconnected to an an-nouncement early on: 'This school is COMPETITIVE I'll have you know, you were wrong about that.' Clearly, for all the need for nice Catholic friends, my mother had felt worried – wrongly – about the level of education in a convent. But the major happiness was created by the discovery of a History teacher who felt as I did about the subject, if possible more passionately. This was Mother Mercedes, IBVM. It was at this point that History stopped being a private matter of enjoyment and became an academic subject – an enthralling academic subject.

Mother Mercedes was Irish and her sister, Mother Perpetua, was also a nun at Ascot. The official history of the school referred to her as having 'blown in from Ireland'; in fact, although born in a little village in Co. Wicklow, she had attended Royal Holloway College to study Latin, Maths and History. But the real point about 'the Merc' was nothing that training alone could give her: she was a teacher of genius and furthermore a teacher with a love of History that matched my own – except that she knew far more about it and in a far more disciplined fashion. She had her favourites – what sympathetic person doesn't? – in the sense of historical favourites: the Empress Maria Theresa was one of them. The Austrian co-monarch had only previously registered with me as the mother of my beloved Marie Antoinette; now I thrilled to the details of her reign, a woman with an enormous family of sixteen children who ruled over vast areas of Europe (we treated the Emperor Francis as a token figure) and was a devout Catholic. It was a tribute to Mother Mercedes that I took the names of Antonia Maria Teresa – I preferred the Latin spelling – at my Catholic Confirmation, finding Maria Teresa infinitely preferable to the dull old Margaret Caroline of my Protestant Baptism. Many years later I discovered that Maria Theresa had been a formidably bossy and disapproving mother to poor Marie Antoinette, blaming the ignorant fourteen-year-old girl, dispatched alone to the French Court, for her fifteen-year-old husband's prolonged failure to consummate the marriage. But as I delineated the relationship as accurately as I could, I sensed the ghost of the Merc standing at my shoulder, emanating reproach from beyond the grave: 'But, Antonia, you know perfectly well that Her Imperial Majesty the Empress Maria Theresa . . .' In life, there was always a special relish with which she pronounced those words.

It would be wrong to suggest that Mother Mercedes, for all her enthusiasm for certain subjects, did not pay attention to historical method. By a piece of good fortune, I happened to read Lytton Strachey's *Eminent Victorians* in the holidays, attracted, to be honest, by the fact that it was on the special shelf at the bottom of the bookcase in the chilly spare room which was never used. I think my mother thought this was a safe place to store books such as Marie Stopes's *Married Love*, not realizing that I would immediately home in on any book with such a promising title. Strachey had been placed there in the first flush of my mother's cultural Catholicism, given his criticisms of the Church; although this severe attitude did not last, for a time she even hid – thought she hid – the book proof of a new novel by the Pakenhams' old Oxford friend Evelyn Waugh called *Brideshead Revisited* in what she believed to be the same safe place. Elizabeth told me later rather touchingly: 'I was frightened that it would put you off Catholicism.' Now I seized the Strachey book, hoping for further revelations: my goodness, what had those naughty Victorians been up to?

I did receive a revelation, although it was not the one I expected. Thanks to Strachey, I entered the world of Florence Nightingale, Thomas Arnold, General Gordon and above all Cardinal Manning. More than that, I realized that writing History was an art in itself as opposed to the bald relation of facts as in my childhood efforts about my various heroines. In short, it could be entertainment as well as enlightenment. There is an irony here: when I read Michael Holroyd's biography of Strachey twenty years later, I learnt that on occasion Strachey had what may be termed an artistic attitude to historical truth. Many of the most vivid touches were in fact the product of his vivid imagination rather than actual research. It was a historian of a different ilk, Hugh Trevor-Roper, who pointed out that General Gordon retired into his tent not with a Bible and a bottle but a Bible and a prayer book. 'Unfortunately,' wrote Trevor-Roper, '"brandy-bottle" is funnier than "prayer-book".'

At the time, I returned to Ascot on fire to talk to Mother Mercedes about the essay on Cardinal Manning (in which the saintly Cardinal Newman was my favourite character). Immediately she directed me to the library where Edmund Purcell's nineteenth-century biography of the rather less saintly Manning languished. It was in fact exactly the kind of book which Strachey, writing in 1918, avowedly wrote to replace: 'Those two fat volumes, with which it is our custom to commemorate the dead – who does not know them, with their ill-digested masses of material, their slipshod style, their tone of tedious panegyric . . .' But I was not to know that. Instead, encouraged by the Merc, I set about comparing the two accounts of the same life, and while at this enjoyable task had some glimmering of what the historical method might be.

As my childish enthusiasm for History developed into something more substantial, I began to feel possessive about it: *my* History once again as I had first felt reading *Our Island Story*. In this way, I devoted intense energy to the project of winning the School History Prize. Some of this energy was spent in the chapel praying, in the course of which I mentioned more than once that, if I won, I would devote my life to History. My subject was of course: 'The Empress Maria Theresa'. Came the great day of the announcement I was trembling with excitement, fear, apprehension, all those things, as Mother Ig mounted the platform in the concert hall in her black garb with her clicking rosary at her side. Beneath the wimple, her thin down-turned lips were set. She smiled: her smile was sweet. Then she addressed us:

'I have to tell you with much pleasure that the History Prize has been won by Antonia Pakenham.' I thought I was going to faint with joy. Then she added: 'I also have to tell you that no one else went in for the History Prize.'

It was a sharp lesson in undue self-esteem as I have no doubt it was intended to be. Now that I was safely a Catholic, Mother Ig had plenty of criticisms of me. One effort to improve my humility could be said to have backfired because it actually resulted in my acquiring what was probably the most useful accomplishment of my entire education. It happened like this. At one point we had to declare our hopes for the future; in other circumstances it might have been called a career meeting. There were modest indications in the direction of marriage and motherhood; even one or two suggestions of a religious vocation (one of my closest friends subsequently became a nun). In spite of my addiction to Hopkins's poem on the nun taking the veil, I personally had no such ambitions. Instead, I saw my chance to create a sensation.

'I want to be a journalist.' Pause for effect. 'On the *Daily Express*.' I should add that the Beaverbrook press was actually banned at Ascot, for reasons I never discovered, so that my public declaration was a deliberate challenge. Mother Ig smiled that sweet smile. She bided her time. A few days later she made an announcement.

'Saturday morning is as you all know a free period. Except for Antonia. She is going to be a journalist on the *Daily Express*. So she will spend Saturday morning learning how to type in the gym, with the benefit of postal lessons supervised by Mother Hilary.' So there I sat, with a kind of iron band masking the keys of the typewriter, beneath which my sightless fingers had to plot their own course. So I learnt to touch-type, touch-type very fast. Mutinous I may have been at the time; I should have felt intensely grateful.

Mother Ig made one other prominent intervention in my life. Senior girls – as I undoubtedly was by right of academic achievement, the early Dragon School boost still working in my favour – were generally made Children of Mary. This meant a broad, pretty pale blue ribbon across the chest with a medal dangling from it. The qualities required were not quite clear but presumed to include piety and general good behaviour. One day Ig sent for me and broke it to me that I had been disbarred from election to the society, not by the nuns, but by my contemporaries: 'They say you are a law unto yourself.'

For a moment I was flushed with pride: a law unto myself! Just what I had always wanted to be. Then the humiliation flooded me. To sit in the front row of the school, the only one without that broad pretty pale blue ribbon . . . But Mother Ig had not finished.

She became brisk. 'Reverend Mother and I have decided that it is unseemly for the head of the school *in work*' – she emphasized the words – 'not to be a Child of Mary. So you will in due course become one.' That smile again as she added: 'But do remember how it came about. A lesson there perhaps for such a clever girl as you?'

CHAPTER TEN

GAP YEAR OR TWO

ELIZABETH STOOD, LOOKING rather warily at my school trunk which had recently been trundled back from St Mary's.

'Won't you need your eiderdown and your sheets at school next term?' she asked after a pause.

'No. Because I've left,' I replied.

'So what will you do?'

'I don't know. I'll think of something.' It was late July 1948: I would be sixteen at the end of August. I felt full of confidence that a glorious future awaited me: I would be a secretary (with my great Ascot-induced typing skills), earn some money and go to parties in the evening. University was very far from my thoughts although intuitively I must have realized that my mother, an undergraduate herself in the Twenties and a strong advocate of female education, would sooner or later point me in that direction. In short I was taking a gap year – or as it turned out, given my youthful age, two.

As for my mother, she had been given some warning of my intention to leave after taking Higher Certificate (the rough equivalent of A level) on the grounds that work-wise, there was nowhere else for me to go since I had reached the top of the school. But with two children under three (to say nothing of the other five) and her own continuing political ambitions, she had other preoccupations. This was after my mother organized that flight from Oxford to Hampstead Garden Suburb, which was animated by resentment at my father leading the life of a Labour minister in London all week, while she languished in 8 Chad. 'Alas, my good friend Oxford, farewell for ever!' I wrote sententiously (and as it happens inaccurately) in my diary.

Now came the first setback. From the start I hated 10 Linnell Drive. It was large – my new room was a decent size – there was a pleasant garden with a view of the Heath Extension and a back door which led out on to it; there was even a tennis court. So what was there to hate? Hampstead Garden Suburb had been planned by Raymond Unwin, with the collaboration of Sir Edwin Lutyens: the gracious low-built houses celebrated the style known as Neo-Georgian. There were to be no pubs, no fences only hedges, ample squares, churches by Lutyens but no church bells disrupting the peace. I did not, could not, hate any of this and had in any case no interest in pubs.

The answer to my dislike lay in the fact that there was no public transport: the Golders Green underground lay twenty minutes' walk away. Furthermore London taxis were allowed to refuse to take a fare there, because it was outside the six-mile limit. Arriving in London with huge excitement, I discovered that I was already a social failure, someone who probably would not be taken home by even the most chivalrous of escorts – and he would have to be remarkably rich to contemplate it in the first place. In short, I felt an outsider. I lived in NW11 (now, incidentally, one of the most expensive residential areas in London). When I learnt that Evelyn Waugh, living as a young man in North End Road, NW11, had walked into Hampstead proper to post his letters to secure the more elegant postcode of NW3, I thought it a perfectly sensible decision.

The problem of my occupation was the next one I faced. There was no such concept as a gap year at the time, although it has now become a familiar term and generally includes exotic foreign adventure for those privileged to have it. That was certainly not an option then. Foreign travel as such, rambling round Europe, Asia or South America with a friend, simply did not exist. Money allowed to be taken abroad was limited to fifty pounds, which in any case was beyond the means of many families. But there was a possibility of a foreign exchange, which did not imply a currency deal, rather the exchange of two young people, roughly the same age, different nationalities, who would live alternately in each other's homes. The experience was often preceded by a lengthy correspondence, postal of course, between the pair in question. The intention was to promote international love and friendship. This enterprise was not always totally successful.

As a matter of fact, I got off quite lightly during the month I spent with a French family in the south-west of France near Bordeaux. There were horror stories: mine was not one of them. It is true that the young people, led by my supposed 'friend' Jacqueline, despised me, despised everything about me, beginning with my clothes. They were right. My clothes were, with one exception, despicable. The exception was an enormous pale turquoise coat, magnificent collar on a Napoleonic scale, which extended almost to the ground. The so-called New Look of Christian Dior had swept France the previous year: in England the yards of material needed to make these swirling skirts were, in an age of continuing clothes-rationing, regularly denounced in the press. But of course everyone desired the New Look. Lucy and I had managed to save enough coupons to acquire one coat each, hers being lichen-green to my turquoise. If these coats looked rather odd contrasted with our plain short skirts and workaday jumpers, it did not bother us. We were confident that we were in the height of fashion.

The French teenagers did not agree. While they did pluck at the turquoise material with Gallic grunts of approval (although such a coat must have been a ludicrous sight in the south in August), they made it quite clear that the rest of my wardrobe was beyond the pale sartorially. They did not seem to care about anything else; or if they did, excluded from their whispered conclaves in French, I had no idea what it was. When I pasted a photograph of myself at the château into my album, about to devour a bunch of grapes which I had suspended above my mouth, the caption beneath read: 'The grapes were the only nice thing about the visit.' There were however two people I found in different ways sympathetic. One was Mathieu, a handsome young man who was supposed to be picking these grapes for the harvest; except that whenever possible he lay down on his back amid the rows of vines, gazed at the sky and appeared to go into a dream until interrupted. The family went into an understandable state of rage at his idleness, but I enjoyed our halting conversations; I was just beginning to watch French films and in my imagination Mathieu amid the vines made a good romantic character.

It was the other sympathetic person who made the whole experience memorable long after I had returned thankfully to England. There was an aged grandfather-figure, generally dressed in the clothes I expected senior Frenchmen to wear from films, including a black beret. Always addressing me as 'mademoiselle', he paid elaborate heed to me, launching into political monologues about England, France, De Gaulle, Churchill and above all the course of the recent war. Gradually I became aware that he must have been a member of the Resistance, and perhaps was not so very old after all. All this reached its climax at my sixteenth birthday celebration on 27 August, which was towards the end of my stay.

There were speeches. Even Mathieu was allowed to rise up from among the vines, although on this occasion he did not speak. Grandpère made up for it. He made an extremely long speech, flowery, rhetorical, grandiloquently polite not only about myself but also about the wartime relationship between our two countries. Then the Resistance seemed to come into it; with my limited French I had the impression that I was forgotten as old issues were being raised, old scores settled . . . There were discontented mutterings from the other older men present, and undoubtedly some of them were disputing what he said, with frequent and furious flourishes of their hands. It was all made worthwhile for me, however, by Grandpère's magnificent conclusion.

Despite all evidence to the contrary, he saluted me as one who had brought peace to the château by my mere presence. 'Just as our English allies did for us during the war,' he added meaningfully, throwing in something in which I could distinguish the word Vichy. There were increasingly angry looks from the unwilling audience of this paean of praise which concluded: 'You, mademoiselle, are coming among us like the goddess Irène, the goddess of peace.' As the sixteen-year-old goddess cast her eyes down, modestly yet peacefully, Grandpère burst into tears and had to be escorted sobbing out of the room. After that, I wish I could report that we gave Jacqueline a really agreeable time when she in turn came to England. Alas, the weather was morbidly wet and cold. Jacqueline retired to her bed and stayed there.

The sense that my Bordeaux visit gave me of an internal

French war not yet finished was a useful historical experience. Up to this point I had imagined that peace in Europe simply meant peace. Everyone loved the Resistance and of course everyone loved the English who came to the rescue of France, won the war for them actually (with a little help from the lovable Resistance). I had no previous conception of the strains that occupation might leave behind. My next experience of foreign travel was very different and infinitely happier; but in one sense it was also a historical experience. I owed it to my father's position in the government and it should therefore be firmly added to the credit account of his political career so far as I was concerned, given that at this age I was liable to grumble tiresomely about the disadvantages of being a Labour minister's daughter, in contrast to the more conventionally social families of my friends.

Alcide De Gasperi, the Prime Minister of Italy and his wife, Signora Francesca, decided that the family would invite from England the daughter of a Catholic Labour minister to spend Christmas 1950 with them. The important element in this was the Catholicism: both De Gasperis were devout Catholics, and in fact lived in a modest flat in Rome very close to St Peter's. Signora De Gasperi certainly went to daily Mass, and probably the Prime Minister as well. Alcide De Gasperi was at this point nearly eighty, and had been the Christian Democrat Prime Minister of Italy since December 1945. With his dignified spare Nordic appearance, Signor De Gasperi was very different from the conventional British picture of a loquacious dark roly-poly Italian (he had been born in the Tyrol when it was part of Austria-Hungary). He certainly did not look his age. Nor did he appear in any way diminished by some of the ordeals he had endured during a long life, including time in prison at the hands of the Fascists, before he became the wartime founder of the (then illegal) Christian Democratic Party. Subsequently he was its first Prime Minister.

Here was a strongly religious man who was at the same time a convinced and ardent politician, standing for social security reform; as well as being demonstrably anti-Fascist he stood out against Communism in the context of the Cold War. I was deeply impressed by him on this level, but also by his gentleness towards ignorant people like myself. He was not without a sly sense of humour, cracking the odd joke about England's Labour government which, once we had found some shared language, was quite sharp and to the point. In writing about politicians later, especially in my book on the Great Reform Bill, I used to reflect on that mixture of idealism and ambition common to the breed to which I had already been alerted by my parents. My mind sometimes went back to that Christmas in Italy and the supreme example set by Alcide De Gasperi.

Signora De Gasperi ran everything in the house and seemed to do all the cooking as well. This was not entirely good news. She had her own ideas on how things should be, which included the fact that English girls needed to eat large lumps of meat daily otherwise they would become restive (like sporting dogs, I suppose). So I was condemned to these large and I have to say tasteless lumps while the rest of the family gorged on heavenly spaghetti . . . Signora De Gasperi's moment of supreme control came at New Year. We travelled down to the south in a special train, with the people standing by to cheer their Prime Minister as we passed. We disembarked with Vesuvius in sight. The welcome was tumultuous. We were shown everything, including the great exhibition of the remains of Pompeii; well, not quite everything. At the behest of Signora De Gasperi, the famously rude sections (unsuitable for modest teenagers) were shrouded off from us. Privilege obviously had its disadvantages, at least in

a Catholic country; it was not until a twenty-first-century exhibition of Pompeian remains in the British Museum that I was able
to see at last those sights which Signora De Gasperi had denied a
nice Catholic Socialist girl.

On my return from France in September 1948, the problem
of what I was going to do next became more acute. (It was felt
that I was as yet too young to embark on job-seeking.) Luckily
my best friend Lucy had also left Ascot. We attempted a session
at the French Lycée in South Kensington. This had the advantage – for me – of being near her parents' stately calm house in
Onslow Square, where Arthur Pollen also had his studio. It was
my aim to get inside this house and stay there as long as possible.
When I managed to be present at the daily family lunch, my
favourite moment was the emergence of 'sculptor Pollen' from
the studio, with both hands extended, politely rubbing them to
indicate that he was not in a fit state to shake hands. It symbolized for me the working artist who also enjoyed a warm family
life. Holidays in the Pollens' house on Lambay Island off the
coast of Dublin were even more agreeable, with a cowrie shell
gathered from the beach serving as a souvenir of the same
hospitable combination.

Where the Pollens were concerned, I was developing that
habit found in certain adolescents, probably members of large
families, which I now call 'cuckooing'. That is to say, I preferred
another nest to my own. I don't think this is altogether a bad
thing: I have observed it since in members of my own family.
It is after all only a rite of passage on the way to independent
grown-up life, as the teenager discovers other preoccupations
from those of her upbringing. In my case, it was the musical and
artistic interests of the Pollens (I don't remember a single word
being spoken about politics) which impressed me. In this way I
discovered the paintings and poetry of David Jones; his magic

and mystic art was first encountered in the shape of a watercolour of an elephant in Lucy's bedroom. Daphne's uncle was the writer Maurice Baring, another Catholic convert; through the Pollens I discovered such novels as *Cat's Cradle,* which I found satisfyingly full of Catholic sophistication.

The French Lycée failed to enchant – a feeling that was mutual – due in our opinion to the monotonous attention to grammar. Already Lucy and I had embarked on a far more interesting endeavour. We were receiving private coaching from a tutor named Louis Bussell and learning about Gothic Architecture as well as History. Mr Bussell's Catholic ardour was an important element in all of this and enabled me to make a connection between the medieval Church and the Gothic, which was deeply exciting to one who had only recently become a Catholic. It also turned me in the direction of the early Middle Ages, after a brief but satisfying fling with Charlemagne, which would have consequences for my future academic career. 'All is worthless after the thirteenth century!' Mr Bussell was wont to exclaim with a mixture of pride and melancholy. In my Progress Book, my mother recorded that I was depressed by this, but she had not read my mood correctly. With my enthusiastic Catholicism, I found it exhilarating to consider, whereas, possibly by temperament as much as anything else, I didn't agree.

The study of History co-existed with my literary efforts, duly recorded in my pocket diaries. There are many starts and no finishes. A typical week would read: 'Monday: Wrote. Tuesday: Wrote. Wednesday: Bought brown pillbox cocktail bag with mirror in lid, same size as gas mask case. Thursday: Wrote. Friday: Wrote. Saturday: Tried to make petticoat out of parachute silk from Butterick pattern on Popie's sewing machine. Disaster.' (Parachute silk was unrationed.) My literary efforts were no more successful than the petticoat. I decided for example that the characters in a children's adventure story written 'to save the family finances' were unreal and abandoned it. Eighty pages of a book called *The Lost Medal* about a group of Catholics (heavily influenced by R. H. Benson, writer of such riveting historical novels as *Come Rack! Come Rope!*) stopped there. In any case, my chief pleasure was not completion but listing book and chapter titles of infinite enticing variety: my literary pleasure, that is. Now that it was agreed that I would attend a crammer called Bendixen in Baker Street for some months before the Oxford Entrance Exam in October, perhaps I could study parties in the gap.

The Bendixen plan came about when my mother noticed at last that I was hanging about the house rather a lot without visible employment, and concentrated her formidable intellect upon her eldest daughter. Now she openly questioned whether I had ever shown any capacity for serious hard work – such as was needed for any girl to get into Oxford in those days, since places in the few women's colleges were so limited. The Dragon School had given me an advantage, she implied, and I had never been tested. She was of course quite right. What sensible schoolchild would do 'serious hard work' if it was made unnecessary by a freak of early education? What Elizabeth hadn't noticed was that I could and did do an infinite amount of hard work where my passions were involved, and my primary passion was History. That pleasant surprise lay ahead. All of this was in considerable contrast to the Labour politics which continued to dominate my parents' lives.

Just as NW11 was not quite NW3 on the social register, so Hampstead Garden Suburb was theoretically not quite Hampstead in the political sense. There was much talk about the 'Hampstead Set' in the Labour government, prominent in it my mother's old Oxford admirer, Hugh Gaitskell and his wife Dora.

Hugh Gaitskell had a slightly pawky appearance, as though a chat with him might not include many laughs. In fact his set mouth and beady eyes, the natural air of a civil servant, belied his amiable and even dashing character: he had a lot of charm. Hugh Gaitskell also loved to dance, as would emerge much later in reports of his friendship with Ann Rothermere (subsequently married to Ian Fleming). All I knew was that he was my favourite of my parents' politician friends. Thanks to him, a great moment in my life followed. I was sitting out, a seventeen-year-old wallflower at a Buckingham Palace dance where, invited as a Labour minister's daughter, I knew no one. Suddenly Hugh Gaitskell swooped by in white tie and tails and whirled me away to the dance floor. We danced and danced. Like Cinderella, I felt myself transformed into the belle of the ball, even if the then rank of my royal prince was actually Minister of Economic Affairs.

NW11 was in fact well represented in the Hampstead Set, which included the Gordon Walkers, also old Oxford friends (Patrick Gordon Walker was Under-Secretary at the Commonwealth Relations Office, later Secretary of State) and in 1948 a younger couple called Wilson. Harold, ten years my parents' junior at thirty-one, had just been made President of the Board of Trade. His wife Mary – 'as I suppose we must now learn to call her,' wrote Elizabeth – had recently given a children's party to which my younger siblings were invited. My mother's faintly scornful comment on the hostess's name in a school letter was due to the fact that Mrs Wilson had apparently once been known by her first name of Gladys, but was now firmly Mary. It also expressed a certain private attitude of condescension to the Wilsons at the time.

The Wilsons were not among my parents' close friends, as I see from my diary record of dinners at 10 Linnell Drive. These were not frequent, although there was one never-to-be-forgotten occasion when the Prime Minister and his wife Violet indicated that they would accept a dinner invitation. Like everything to do with the Attlees – with one notable exception – the occasion was to be formal in the pre-war fashion which they seemed to prefer, which combined so strikingly with Clement Attlee's strong feeling for social welfare and made him at the time an underrated leader. There were even dinner jackets. Both Elizabeth and Violet Attlee wore what looked like discreet velvet tea gowns.

In the same way a little dance given for the Attlee daughter Alison, at No. 10 Downing Street, might have been hosted by any of the previous incumbents. The pleasant fair-haired very young man with blue eyes and regular features who danced with me would have fitted into any Conservative ballroom; I thought we got on well as he chose to tell me the history of No. 10 at some length as we danced. In fact he turned out to be called Anthony Wedgwood Benn, and was soon claimed, rather to my surprise, by an equally sweet-looking young American wife. (The future Tony Benn would have been in his mid twenties.)

The exception in the public *persona* of Mr Attlee was our memorable family visit to Chequers for a Boxing Day party. A vast Chinese screen was prominent in the great hall; behind it lurked an enormous fireplace. Lo and behold! From behind the screen stepped out the figure of Father Christmas! He looked immensely confident, even commanding, after his presumed Arctic journey: but . . . for a moment I thought the new spirit of internationalism had gone too far and he was actually a former enemy, a Japanese. Of course it was our host, Mr Attlee, who in Father Christmas gear, with his dark slanting eyes under his scarlet hood, did have a certain Asiatic look. After that, I rejected all the fashionably snide Society stories about Mr Attlee: 'an empty taxi drew up at No. 10 Downing Street and Mr Attlee got out' was typical. Anyone who could convincingly come down the chimney at Chequers and retain his dignity was a great man. That was quite apart from his unfailing kindness towards the children of his colleagues such as myself: there was none of that legendary taciturnity for which he became famous as a leader.

When my parents' dinners did occur, as for example on my father's birthday in December 1948, they would typically feature the Gaitskells, Aidan Crawley with his celebrated war reporter wife Virginia Cowles, Douglas and Peggy Jay. Douglas Jay was a brilliant man who had in addition demonic good looks; despite this combination, or perhaps because of it, my pretty girl friends who stayed at Bernhurst were careful not to be in a Sardine situation with him when playing after-dinner games, as one or two of them explained to me. I did not experience this; in any case I much preferred Peggy Jay, a high-minded woman with a strong conscience on which she acted. My real reservation about Douglas Jay, which applied to various of my parents' political friends, was his arrogance.

There was a famous utterance of my parents' friend Sir Hartley Shawcross, then a Labour MP, in the House of Commons in 1946 during a debate on anti-Union laws: 'we are the masters now.' As a matter of fact, like many famous utterances, it was misreported in the first place. Shawcross actually said: 'We are the masters at the moment', which has a very different connotation. Unaware of the truth, I did find the phrase summed up a certain Labour attitude that made me uneasy. My loyalty to Labour was as yet undiminished. But I was brought up on Frank's belief in the Christian doctrine that 'we are all of equal importance in the sight of God', which, as he put it himself in his autobiography, animated his Socialism. So I was similarly disquieted by the notorious outburst of Jay himself. Once again I was misled by the press. There was no outburst. Jay, now

Economic Secretary to the Treasury, had written in a pre-war book: 'In the case of nutrition and health, just as in the case of education, the gentleman in Whitehall really does know better what is good for people than the people know themselves.' It was now quoted in a much cruder form: 'the man in Whitehall knows best.' With my ignorant but enquiring mind, I asked myself: was this really an expression of the philosophy of the beloved Labour Party?

I fared much better being swayed by oratory, as the ignorant but enquiring tend to do. There were two significant occasions. Once my parents took me to hear their friend Richard Crossman give a rousing talk in Headington; I think they intended to excite me about politics. As it was, I was indeed excited by Dick Crossman, rather more than they expected or even hoped. His ebullient style, his flashing eyes behind their enormous glasses, his thick wedge of hair above all made him an evangelical figure. I did not realize that my parents considered him in some way unreliable, although they were very fond of him personally. My ingenuous enthusiasm took them by surprise.

'Dick is a good speaker but he's not Gladstone,' said Frank rather grumpily. Gladstone was one of his heroes. In private life, Dick was a man of enormous personal warmth as I discovered later when married to an MP, even if a Tory one; Hugh often remarked that he preferred the company of Dick Crossman to most of his fellow Tories.

The second speech was given in a hall in Hampstead Garden Suburb by Victor Kravchenko, who had escaped from Soviet Russia and written a bestselling book, published in 1946, called *I Chose Freedom*. Ukrainian-born, Kravchenko had been a Soviet official, before requesting political asylum in the United States when he was posted to Washington. The Soviet Union demanded his immediate extradition, which President Roosevelt declined to carry out. Here was an even more captivating speaker, in the literal sense of the word. Coincidentally this experience came at roughly the same period as I was reading about the ordeal of the Hungarian Catholic Cardinal József Mindszenty, tried and imprisoned under the Communist regime, with a false confession forced out of him by torture (having already been imprisoned during the war by the pro-Nazi authorities). Together with my parents' resolute opposition to Stalinism, and their equally resolute adherence to Socialism, I was never in any danger of confusing the two; my Catholic loyalty, exemplified by the fate of Mindszenty, was the third element.

I was certainly proof against the teasing of my uncle John Harman, my mother's much-loved brother who conspicuously did not share her politics. For some reason, I had to have my tonsils out in a London nursing home when my parents were stuck in Oxford. Uncle John showed great kindness in visiting me (he was already a busy doctor and must have had a demanding schedule). One day he arrived and with a mischievous smile held out a copy of George Orwell's *Animal Farm*, which had been published eighteen months previously.

'Read this,' he said. 'This is what will happen to this country if your parents have their way.' I had never heard of either George Orwell or *Animal Farm*. Reluctantly, I put aside salacious *Forever Amber*, which I could never have read at home but was being serialized in the *Sunday Dispatch* and obtainable at the nursing home; I had hidden it under the bedclothes when Uncle John arrived. Immediately I was hooked and *Animal Farm* remains the most gripping horror story I have ever read, which I have always rated much higher than *1984*. But never for one moment did I think it had any relevance to the idealistic Socialist Britain of my parents.

All this amounted to the fact that, at the age of sixteen, I was naturally interested in public affairs, while preferring action over issues to party politics. A few years later I would find with relief a straightforward cause about which it was possible to feel passionately and that was the abolition of capital punishment, acting as an usherette at Gerald Gardiner's Fifties meetings arguing for the reform. But I was also inquisitive (and already of course an inveterate newspaper reader). In short, I liked to know what was going on. It was in this mood of high-minded research that I decided to bunk off from the Lycée in December 1948 in order to attend the proceedings of the Lynskey Tribunal. This concerned possible corruption in political life and it involved a member of the Labour government.

I had to queue for five hours to do so. To see the chief witness in the investigation, Sidney Stanley, a flamboyant adventurer if not outright conman, born in Poland as Solomon Wulkan, more than made up for the temporary inconvenience. In any case I was used to queuing and found my fellows outside Church Hall, Westminster much more interesting than those in my usual Golders Green queue for nylon stockings: they all had strong political views, I discovered, but no single person agreed with anyone else; there were quite a few Poles among them, but they were not necessarily on Stanley's side. Most people disapproved of John Belcher, a junior minister at the Board of Trade who had been a railway clerk, for what seemed like shocking corruption in those austere days – a hotel in Margate! For his family as well! Horrors! With hindsight, Belcher's well-meant efforts to involve business with Labour, never an easy task, seem more pathetic than corrupt. In the event there was no prosecution, but Belcher resigned from Parliament and went back to being a railway clerk. However, if you were not involved in the allegations of corruption, it was all good fun. Stanley proved to be what I can only describe as a Pinteresque character before his time, with something of the panache of Max in *The Homecoming*. You had to believe him with that wicked smile, those inviting gestures, that air of cheerful self-confidence. Perhaps he should have played the part of Max: at all events, a potentially fine actor was lost to the English stage when Stanley, transformed into Schlomo ben Chaim, spent the rest of his life in Israel.

Later I boasted to my parents what I had done: apart from anything, I needed a letter of excuse for the Lycée. In my mother I saw a certain admiration for my boldness struggle with parental disapproval for skipping school. In the end, parental disapproval won.

Elizabeth said: 'You know I can't possibly write a note for you which isn't true.' I made no comment. Like any girl of spirit, I had perfected my mother's clear, flowing signature years ago and my little portable typewriter, my sixteenth-birthday present, would do the rest.

Frank looked up from his reading and merely said in his mild way: 'John Belcher is an unfortunate man. He deserves our pity.'

The spectacle of corruption in politics, the law-givers negligently tossing the laws out of the window, however petty, is always upsetting. This was my glimpse of it at an early stage of my personal interest in politics, as opposed to the political background endowed by both my parents; it was all a long way from the intellectual arguments of the Hampstead (Garden Suburb) Set. In my case, I must admit that I felt more fascinated by the characters involved, especially Sidney Stanley, and their motivation, than the tricky delineation of political corruption. It would be possible to deduce from this that I was a lawyer *manquée:* certainly I have retained a fondness for attending trials out of curiosity and reading law reports, also deriving enormous vicarious pleasure from the flourishing careers of family members who have gone to the Bar. But I believe the truth is slightly different: a biographer has something in common with a barrister making a case, and it was the biographical impulse which finally was driving me.

One possibility never remotely crossed my mind (either then or since) and that was becoming an active politician myself. I suppose having both a mother and a father who aspired to enter Parliament, and a first husband who was an active MP, might have inclined me either way. In fact there was no question of me being persuaded by outside factors like these. I had always known exactly what I wanted to do, which was to write History, although very far indeed from knowing how to do it.

This did not preclude me from feeling fascinated by the political process. I particularly enjoyed attending debates in the House of Lords when my father first joined, although it should be remarked that members were still strictly men only in the late Forties and most of the Fifties. One was used to serried ranks of male faces in dark suits when not in red robes and white wigs. This was in contrast to the House of Commons where Joan Vickers, the elegant middle-aged Tory MP elected in 1955, who displayed an immaculately coiffed head of silver-blue hair, could never have been mistaken for a man. Then there was the unmistakable voice of the Bevanite Labour MP Barbara Castle. It was a high voice and rather screechy to the critical ear, but then what else could she do to be heard above the deep baying of the male hounds at her heels? Women peers were not actually allowed into the Lords until after the Life Peerages Act of 1958, that act provoked into being by Tony Benn, whereas they had been admitted to the Commons for the first time forty years earlier. But then women were not yet admitted as members of the Oxford Union in the Fifties: even charismatic future leaders like Shirley Catlin, later Williams.

In the Lords at that date, as a peer's eldest unmarried daughter, I was allowed to sit in the gallery among the peers' wives. I celebrated my status by sending my roving eye across the serried ranks of noble faces. I had in mind a diary entry around this time about my future husband: 'Mine must be Catholic or convertible, a peer if possible, clever, intellectual and literary, interested in his surroundings. Either Labour or amenable, having a house in town and ancient family seat, fond of children and wanting them.' Somehow I doubt the sincerity of the next sentence, given the people who were my current heroes: 'He need not be good looking, must be a *nice* person of moral worth.' I added: 'Also wealthy and tall.' There spoke my beating sixteen-year-old heart.

There was little positive sign of this paragon in the House of Lords of the Forties although I did rather fancy the look of my father's friend Victor Rothschild, who had apparently chosen to sit as a Labour peer. I also understood him to be a war hero for his work with unexploded bombs. (I had forgotten to add 'courage in war' to my diary requirements.)

When I came to study the early-nineteenth-century Parliament, I became aware how privileged I had been in my youth to sit right there inside the House of Lords and House of Commons: the Whig ladies who were keen on politics had to lean forward and peer down a sort of ventilator and in any case the old Houses of Parliament, before the fire of 1834, were intolerably stuffy, crammed and uncomfortable. The parliamentary debates – in both houses – were crucial in the cause of Reform and researching; I read and reread the Hansard accounts, trying to picture them and recreate them in my mind. The spur to my imagination was the memory of those early sessions.

Life at the Bendixen crammer was not quite so glamorous, and in fact consisted of a lot of concentrated hard work, but it was not entirely without its pleasures. This was because Bendixen was next door to the Classic cinema in Baker Street. In those days, no questions were asked, and no new ticket requested, if you elected to spend all day in the cinema, attending three or four performances of the same film. It was vital that the prices were so much cheaper than in the West End, where we could only afford the noxious front row. (As a result, the memory of the unhappy looming face of Richard Attenborough in close-up as a tobacconist's son sent to an exclusive public school in *The Guinea Pig* disturbs me to this day.) At the Classic, Lucy and I were able to make a thorough study of *The Lives of a Bengal Lancer* (1935) as part of our larger project of investigation into the career of Gary Cooper.

This was so important that Lucy actually telephoned Linnell Drive – a rare occurrence, our single telephone being in a tiny lobby under the stairs – to give me some news from a magazine centred on movie gossip. Gary Cooper had been asked why he had been at the top of his profession so long. 'People with big feet is hard to move,' he replied. This, as Lucy pointed out, effectively contradicted the dreadful rumour that Gary Cooper was dumb. It had been derived from some other gossip magazine, which we would now never buy again.

The Oxford exam came, proved very difficult according to my diary, and then there was the prospect of the interview. In theory, not everyone got an interview, but it was obviously un-likely that Lady Margaret Hall, my mother's old college to which she remained much attached, would not give her daughter a chance. Besides, Elizabeth herself had taken a keen interest in my campaign, as she saw it, but which was frankly quite as much her own.

First of all, she instructed me to read Arnold Toynbee, and not the abridged version, by the way. 'Read the whole thing,

Antonia, and at the interview when they ask you what you have been reading, be careful to make references to passages which are not in the abridged version. That means you had better read the abridged version as well and make notes. You can do it.'

Yes, the quick reader she had involuntarily created (she always said she was not a particularly quick reader herself) could do it. But I didn't much want to do it. I preferred Lytton Strachey to Toynbee, although I had enough sense to keep that judgement to myself. As it was, I plastered my interview with interpolations from Toynbee. Afterwards I realized my behaviour had been like that of Bertie Wooster who, when told in advance that a certain attractive young lady admired Tennyson, managed only to read *The Princess*. His conversation with her at dinner led at all points inexorably to quotations from that poem, while the young lady tried in vain to invoke other works: 'You *do* seem to be fond of *The Princess*,' was her final comment.

Elizabeth's second instruction was along different lines.

'Antonia, you will read PPE,' she said.

'Not History?'

'No. All girls nowadays want to read History. That is, if they don't read English. I want you to get a scholarship. Hardly any girls read PPE. If you take the History exams, but say you hope to read PPE at university, you will probably get an award.'

Dutifully, I did as she suggested. And sure enough, the great day came when an orange paper telegram, prepaid reply possible by telephone, arrived at 10 Linnell Drive. 'Lady Margaret Hall offers Exhibition . . .' I dashed into the tiny dark lobby, seized the instrument and dictated my reply at high speed which went something like this: 'Yes, yes, dear Lady Margaret Hall, I would love to accept your kind offer, in fact I would love to come to Oxford altogether . . .' At this point the sour voice of the telephone operator to whom I was dictating these rapturous words broke in: 'You have used up all the prepaid message. Do you want to pay for more?'

There was one question that I had never thought to ask during all this time: what is PPE? Now I had about ten months to find out before I went up to Oxford in the following October. My airy plans for the next year did not however include making simple academic enquiries like that.

CHAPTER ELEVEN

BRINGING MYSELF OUT

'**M**ISS PAKENHAM IS TAKING HER debut seriously,' wrote the *Bangkok Post*. 'She has given up her job to devote more time to social affairs.' I was seventeen and a half. I still don't know why the *Bangkok Post* elected to share this news with its readers. Did the fact that my father was Minister of Civil Aviation in the Labour government really make this a news item in faraway Bangkok? At all events the tattered cutting sent by some well-wisher overseas was preserved in my Progress Book.

Unfortunately, although Miss Pakenham was undoubtedly taking her debut seriously, the rest of the world was not. In particular, Elizabeth was evidently irritated that as an active Socialist and a Socialist minister's wife, she was being plagued by me to act the part of a debutante's mother. One can see her point – or rather I can see her point now; at the time I merely thought being a debutante was an enchanting idea, something that admittedly needed a bit of work to achieve. I had hoped that my mother would do some of this work (as other people's mothers did) but if for some strange reason of her own she was unwilling to do so, I would apply myself to the task.

I should make it clear, with regard to my mother's Socialism, that she was not irritated by the Court itself let alone the monarchy; she was a Socialist but not a revolutionary and enjoyed the royal outings to which Frank's political offices entitled her. (This was incidentally long before she became famous as a royal biographer: Elizabeth's ambitions were still political in the late Forties, and as mentioned earlier, she would stand for Parliament for the last time in 1950.) It sums up my parents' attitudes, which were far from exceptional for Labour ministers at the time, that their children went to private schools of one sort or another at some stage; all the four boys, for example, went to Ampleforth. On the other hand we used the National Health Service from the start. When it came to so-called presentation at Court it was the frivolous work involved which appalled Elizabeth, when there were so many much more interesting things to do. She after all had allowed herself to be presented after her marriage, photographed in the full Thirties rig of long white dress, train and ostrich feathers (since the war, reduced to afternoon dress plus hat). Someone had sent her the news clipping, adding the jokey comment by hand: 'All I learnt at Stoke', referring to her highminded WEA lecturing in the Midlands. To Elizabeth's credit, she stuck the clipping in her photo album.

Elizabeth did not understand that her frivolity was my serious glamour – the glamour of the aristocratic past brought to life. I expected to meet the new Whigs, the new Lady Georgiana Spencer, future Duchess of Devonshire (from reading *The Grand Whiggery* I might have remembered that the original Georgiana was married off on her seventeenth birthday). Then my favourite fiction figured as well. An intense study of Jane Austen and Trollope, whom I loved even better, had left me hungry for Society, as I imagined it to be. In Trollope, for example, it will be remembered that since Dragon School days onwards I had identified myself with Lady Glencora Palliser of *Can You Forgive Her?* – she who inadvertently introduced me to the real facts of life. At the age of seventeen, as a role model I still preferred her to Dorothea in *Middlemarch*.

There had not been many Whigs about in the first job I managed to get after I had secured that place at Oxford in the autumn. But I was determined to earn money, and be my own mistress in that respect (hoping to spend most of it on clothes) since there didn't seem to be any other money around at home. The job was as a typist in a pool in the accounts department of a leading advertising agency called Pritchard Woods, off Bond Street. The typists' room was our world: I never had any contact with the suave gentlemen who were actually creating the advertisements for which we typed out the bills. They wore suits, had thick hair slicked back, and seemed much preoccupied if one passed them in the corridor. I like to think that the ability to type an intricate bill correctly with six carbons beneath is one which will stand me in good stead when some kind of retrograde anti-technical revolution arrives, and with it once again the need for such things. And I suppose I must have carried out my work more or less correctly, otherwise there would have been trouble. What I remember chiefly is the rich private life which was outlined by my fellow workers every morning, all married as I recall it, and one at least trying for the baby which would release her from the workplace.

I was never asked about my private life, out of sensitivity I believe, because it must have seemed rather unlikely from my appearance that I actually had one – at any rate one that would interest them. These were smartly dressed, well-made-up women at all times, whatever their difficulties and whatever the journeys they had to take to reach the office. Compared to them I was a hobbledehoy.

My next job should have done something to solve that particular problem. This was selling hats in the ground-floor department of Fenwick's in Bond Street. Here I was known as Miss Tony, the only time I have ever permitted this sobriquet: in this case I had no choice as it was simply announced that no one could work in Fenwick's hat department with such a ridiculous long name as Antonia. I certainly had a very jolly time as Miss Tony. The trouble was that, as time passed, it got rather too jolly. I was by now beginning to have nice London friends, to add to my nice Catholic ones.

First of all, I got to know Raymond Bonham Carter, then doing National Service but stationed in London at the Guards Barracks. This was arranged by my parents via his parents, the formidable Lady Violet Bonham Carter, and her husband Sir Maurice, always a kindly man in the short conversations one managed to have with him. Lady Violet had a long, horsey face which she had a habit of sticking close to yours, while she confided fascinating things in a low and thrilling voice that seemed to derive from some marvellous society before the First War; unfortunately I was generally too frightened to listen. She was the daughter of Prime Minister Asquith, a fact of which one was not kept in ignorance. Raymond too was suitably proud of this descent.

I found him the most agreeable company; as a person he was a credit to the sort of super-intelligent conversation he had listened to all his life, without any of the loftiness of his mother. So it was natural that I should confide in him about the two problems I had with my life at Fenwick's. One was the need to sit down from time to time due to my uncomfortable court shoes. The other was the need to get away for the weekend instead of working on Saturdays, in order, as I put it, to go to hunt balls. The latter need was pure fantasy on my part. What hunt balls? I had never been to a hunt ball. But somehow I believed that, if I were free, invitations would waft magically in my direction. Raymond was extremely sympathetic.

'My grandfather, Mr Asquith, passed a law saying that shop-workers had a right to sit down. Insist on your rights!' I didn't quite do that. I did the next best thing, which was to confide in a beguiling man from the *Evening Standard* Diary who seemed interested in anything I had to say.

The first result was an entry headed: SITS AND NO SATS SAYS MISS TONY. The second result was a ticking-off from the head of the department, who took the opportunity to sug-gest that where my unkempt long curly hair was concerned, I should have what she called a 'Fork-me-all-off'. Then I would at least look the part of a smart saleslady. It seemed wise to do as she suggested; so the third result was a head of soignée but unflatter-ing short curly hair, visible in photographs of me aged seventeen, which if it was revenge on the part of the head *vendeuse* must have been a satisfying one.

The next episode was not resolved, unfortunately, with a mere haircut. As part of my parents' new Catholicism, which they were taking so seriously, they had purchased tickets for a Catholic charity event called the Rose Ball. This was a remark-able departure from their usual parsimony (as I saw it, although practical economics might have been a fairer description). At all events, here was a rare opportunity for them to behave as phil-anthropic Catholics and please me at the same time. Elizabeth even secured a partner for me, a suitable Catholic young man, the son of the painter Simon Elwes, grandson of the diplomat Lord Rennell. Dominic Elwes was eighteen. He had fair hair and brown eyes, and was startlingly good-looking. Besides that, he had extraordinary charm.

In view of Dominic's subsequent career, which included elopement with a beautiful girl, and an eventual sad suicide at the age of forty-four, it is easy to see now that a suitable Catholic young man was the last thing that he was. At the time, I had some warnings of his erratic but romantic nature since he took me to meals at the Hungaria restaurant, merrily signing the bill 'Simon Elwes'. It was the kind of thing that many young people might secretly want to do, but wouldn't have the courage. Dominic Elwes certainly had daring spirit enough to do anything that suited him. I was bewitched by him without being in love. Alas, my brief diary entries show that our meetings were generally 'unsatisfactory', which referred to unpunctuality and even outright forgetfulness. But then Dominic and his friends did rescue me from Fenwick's, leaving me to concentrate, in the words of the *Bangkok Post*, on 'social affairs'.

Dominic loved any kind of outrageous exploit, especially if it involved the flouting of authority. So, in order to amuse me, as he said later, he gathered together a body of his friends and invaded the hat department of Fenwick's. Under the pretence of buying hats for other people – 'My mother,' said Dominic boldly, when challenged – they began to throw the hats about with increasing abandon. I was powerless to stop them, and I don't think anyone in the department really blamed Miss Tony. But soon afterwards I was gently encouraged to slink away, and slink away I did.

In all fairness, I should balance the introduction of Dominic Elwes into my life by my parents against their other very different social introduction, which also involved a ball. My father's interest in Germany had by no means waned with his appointment as Minister for Civil Aviation. The need for practical reconciliation in the post-war world had been, and remained, a passionately held belief. As a mark of respect for Frank's position, I was among those chosen to be presented to Dr Adenauer when he came to Oxford in 1951. I was honoured to meet the Chancellor of West Germany. After that, things did not go quite so well.

Dr Adenauer, evidently primed, asked me how many children my mother had:

'*Achtzig*,' I replied proudly.

'*Achtzig!*' repeated the great statesman in astonishment.

'Do you realize what you have just said?' whispered the man from the Foreign Office in attendance, gazing at me in disgust. At that moment, I just did: even my mother didn't have *eighty* children. But while the diplomat sneered, the Chancellor continued to beam at me, repeating once or twice: '*Achtzig, achtzig*,' in good-natured amusement, before he was moved on.

Later, the foundation of some kind of Anglo-German Society was another progressive step on the part of my father and his fellow believers in reconciliation. It owed a great deal to the activity of my father's friend Victor Gollancz – 'Jolly Golly' as he sometimes referred to himself – who, being both Jewish and fearless, was in a strong position to see off any possible opposition. Other people joined in; then the exciting news came that T. S. Eliot wished to be part of the enterprise in some way. This was a huge honour. His mere name was an enormous asset. He was not expected to attend an event such as the Anglo-German Ball, a friendly small-scale affair held at the German Embassy.

The next exciting – but unexpected and slightly daunting – news was that Mr Eliot had every intention of attending the Anglo-German Ball. Mr Eliot's manners being perfect, in due course he asked me to dance. It was in this way I considered that I entered literary history, able to point out to future partners that they were dancing with a girl who had danced with, not so much the Prince of Wales, but the greatest poet of our time. Apart from that, Mr Eliot was an excellent, firm dancer and showed every sign of enjoying the activity while my father (not interested in the subject of dancing) was optimistically trying to adapt the talents of the rugby field to the dance floor.

My campaign to become a debutante did not take place at quite such a high level. At least the problem of getting home to NW11 after the dance had recently reached a delightful solution. Moved to pity by my social dilemma, my father's younger sister Violet Powell offered a periodic refuge at the house she lived in with her husband Anthony Powell in Chester Gate, off Regent's Park. This was NW1: and what a wonderful postal district that was since one could post anything there with pride. More to the point, any young man would be willing to drop a girl back to the Regent's Park district. Inclusion at last in the London whirl! This was my first reaction to the imaginative generosity of my aunt. In fact, my friendship with the Powells – as it became with time, way beyond the family ties with which it originated – was far more important in my life than mere convenience for a taxi ride.

Violet Powell was an extremely tolerant person. As a result of her acute interest in social life in all its forms, she had no time for dismissing people as dull; no one was dull for Violet, there had to be some connection and she would find it. Of course the result was that no one *was* dull in Violet's company; I found myself relating the details of my encounters at parties with new relish. She was not a substitute mother, although she performed some of the functions another kind of mother might have performed, such as listening to my tales of social derring-do with apparent interest (did they lose anything in the telling? With an audience like Violet, definitely not). Besides, I had a mother, a mother I loved and admired.

What Violet was, I realized afterwards, was my first 'grown-up' friend; that is to say, she was the staging post between the friendships of early youth, of necessity always with contemporaries, and the wide-ranging friendships we enjoy later on. It helped that there was something infectious about Violet's enthusiasms. I note from my pocket diaries that an evening spent at Chester

Gate would quite often be followed by a visit to a picture gallery, not out of duty, but for the sheer possibility of pleasure it offered. Her elder son, Tristram, then eight or nine, sometimes accompanied us, showing remarkable equanimity and even enjoyment.

Anthony Powell exerted a different kind of influence. To me in those days he was simply the benevolent man who sat down every morning after breakfast and wrote. He had a handsome head, with fine Roman features that could be well portrayed in busts (as happened later). This god-like but friendly figure obviously enjoyed what he was doing: that was my strongest impression; and then there was the regular discipline with which he appeared to write. Somehow I began equating writing, discipline and a good life. I had no idea at this point what he was writing: in fact this must have been the early stages of *A Dance to the Music of Time,* the first volume being published after the Powells moved to The Chantry in Somerset in 1950. At other times of day, Tony was definitely up for gossip based on the coloured-up details of my social life.

Anthony Powell had a great interest in genealogy, which of course I shared in a humbler fashion. It was however far from being centred on famous dukes and the like: it was family history that fascinated him. He took for example my decision to write about Cromwell as a personal challenge to involve me in the details of the Cromwellian Welsh ancestry that Tony had thoughtfully traced for me. Whereas Cromwell's eighteenth-century biographer the Revd Mark Noble had dismissed these ancestors with English condescension – 'their history could afford no pleasure, and but little knowledge' – Tony took the opposite view. To sum up a long and intricate tale, Cromwell's true family name was Williams. His father, Richard Williams, was the nephew of Thomas Cromwell through his mother. Opportunistically, Richard proceeded to change his name to Cromwell while the influence of his famous uncle was paramount, and the change survived Thomas Cromwell's fall from power.

'Why not refer to him as Williams throughout?' suggested Tony at the end of his helpful and detailed letter. The trouble was that, apart from anything else, I had already decided to call my book *Cromwell, Our Chief of Men,* inspired by Milton's sonnet which begins with this acclamation. I replied diplomatically to Tony that I did not think that *Williams, Our Chief of Men* had quite the same ring.

With time, I became a prodigious fan of Anthony Powell's great sequence of novels. Just as my favourite pieces of instrumental music, string quartets, can be heard for ever, I find that his 'music of time' bears endless rereading. While he was creating the novels, I had the added pleasure which all fans share of trying to distinguish reality from fiction. Perhaps it is an ultimately pointless exercise. I certainly came to think so when married to Harold, sometimes wanting to mutter: 'What's wrong with the writer's imagination?' when claimants to be the original of this that and the other character stepped eagerly forward. Nevertheless, the exercise is undoubtedly an irresistible one. My favourite tutor at Oxford, Anne Whiteman, was proud to consider herself the origin of the claret-loving scholar Dr Emily Brightman in the later books. Was Pamela Widmerpool or was she not Barbara Skelton? And where did Georgina Ward, actress in the dramatic version of *Afternoon Men,* fit in all this . . . At one point I was encouraged to enquire of Tony whether I myself might not one day feature . . .

Tony gave his genial laugh which very often preceded a polite contradiction of what one had just said. 'Oh no, Antonia,' he said. 'You are a resolved character. I don't write about resolved characters.' At the time I was innocent enough to be flattered: a resolved character! Like the *bourgeois gentilhomme* speaking prose all his life without knowing it, I had never even noticed my 'resolving'. Later I realized that it was Tony's elegant way of avoiding a discussion with which he must have become all too wearily familiar over the years.

One of the most agreeable aspects of conversations with Tony was his deep interest in the work of other writers; these talks were precious. There could however be traps here for the unwary – or the less well read. I once went on a Hellenic Cruise with the Powells. The company of fellow passengers was grist to Tony's mill (in fact the Powells became inveterate cruise-goers). It was in this way that he suggested that we should assign them code names, using characters from Scott Fitzgerald, so that if necessary we could carry on our enjoyable discussions in public without offence. Somehow I allowed it to be understood that I was as expert on the work of Fitzgerald as the Powells were. The scene where I waxed eloquent on the subject of Jordan Baker, Daisy Buchanan's girl friend with the 'autumn-leaf' yellow hair, except I assumed from the name Jordan that he was a man, can still occasionally trouble the noon's repose. The situation was saved by Violet, who gallantly continued to make gender-correcting references until I got the point and shut up; after that, by mutual agreement, we transferred our allusions to the works of Dickens.

There were no such perils during my happy visits to The Chantry, unless you counted walks round the lake with Tony swinging a billhook and occasionally pouncing on an errant shrub in our path. Even Tony cooking his famous curry did not make me nervous because I was confident Violet's benign spirit would somehow ensure that everything would turn out all right.

The season of 1950 was the one into which I now launched myself, having bettered my social life from the landing-stage of Chester Gate. My parents survived in the NW11 suburb until the end of July when they returned to Bernhurst, a year or two later

Right Great-Uncle Eddie, as the magnificent eccentric Irish writer Lord Dunsany was known to us.

Below A poem written to me by Great-Uncle Eddie with his characteristic quill pen; it was subsequently published in *Punch* to my great pride.

Lines to Antonia.

Come when the hay has grown
  And visit us, Antonia;
When all the lilac's flown,
  But there is still begonia.
Come when the midges drone
  (Better bring some ammonia),
And our new gramophone
  Shall play you a sinfonia.

Left Our uncle, Edward Longford, painted by Henry Lamb, his brother-in-law.

Below left Christine Longford by Henry Lamb.

Above right Lady Margaret Hall first-year students, 1950. Front row 6th from l.: Marigold Hunt. 3rd row 1st l.: Sabel Desta, grand-daughter of the Emperor Haile Selassie of Ethiopia. Back row 6th from l.: Antonia.

Right New Year, 1950, with the family of Alcide De Gasperi, Prime Minister of Italy; Signora Francesca De Gasperi, Paola, Antonia, Lia. We are on Monte Faito in southern Italy.

Left A visit to Bernard Berenson at I Tatti, arranged by Patrick Lindsay: l. to r.: Vanessa Jebb, B.B., Antonia, August 1950.

Below left Engagement photograph taken by Thomas in the back garden of Cheyne Gardens, August 1956.

Right Wedding photograph, the gift of Cecil Beaton for whom I worked, taken outside our reception at the Fishmongers Hall, 25 September 1956. My headdress, a childhood dream, was inspired by Mary Queen of Scots.

The monument to Mary Queen of Scots in Westminster Abbey erected by her son, King James I. I ended my biography of her with this powerful image.

Above George Weidenfeld, for whom I worked immediately after Oxford University. He then became (and remains sixty years later) my publisher: we are at a party to celebrate my book *A History of Toys*, 1966.

Right The cover of the first Weidenfeld & Nicolson edition of *Mary Queen of Scots*, published 15 May 1969.

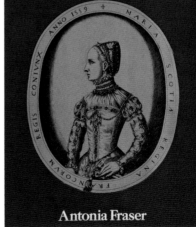

Mary
Queen of Scots

Antonia Fraser

The illustration from *Our Island Story* which first drew me into the story of Mary Queen of Scots when I read it as a child.

adding a sparsely furnished house in Chelsea to the equation to save my father commuting. It seemed peculiar to find something like the debutantes' season still in place in 1950: wartime attitudes had not altogether vanished in the past five years. Petrol-rationing only ended in late May, clothes-rationing having ended a year previously; sweets and sugar remained rationed for a few years, and the final end of all rationing did not come until July 1954. In social life generally, at the start of the Fifties, there appeared to be a harking-back to the remembered rituals of the Thirties, and no impulse that one could discern towards breaking with the past. The ceremony of presentation at Court, for example, continued placidly for the next eight years. Change, when it came, was for the Sixties.

In this apparently retrograde world, I had developed expectations. Those wartime holidays staying with Aunt Mary Clive at her cottage at Whitfield had been enlivened by obsessional reading of old copies of the *Tatler* in the attics of the dust-sheeted big house nearby. I expected therefore race meetings, felt hats for gentlemen and suits with rather baggy trousers, dances with heavy lipstick and ropes of pearls for the ladies. Names would be mainly double-barrelled, with both names quite long and difficult to spell. (Any yearning I might have had for a double-barrelled name was, however, quickly removed by finding my own name difficult enough for anyone formally announcing it at my entrance to a ball. 'Miss Alethea Buckingham has arrived,' was one memorable stab at it.) In fact, the season of 1950, in so far as I managed to infiltrate it, was a shabbier and thus cheaper version of the Thirties seasons.

I was certainly not the only one who made her own ball dresses, my masterpiece being made of layers of coarse cotton net, cheap and surprisingly easy to fashion into an off-the-shoulder number with a huge skirt. Daringly, the colour was black, but I softened the effect with an enormous pink velvet rose plonked in the middle of my *décolletage*. Queen Victoria was known to have suggested to one of her granddaughters, wearing a plunging evening dress at dinner, that she should poke a flower into her bosom, for the sake of the footman who was standing behind her chair in the direct line of vision. My pink velvet rose would hardly have saved the sensibilities of a footman since it tended to weigh down the whole edifice, with its inadequate structure beneath.

A different kind of danger was posed by petticoats: in the evening they gave a crinoline effect, being made of cheap material and held up by rings of whalebone. But petticoats were wayward things: if the fastening broke, or the emergency safety pin gave way, the gleaming white structure could sink without warning to the floor at one's feet, say, during a Scottish reel. The so-called Merry Widow corset which held one in to an improbably small waist was on the other hand a loyal friend, but was not launched on a grateful market of young ladies until a few years later. This was the one period when I kept elaborate accounts at the back of my pocket diary of what I spent on clothes – probably because I was trying so hard to be something I wasn't. In my tiny budget, there was inordinate expenditure on pairs of white gloves, which certainly proves the point.

I had two dresses made for me by a dressmaker. One was of startling lime-green silk with white stars on it, material bought at Jacqmar; this was for my garden party dress, the garden party at which I would be presented. With it went heavy white court shoes and a shiny white plastic handbag, modelled on one carried by Princess Margaret. A large white straw picture hat with a carefully matching lime-green ribbon completed the picture. The saleslady at Jacqmar, a large building just off Bond Street, said brightly: 'What an interesting colour! I'm sure no other debutante will be wearing this colour green.' I did not tell her that my uncle Henry Lamb had recently drawn me and flatteringly discerned exotic green lights in my skin; he suggested green would be a good colour for me to wear, but bearing in mind the mysterious greens in his own pictures, probably did not have in mind lime-green-patterned Jacqmar. The other dress was of cream-coloured faille, once again adorned by a large pink rose, but a better-behaved rose that did not weigh anything down. I was photographed wearing this by Baron, the famous Society photographer, looking uncharacteristically soulful after he told me sharply not to smile.

In giving an account of my appearance at the time, I am tempted to imitate the example of the Marquise de la Tour du Pin in her eighteenth-century memoir of her life at the Court of Marie Antoinette: as an exercise in false modesty it is hard to beat. 'I think the moment has come to describe myself,' she wrote. Despite her reputation for beauty, 'on paper, the portrait will not be flattering . . .' After this preamble, Madame de la Tour goes on to list her features in the most favourable terms, including the beautiful fresh bloom of her mouth, and her very good teeth, before observing that she herself always considered herself – and any woman said to look like her – as 'hideous'. She ends: 'Perhaps it was my dazzling clear and transparent complexion which made me outstanding in any gathering . . .' Unfortunately a dazzling clear and transparent complexion would not have made a girl of my generation in England in any way outstanding since the cliché about the famous pink-and-white English skin was broadly speaking true. A compliment to the complexion always sounded suspiciously like the compliment of last resort, when there was nothing else to say.

My own looks, including what was seen as an over-large mouth (as Baron had pointed out when he told me to purse my lips), were not at all fashionable at the time. The contemporary ideal was the Deb of the Year, the Hon. Sally Ann Vivian, with her exquisite fragile appearance: cute blonde curl in the middle of her forehead, little beanie hat above (my head looked ridiculous in a beanie hat) and delicate rosebud mouth. She was indeed ravishingly pretty and I longed to look exactly like her. It was not until the Sixties, once again, that the wheel of beauty turned, as it does from decade to decade, and a new type emerged with film stars such as Julie Christie and Marianne Faithfull. I was able to benefit from an imagined resemblance to Julie Christie, especially after her success as Lara in *Dr Zhivago*.

It was a comparison I heavily encouraged. My hair had somehow grown longer and blonder in the interval, and may even have been reinforced by the strategic positioning of hairpieces (sometimes I still discover these relics of that time in an old cupboard and gaze at them with a mixture of nostalgia and amazement). I swept it up into Lara-like styles whenever possible. Of course when I got to know Julie Christie, associated with Harold on Human Rights issues, I realized that the comparison was absurd. We were not really at all alike. It was the illusion of the huge fur hat (naturally I had bought a huge fur hat to peer from under) and the make-up. Apart from anything else, like many film stars, she was not only intensely beautiful but tiny in real life, a Pocket Venus. I only hope that those people to whom I nodded in gracious acknowledgement at the opera in New York when they questioned me respectfully from the next box with the words: 'Miss Julie Christie?' never found out the truth.

The contemporary values for good looks became of particular interest to me when I was writing historical biography. One was faced with the inevitable contrast between the reports of the day and the illustration on the page which seemed to be contradicting what I had written. Mary Queen of Scots for example was regularly described as the most beautiful princess in Europe; looking at the statutory pictures of her, long beaked nose, small pursed mouth, eyes which were certainly not large, one wondered what the other princesses must have looked like. Soon I came to realize that my role was not to pass any kind of judgement based on my own values but simply try, by quotation, to establish how she was seen at the time; readers could then interpret the pictures for themselves.

When it came to the question of Marie Antoinette, I understood further that grace of deportment and dancing was something that was vital to the image of an eighteenth-century French queen; but I could hardly experience it first-hand. This was where a report by Horace Walpole, paying a visit to the French Court, was a wonderful discovery for me. He wrote that he would never forget seeing her follow Louis XV into the Royal Chapel, how she 'shot through the room like an aerial Being, all brightness and grace and without seeming to touch the earth'. After that, I found that Marie Antoinette was several times compared by eyewitnesses to Venus, in that passage in the *Aeneid* where she appears incognito to Aeneas. But as Venus turns away, 'by her gait she revealed that she was in truth a goddess' (*vera incessu patuit dea*). All this was worth far more in evoking her aura than discussions of the 'Habsburg' lower lip she had inherited, which contemporary observers took for granted.

The failure of the modern eye, unless it is guided properly, was quaintly illustrated for me when I visited Hever Castle in Kent. This was where Anne of Cleves, the fourth wife, held sway following the collapse of her marriage to Henry VIII due, as every schoolchild knows, to his instant physical distaste for her person, dubbing her 'the Flanders Mare'. A party of schoolchildren who did of course know this were going round at the same time as myself. In this way I was privy to the following piece of dialogue:

Schoolchild A – 'There she is. The ugly one.'

Schoolchild B – 'Yes, there she is. Plug-ugly.'

But they were actually gazing at a portrait of Anne Boleyn! The captions had confused them. Anne Boleyn: she of the fascinating black eyes which she knew how to 'use with effect', sending a silent message that carried 'the secret testimony of the heart', in the words of a contemporary. Anne Boleyn: the siren of a second wife, who with her sensual appearance gathered Henry VIII into her toils. I looked again at the second wife: if I had not studied the evidence of eyewitnesses, would I really have understood her magnetism? In the same way, the portrait of Anne of Cleves, along the line, looked perfectly attractive to the outward eye, unless you knew what happened – or rather didn't happen – on her wedding night.

In the summer of 1950, there were lunches given by debutantes' mothers at which important social matters were ironed out; it was of course out of the question for Elizabeth to attend such things. Dances were arranged but also cocktail parties for those who could not afford a dance: some of these were shared conveniently between two families. The problem I faced was how to get myself on to the invitation list. There was only one answer. Since my mother was no help, I would bring myself out.

I did not realize at first that, as a future student at a university, with an assured place, I was a rarity among the debutantes. I was to discover this when I began to acquire some dancing partners who would politely ask me about my autumn plans: 'Are you going to the shoot at Stately Home X on November twenty-fifth . . . ?' 'No,' I would answer brightly: 'I'll be shooting down undergraduates. I'm going to Oxford.' After a few uncomprehending stares, I abandoned that line of chat and let it be understood that I was going to take a secretarial course, like the others. All the same I began dimly to understand the inestimable advantage I had in 1950 in having an ambitious mother – ambitious for her daughter academically, that is, and not like Mrs Bennet seeking an advantageous matrimonial bargain.

In truth, this instinct was the first small indication that a highly prized and successful relationship with my mother might lie ahead. My late teens were definitely the time when we were least in accord: to sum up, she only thought about Politics and Small Children, and I only thought about History and Romance. At the time, Elizabeth did give way to my wishes in one respect. She consented to host a modest cocktail party at the Allies Club in Park Lane, which had been fashionable during the war, I believe, but certainly wasn't now. I achieved this by making it clear that agreement would be less trouble than prolonged argument. The rest was up to me.

So it was a challenge that was all about winning and losing; although I did not attempt to scale the heights of the fabled Queen Charlotte's Ball, where debutantes were said to curtsey to a cake in the absence of the monarch. It was as though Marie Antoinette had withdrawn from the courtly fray and issued the directive: 'Let them curtsey to the cake.' That, I felt, would be a step too far for my mother and even, to be honest, for me. Sometimes I won when I managed to get to a dance because I had been at school with the girl concerned and discovered a spurious past intimacy between us. Sometimes I lost through trying to scale the heights, as when I failed to get to the ball at Holkham for Lady Anne Coke, a modern Gainsborough beauty. I won when I was invited to a shooting weekend in Hampshire by one John Baring, a quizzical fellow with a good sense of the ridiculous. He would have appreciated the entry in my diary noting the future event, with its order of priorities: 'I am terrified of doing the wrong thing,' I wrote. 'Also of getting shot.'

At this distance of time, I remain intensely grateful to all the hosts and hostesses who received me and – more or less – philosophical about those who didn't. Fortunately at least one event followed conventional lines of mother and daughter bonded together in attendance and that was my presentation at Buckingham Palace. Debutantes had to be presented by someone who had been presented herself, which category included of course Elizabeth, despite her lecturing at Stoke. I was even able to boast later of exchanging a few words with the Queen herself. This honour could hardly have been accorded to every single debutante at the packed occasion, although I'm sure the perpetually smiling Queen Elizabeth did her best. I was evidently the beneficiary of my father's official position as a Labour minister. Once again, this was something to set against his basic disinclination to attend any social occasion designed for my self-promotion.

'What would be the point, darling?' said Elizabeth sensibly. 'Dada would only go to sleep.' This was so obviously true that I had to hold my peace. It was an exchange I bore in mind much later when Harold entrusted me with the delicate mission of stopping Frank coming to his first nights: not only did my father fall asleep almost at once, but his prominent, highly recognizable slumbering figure gave, Harold felt, the wrong impression to the critics.

'So you are going to Oxford,' said the well-primed Queen Elizabeth in a friendly manner, after I had made my curtsey. 'Well, you must have a fling first.' Actually a fling was the last thing I wanted: on the contrary I wanted True Love, the sort I read about in books, not all of the high standard of *Pride and Prejudice*. It is a fact that, being a quick reader, apart from enabling a person to study good books such as Macaulay and Gibbon, enables a person to read a lot of bad books as well. It would however be ungrateful to pick out the titles that gave me such pleasure and stigmatize them as bad books; besides, I would maintain that such books can teach you narrative skill, which certainly never comes amiss in writing History. I made this point in the very first interview I gave to the press after writing *Mary Queen of Scots*, acknowledging my debt to Barbara Cartland for whom I had had a teenage addiction. The next day the doorbell rang and a chauffeur stood there with a huge parcel of books.

'With the compliments of Miss Barbara Cartland, my lady,' he said. 'The mixture as before,' read the engaging note which accompanied the books, signed by the author herself.

At the age of seventeen I had not yet found True Love (that would in fact turn out to be many, many years ahead). But I had got to the first stage: I had met my First Love. Patrick Lindsay was the dashing younger son of the Scottish Earl of Crawford and Balcarres. Extraordinarily handsome, with his thick black hair, eyebrows which met in the middle – 'a sign of jealousy,' he told me complacently – and his large compelling green eyes, Patrick Lindsay was every maiden's dream. Besides, with Patrick, the word dashing meant exactly what it said: he dashed in every possible sense of the word, dashing very fast down mountains, dashing about very fast in cars, and finally taking to aeroplanes where no doubt he dashed about the air as a pilot. Patrick's interests were not limited to fast sports, however. He would take me later to my first opera since that disastrous *Tales of Hoffmann* at which I had howled the house down on witnessing the death of Antonia. This was *The Marriage of Figaro* at Covent Garden with Geraint Evans as Figaro. The combination of Mozart, First Love and opera was irresistible: it seared me for ever. I still cannot hear the overture without feeling some welcome residue of romantic excitement.

I first encountered Patrick at a very different occasion, a hunt ball – how right I had been to fantasize about them when at Fenwick's! – and my behaviour was in no way elevated to Mozartian standards. Somehow I planted a sticky kiss on the shirtfront of his evening dress. Patrick was not best pleased by this: in fact I learnt later that he had quite a puritan attitude to make-up and smoking. At all events the lurid pink lipstick I favoured appeared to make more impression than I did. Besides this maiden's dream was said to be in love with a girl who was both a skiing champion and the niece of a duke. I could compete in neither category.

All the same, I had met my First Love and I knew that somewhere, somehow, as in books, we would meet again. In the meantime I was going to Oxford to study History. No, wait, I was going to study – what *was* the name of that subject? I would shortly find out.

CHAPTER TWELVE

OXFORD MISS

THERE WE WERE, WE FIRST-YEAR students, assembled in the Junior Common Room of Lady Margaret Hall
to be wised up about all that was hopefully to come. We were
told we could ask any questions we liked about the way things
worked in our new life. There was briefly silence. Then a very
small, very pretty girl, sitting in the front row more or less envel-
oped by her huge scholar's gown, said in a loud, confident voice:

'I have a question. What can we ask the scouts to do for us in
our rooms? Will they do some ironing?' These were the college
maids, known as scouts in imitation of the servants in the men's
colleges. I remember a gasp. Someone nudged me.

'That's Marigold Hunt. The Headgirl of Benenden.' It was
in fact my first sight of the future Marigold Johnson, who filled
me with admiration for her boldness: it was to inaugurate a
lifetime's friendship. At the time, being both domestically inadequate and terrified of my scout, I badly wanted to know the
answer.

My neighbour in the back row quizzed me: 'What are you
reading?'

'History,' I replied without thinking, *my* History. Then I had

to correct myself. 'Actually I got in on History, but now I'm reading Politics, Economics and . . .' My voice tailed away.

'Philosophy,' concluded my new friend helpfully. 'PPE.
You forgot Philosophy.' Everybody at LMH was clearly very
kind. Apart from this general atmosphere of kindness, the college, given its punitive rules, conveyed the impression of being
an enormous ladies' boarding school, more Godolphin than St
Mary's Ascot. Girls, or I should of course say women, were not
allowed to . . . the list was endless, many of them positively encouraging defiance. No man in your room before 2 p.m. or after
7 p.m.; no student to come back into the college later than 10 p.m.
The latter rule certainly led to some strange solutions, of which
spending the night out was the simplest; I developed a habit of returning for breakfast, carrying a black veil and a Missal, with the
smug expression of one who has recently attended early Mass.

Climbing in was another more exciting option, needing the
hefty arm of a man, from Christ Church perhaps, one who was
used to beagling, with oneself as the hound. That still did not
overcome the problem of the movable crinoline petticoat, alluded to in the previous chapter; after a dance, sporting girls
tended to throw the petticoat over first in a merry gamble that
the petticoat would not be stuck one side and the owner the
other. Another rule that visits to London were not permitted in
term time probably affected me more than most, given that my
social life, including my unrequited love, was still focused there.
I shall always bless the memory of the LMH tutor (not my own)
who happened to coincide with me on the platform of Oxford
station.

'Good afternoon, Miss Pakenham, an emergency dentist's appointment, no doubt.'

'Yes, definitely an emergency,' I gulped. It certainly was now,
if it had not been one originally. As equivocation, it was rather

clumsy: this was the art of not telling a positive lie while not conveying the truth either, which I came to study later over the Gunpowder Plot. But it satisfied both our consciences, the charitable don and the wayward student. I heard no more about it.

The original fine red-brick buildings of Lady Margaret Hall, named for Margaret Beaufort, scholarly mother of Henry VII, had been constructed before the First World War, and Deneke, rather less agreeable because the rooms were so small, designed by Giles Gilbert Scott in the year I was born. They were utterly different from the ancient and august stone structures which constituted my childhood memories of Oxford: that freezing room in Tom Quad where Frank taught had little in common, including the temperature, with the cosy sitting rooms in which the LMH dons resided. All this increased the impression of a boarding school, whereas Christ Church was what was meant by a college. Of course in yearning for icy-cold stone and tramps in the rain, instead of warm red-brick and bathrooms, I was being perverse. I was deeply impressed when my daughter Flora got a place at Wadham College to read Greats not long after girls were first admitted – three hundred and sixty-four years after its foundation in 1610. (Shades of the august Maurice Bowra of my youth!) I soon found out the discomfort which went with a greater sense of historical presence.

The gardens of LMH on the other hand were a joy. They were beautifully laid out and tranquil, rolling down towards the Cherwell – that river in which I had already immersed myself so often while living at 8 Chad and at the Dragon School. In fact, geographically LMH was virtually part of that North Oxford suburb in which I had grown up. I did not see it like that at the time, and it never occurred to me to wander in the direction of 8 Chad, down the footpath which skirted the Dragon School. The sound of bells which was the music of my childhood still came at evening from the chapels in the colleges; now the bells drew me towards the centre. My footsteps (and my bicycle) were firmly pointed in that direction.

I was however actually there to study. It was clear that academically things were already off to a bad start: there was something Freudian about my forgetting – yet again – what PPE stood for. Within the next few days they got worse when I attended my first lecture in . . . Philosophy, I suppose. At any rate, it was given by the future Waynflete Professor of Metaphysical Philosophy, Peter Strawson; the site was University College in the High Street. The first sight which greeted me was a blackboard. And the lecturer almost immediately began scribbling figures on it in chalk.

I felt the kind of desperate impulse which must animate a bride who bolts at the altar, regardless of all the actions that have got her there in the first place – because it's her last chance to escape. What had happened to *my* History? This was not why I had come to Oxford, to gaze at a blackboard covered in chalk figures. There and then I fled from Univ, into the High, dived towards the back streets of Christ Church, found my bicycle, and peddled frantically back to LMH. An awkward period of negotiation followed.

At some point, one of the dons involved murmured in a reasonable voice: 'If we had known you wanted to read History, not PPE, we would not have awarded you an Exhibition . . .' The implication was that there had been other more worthy candidates in a fair fight over a History award. So my mother had been right about that, I remember thinking. That didn't help me in my present fix.

'So are you going to take it away?' I burst out, thinking that would be the second piece of bad news, apart from my change of subject, I would have to confess in a letter to Elizabeth (I had no intention of risking a call from the single available telephone, a pay box in the porter's lodge). There must have been some kind of conference. The dons were essentially fair-minded women. I had been given an Exhibition without a condition publicly attached. I was allowed to keep it.

I should like to relate that this crisis and its generous resolution turned me into a model student. My love of History was genuine enough; the trouble was that in other ways I lacked seriousness. Or at any rate the kind of seriousness demanded of a girl student in 1950, who incidentally would be writing two essays a week to the one essay that the men wrote. Any girl who looked as if she might have pretensions to a social life was deliberately given a 9 a.m. tutorial to keep her alert to her real mission – or so we believed. Certainly my sessions on medieval History with Miss Naomi D. Hurnard, my so-called Moral Tutor, always seemed to take place at this antisocial hour. It was not the hour itself to which I objected, by nature being a lark rather than an owl (like my father). It was the fearful temptation it presented of doing nothing about my essay during the days before, and then getting up with that famous lark and writing, fast, very fast . . . This was no way for an aspiring historian to come to terms with her subject.

The trouble was compounded by an unhappy juxtaposition of teacher and pupil. Admiration for Mr Bussell, the man who believed nothing good had happened after the thirteenth century, convinced me that I wanted to study medieval History in particular (apart from the whole of English History, which we had to do as a matter of course). It was this which brought me into the orbit of Miss Hurnard, who would certainly have agreed that this match thrown up in Oxford was not one made in heaven.

Then in her forties, very pale, with black hair screwed into a bun, Miss Hurnard had long white hands which she extended together in the general direction of the fire. She looked remote; one has to bear in mind however that she was the author of violently learned articles about legal History which would culminate in the publication of *The King's Pardon for Homicide Before AD 1307*. Sometimes the hands appeared as if they might pick up the metal toast rack lying by the hearth; and what would they do with this sharp instrument? In the meantime Miss Hurnard never looked in my direction, only talked in elegantly composed sentences as she gazed into the flames. On the hearth lay her dog, a large, equally pale lump of Staffordshire bull terrier. When the dog, unlike the don, did look in my direction, I got an uneasy impression of transferred hostility.

Miss Hurnard's obituary in the LMH *Brown Book* would refer to 'the wintry warmth of her conversation': I experienced the winter but not the warmth. 'I was one of Sir Maurice Powicke's young ladies,' she sighed on one occasion, still looking firmly in the direction of the fire. The dog stirred, perhaps at the mention of the hallowed name, which was that of the immensely distinguished medievalist who had recently retired after twenty-odd years as Regius Professor of History. The impression given was that I would certainly never have fitted into this category.

I had several other tutors, both at LMH and elsewhere, with whom I got on better. Anne Whiteman, she who prided herself on being the model for Anthony Powell's Dr Emily Brightman, was a jolly woman, squarely built, not very tall, with short frizzy hair who generally wore square-cut tweeds. At all times she seemed determined to enjoy the teaching of History: naturally the student opposite also enjoyed the experience. Then there was the delightful Karl Leyser at Magdalen who subsequently became Chichele Professor of Medieval History. With his brooding dark looks and heavy brows he was a refugee from Hitler's Germany who, after a period of internment at the beginning of the war, was rightly proud of going on to serve in the Black

Watch. Although Karl's lessons could be incomprehensible to those not listening keenly, he felt an excitement about his subject which was inspiring if one was sensible enough to pay attention.

'Matilda of Tuscany!' he once exclaimed at the beginning of a tutorial and then paused for a long time as though in ecstasy at the mere thought.

Hugh Leech, a young don at Balliol, was a man of great sweetness who once took the trouble to visit my mother in London and warn her against my wild ways. He believed that I *could* get a First but feared I would do something outrageous and be sent down. (In theory, I suppose anyone who received an award on getting into the University must be in line for a First.) Touchingly, Mr Leech had developed a theory that I was rebelling against Catholicism. This was far from being the case: I was a keen Mass-goer, quite apart from those spurious visits which were supposed to explain my breakfast return to LMH.

The truth was that I was not very wild, even those forbidden overnight stays being more the product of LMH rules and a wish to prolong the party than any more exciting developments. But I rather wished I were. Or at least, I wished to be seen as such, without the more testing task of following through. As we of the early Fifties inched slowly towards social freedom, we were in many respects essentially respectable tortoises who wanted to be seen as madcap hares; except, in this case, it would be the madcap hares of the Sixties who won the race. The shadow of the Bright Young Things of the Twenties – we'd all read Evelyn Waugh – fell athwart us, but in a time of clinging austerity there was nothing particularly bright about us (hardly any undergraduates had cars and they tended to be both male and older; I never met a girl student who owned a car).

One episode sums up my own rather inept attitude to all this. Tom Stacey was one contemporary who was notably more enterprising than the rest of us, as his subsequent career as explorer, politician, publisher, writer and penal reformer, just for starters, would go on to demonstrate. In the Festival of Britain year he conceived the idea of Undergrad Tours: put simply, we, the impoverished undergraduates, were to make a great deal of money out of the wealthy tourists by showing them round the sights of Oxford. I was all for it, the money side of it, that is. I was more uneasy about Tom's ebullient way with publicity, but unable to resist it since I was assured publicity was essential to our success. In the event, my diary records only one tour by three allegedly wealthy tourists, and then I paid for our lunch myself.

You could say that the publicity side of it all was more successful, especially if you believe that there is no such thing as bad publicity. To promote us, in a group which included Tim Renton, a future Tory Chief Whip, I agreed to smoke a cigar despite the fact that I had never smoked cigarettes, not out of any principle (which would have been rare at that time) but insecurity mixed with vanity: I thought I looked ridiculous with the minute white object stuck in my mouth, especially when it dropped on to the Bernhurst sofa by mistake. None of this prevented me freely posing with the cigar in the interests of fortune if not fame. As for the rest of my appearance, I wore a blue velvet pixie hat, with a grey suit and pearls, a sophisticated fashion statement as I saw it, which made for difficult bicycling. In the end, it was my lack of any true sophistication which found me out. Anthony Powell summed it up in the card he sent me when he saw the photograph in the press: 'Take the band off the cigar next time when you smoke one,' he wrote.

The fact was that I had not yet discovered that truth so perfectly expressed in a line of verse by Hugh's old friend, the poet-diplomat Sir Charles Johnston: 'Having fun is such hard work.' In time I would discover the truth of the exact opposite, that working hard on what you really wanted to do could be the greatest fun in the world; but that was in the future. It is essentially a grown-up truth and I had not yet got there. Meanwhile, I had occasional intimations of what intellectual pleasure might be, as opposed to the elusive other sort. These intimations did not however occur during my infrequent attendances at lectures. When it came to living historians, I much preferred reading their books in a library to listening to the spoken word; so I only attended grumpily when I was assured that the research concerned had not yet been published. (Oh, why wouldn't Bruce McFarlane get on with it?) I tended to concentrate on my parents' friends, like Isaiah Berlin and David Cecil, who were of course the famous lecturers of the time.

'You're just a tourist looking for sensations.' When Isaiah Berlin spoke these teasing words to me in his rapid glottal voice, he got it absolutely right. Lord David Cecil's lectures were a particular delight: he would rush in rather late, in a flurry, and proceed to read aloud from, shall we say, Jane Austen. That occupied about twenty minutes, by which the prescribed hour's lecture was nearly gone, and the rest of the time would be occupied by David, in his equally characteristic voice, the voice of an aristocrat in love with literature, giving us pleasant insights. The most celebrated lectures all the time I was at Oxford were given by the art historian E. H. Gombrich. And they took place at the Ashmolean Museum.

'Tea after Gombrich?' was the kind of smart invitation you hoped to get, especially from someone at nearby St John's in St Giles or Worcester College, down the road. I wish I could remember one word of what I heard before these wished-for teas took place. Compared to the thrill of reading a book by Gombrich, the mind ungratefully blanks out.

So the first real intimation of the pleasure of historical research
– in the proper academic sense – came with a special small class
held at Merton College: there were three of us, and the two men,
Alan Brownjohn and Jon Stallworthy, went on to become well-
known poets. I on the other hand went on to become someone
who adored digging into historical documents with my mental
spade. I had a double task. First I was to investigate one volume
of the manuscripts held at Hatfield House, seat of the Marquess
of Salisbury, whose ancestors were advisers to Queen Elizabeth
I, printed by the Historical Manuscripts Commission. Secondly
I was to write a paper about what I found. For once, this was no
hasty how-fast-can-I-do it job. I revelled in the task.

In the Sixties I was able to read some of the originals when
I was writing about Mary Queen of Scots, and the Marquess of
Salisbury allowed me into his library at Hatfield. This was an
honour for an as-yet-unpublished historian and even the formidable Lady Salisbury's greeting did not diminish it.

'Why are you writing about that silly woman Mary Queen
of Scots?' she demanded. 'Why not write about Queen Elizabeth
instead?' (Many years later I did attempt it, but, finding that I
personally had nothing new to say about this fascinating woman,
gave it up.) At the time the excitement of fingering respectfully
the letter which Mary Queen of Scots had once touched – this
was an age before gloves were requested – equalled but did not
exceed that original dramatic discovery at Merton: this was
something I wanted to do, was determined to do, and hoped to
do for the rest of my life.

I could not see into the future. I did not know that I would
one day be sitting in the Archives Nationales in Paris, this time
fully equipped with white gloves, gazing at the only copy of the
Wardrobe Book of Marie Antoinette which had survived the
French Revolution, watched by two armed French gendarmes,

feeling almost as terrified as I felt excited. What would happen to me if I left a blotch? Was the Bastille still in use? At the time in Oxford, it was enough that this was another Keatsian moment, as when I first learnt to read: once again magic casements opened. By chance, I subsequently came across that exact volume of the Historical Manuscripts Commission looking unloved on a dusty back shelf of a second-hand bookshop. It cost three pounds. Naturally I bought it.

Given this revelation, and the pleasing welcome accorded to me by my parents' Oxford friends, it seems strange that at the time I felt that Oxford was more of a miss than a hit. Of the friends, Hugh Trevor-Roper was particularly hospitable to Frank's daughter, although I saw him more in the light of a bachelor don in a dark blue velvet evening jacket who went hunting in the day and entertained at night, than as the celebrated historian he already was. (*The Last Days of Hitler* came out in 1947.) David and Rachel Cecil, still in Linton Road, frequently asked me to dinner; the spare man who was chosen to balance the numbers was, more often than not, John Bayley. Looking like a substantial owl, he was not my idea of Prince Charming and, given that he would go on, famously, to marry Iris Murdoch, he would no doubt have said the same about me. But I much enjoyed his company: somehow he managed to be both cheerful and lugubrious at the same time.

It is possible that in this privileged access, due to my parentage and my North Oxford upbringing rather than my own efforts, lay one reason for my slightly disconsolate reaction to university. I experienced none of the wonder that my mother described to me on her first day at Oxford University: how whirling up to LMH alone without her dominating parents was the most liberating experience of her life. How could I? I had whirled nowhere; or if I had, I had certainly not left my parents' world behind.

It is perfectly true that there is one advantage of a university education, whatever one's background, for which I will always be grateful. That is the unforced encounter with people of different nationalities, especially important perhaps for wartime children. Friendships could and did exist which illumined the vast world outside. There were two cases in point at LMH, two intriguing girls who were roughly my contemporaries.

Alia El-Solh, like Masha in *The Seagull,* always wore black (except for her dressing gown which was red, but that was in private). She explained to me the reason with simplicity: 'They killed my father.' I learnt that this was the former Prime Minister of the Lebanon, assassinated in July 1951 shortly after his second term of office. Up to this point, I had never paused to think about the Middle East (except in biblical times) and occasional forays into reading newspapers about the military campaigns of the war. Now I made a few nervous attempts to find out *something* in order to get to know Alia El-Solh better and not make a fool of myself.

With Sabel Desta, granddaughter of Haile Selassie, Emperor of Ethiopia, time was to bring about a closer connection. In the LMH first-year photo Sabel stands on the sideline (I am at the back, Marigold at the front, an excellent guide to our standing in the college). Sabel's aristocratic features, her high cheekbones and large black almond eyes give an impression of *hauteur*; this was very far from being the case. Cheerful and hard-working, she hardly deserved to be imprisoned after the fall of her grandfather's regime, along with her five young children. By then a visit to Ethiopia while Haile Selassie was still in power, and a long rugged trip up mountains where no mule foot had ever trod (or so it seemed) under Thomas's auspices had made me feel close to the country and Sabel's family. I ended by protesting outside the Ethiopian Embassy against Sabel's and others' long incarceration (fourteen years altogether): Sabel, the cheerful young woman first encountered at LMH.

Another obvious reason for my ungratefully tepid reaction to Oxford lay in my love life at the time. Things had come right between Patrick Lindsay and myself – as I saw it – and unrequited love had turned into grand passion – once again in my version. But Patrick, destined for a job in the art world, had first of all studied with Bernard Berenson in Italy, and then, giving vent to his other more extrovert side, decided to sail the Atlantic in a yacht. Of course, the love object being at a distance, even on a yacht in mid-Atlantic – oh the perils! oh the privations! – has never yet dimmed a first-rate passion. The situation seemed to me vaguely operatic, that new pleasure to which Patrick had so successfully introduced me.

Before and after these *sorties,* typically adventurous in different ways, Patrick took me to his home in Scotland, Balcarres in Fife. It was an introduction to another side of Scottish History, not so much the character of her romantic Queen, more about the nobility who had been prominent in her reign. Patrick had an immense pride in the family history of the Lindsays, who, he assured me, had once been known as the Lightsome Lindsays, although at what period was not clear. His father Lord Crawford was certainly not lightsome: his record of public service to the arts included the trusteeship of every museum you could name from the National Gallery and the Tate, to the British Museum and the National Galleries of Scotland. His huge head of silver hair held high and his fine Roman nose also aloft, he might have given an impression of pomposity; his courtesy to all and sundry quickly corrected that.

'I'm so glad you're able to see our Stanley Spencer, *The May Tree,*' he said to me. 'As you know, it's generally away on exhibition. You understand the problem one has in refusing these requests.' I was taken aback but flattered at being included among those who had this particular problem. Lady Crawford, small and private, was not lightsome either. She appeared to regard me, and indeed the rest of the world, with a certain suspicion. When I came to listen to her dry comments on her various relations including her husband, I realized that, quite as much as the great Lord Crawford, she lived life on her own terms.

The lightsome one was of course Patrick: it was in fact the combination of his dashing ways and his true fascination with art history – he ended up as Head of the Old Masters Department of Christie's – which held me in his spell all the time I was at Oxford. My diary resonates with good days when I saw or heard from him, and bad days when the brief entry 'Miz' probably meant that neither had taken place. There were plenty of visits to the opera. Our relationship reached its height in a trip to Italy, Patrick driving his ancient car with two other passengers. These were my brother Thomas and the beautiful Vanessa Jebb, admired generally by all at Oxford and the particular object of my brother's affections. Thomas had arrived in Oxford to read Greats at Magdalen the year following me. As has been mentioned, he had failed the test for National Service because of his childhood attack of polio and was thus in the small category of undergraduates (male: women did not do National Service) who were about eighteen when they came up.

Comparative youth did not faze Thomas, any more than the spirit of the boy once famous for asking 'Hujamean' and 'Wajamean' at every conceivable opportunity had been dimmed. One of his early actions was to buy a very cheap decommissioned taxi, which he baptized Pythia, after the Delphic oracle. Pythia certainly manifested much of the unhelpfully enigmatic spirit of the original for whom she had been named. On one famous occasion, Pythia gave a few grunts.

'You hear that rattle?' said Thomas carelessly over his shoulder through the glass window to Henrietta and myself, deposited in the back seat. We were in full finery, scanty shawls over our off-the-shoulder dresses. My home-made black tulle was still going strong even if I had to cut off the ragged pieces at the bottom of the skirt where energetic dancers had trodden on them, so that the dress was now somewhat shorter. We were all three attending (without permission) the coming-out ball of Caroline Child-Villiers in London, determined not to miss such an august occasion hosted by her father, our cousin Grandie Jersey. 'It sounds like the big end going,' said Thomas. 'Of course it isn't.' But it was. The rattle had been a message from the oracle, once again misinterpreted.

I cannot remember how long we lurked in the black depths of the Pythia on the edge of the dark road before rescue came. I do know that we proceeded to London by hitchhiking, despite our unsuitable clothes, and that finally we tagged in wearily to the ball. 'How did you come from Oxford?' 'By taxi' – well, it was partly true. Thomas was the only one who was in no way put off by all this, occasionally commenting with surprise on the extraordinary coincidence of the big end actually going at the same time as it sounded like it.

On our Italian trip, the fact that the knowledgeable Patrick was our guide and driver did not put Thomas off either. He had his own sturdy independent views, in this case mainly from the back seat. Patrick owned the car, a Triumph which seemed very grand to us, and had a little money to pay for petrol, but the rest of us could contribute practically nothing. As a result, all four of us camped out every night in sleeping bags, for economy's sake, except when we could winkle our way into the grand Italian house to which Patrick had an introduction. We were on the cadge throughout our journey, including the moment in a small

Italian town when Patrick spotted a friend of his father's sitting alone at a table across the square.

'At least he'll give us all some coffee. He's always coming to Balcarres.' But the haughty individual sitting in solitude at the café showed absolutely no signs of entertaining us; in fact, by his body language alone, he displayed a strong preference for the rapid departure of this little ragged party. It was Sir Anthony Blunt. Afterwards, when his career as a spy was exposed, I worked it out from the dates that he must have been waiting for some kind of illicit contact and I felt a vicarious thrill. At the time we were disconsolate, except for Patrick, who was indignant when he thought about all the Balcarres hospitality. We sloped back across the square like unwanted dogs.

So that was a failure. The success was our visit to Bernard Berenson, for whom Patrick had worked at Villa I Tatti before his yacht trip to America. It was a success, that is, for Vanessa and myself; I'm not sure that Patrick and Thomas in their different ways shared this view. The great man was now in his late eighties, a small but very dignified figure, with a well-trimmed silver beard; he was wearing a lot of clothes for such hot weather, as well as a hat, but that only added to his impressive aura. 'B.B.', as he was known, was presented to us as the pre-eminent authority on Renaissance Art, and Patrick's hero; I knew nothing of his more controversial history with the art dealer Joseph Duveen. Vanessa and I found him to be extremely benevolent in a delightfully paternal manner, as though it was an especial pleasure to encounter young ladies like ourselves. We were placed on either side of him at lunch; he smiled warmly at us. B.B., however, showed no similar desire to be paternal towards my brother Thomas, who was put at the bottom of the long table under the arches; either that or Patrick, scenting trouble, had influenced the placement.

Patrick, if it was indeed his initiative, was right. Towards the end of lunch, Thomas leant forward – he had to lean a long way to make himself heard – and said in a loud voice: 'Mr Berenson, you have made a pretty good thing out of the Renaissance, haven't you?' B.B. did not miss a beat. He continued to smile, a smile that included Vanessa and me, and might even have included Thomas. He gave no acknowledgement whatsoever of the importunate question. Twice more, the demanding voice from the bottom of the table was heard. Each time B.B. smiled on. Eventually Thomas gave up. Yes, a great man indeed.

My romance with Patrick did not last, not because of the importunities of my brother, for whom he retained a strong if exasperated affection. (In later years, in arguments over family pictures, Thomas probably felt the same.) For all my hopes and sighs and wishes, his ardent protestations and plans, Patrick and I were simply not meant to spend our lives together. The trouble was that we both found difficulty acknowledging the fact to each other, given the heady relationship we had enjoyed while I was at Oxford. It was understandable – I was still only twenty when I left and Patrick four years older.

There was undoubtedly a certain amount of deception on both sides, due to this shared reluctance to say goodbye. For my part, those summer nights in Oxford, my last summer term, could not really pass without romance of some sort; and as for summer days, what are punts *for*, if not for gazing upwards in rapture at the manly figure in charge? From Patrick's point of view, he was now in London, and once more every maiden's dream.

In any case, in a mysterious but timely fashion, my historical work had suddenly returned into my life with renewed significance. Having malingered over medieval History, on a sudden impulse I chose a completely different special subject. This was known as 'The Making of the Ententes' and referred to the period in the first decade of the twentieth century, in which various diplomatic alliances were constructed in Europe; arguably these Ententes would lead up to the First World War, although the precise connection is still debated. I cannot now remember why I defiantly chose a special subject so far from my earlier declared medieval interests. And it was defiance: I was delicately warned that it might harm my academic prospects. The implication was that I would be regarded as a historical flibbertigibbet. I suspect that in the first place I got interested in the character of Edward VII, who played a major role in these events. (Did that define me as a flibbertigibbet?)

What I did not know at the time of my choice was the fact that this whole period was a special interest of my father's. To me, Frank at this point was a dedicated politician, and I had not cared to investigate his academic career. The final job he held in the first post-war Labour government was that of First Lord of the Admiralty. By his own account, Frank hesitated before taking it: it was his past which still haunted him. 'Was it really possible that I, with my own inglorious war record, could supply leadership and inspiration to the finest Navy in the world?' Mr Attlee persuaded him to accept with the cheerful reflection: 'The Navy survived Winston and Brendan – it will probably survive you.' Five happy months followed, in which we had the use of Admiralty House, remarkable for harbouring in winter the so-called Fish Furniture, the wondrous Regency suite in the shape of dolphins from the Brighton Pavilion. This coincided with the Oxford holidays. All too briefly, my entertainment of my friends in London took on a remarkable lustre.

In the General Election at the end of October 1951, Labour was defeated and Frank's spell in the government came to an end. He returned in due course to Oxford, the place he really loved, and thanks to the influence of Robert Blake (so Frank always said) resumed teaching at Christ Church. It was in this way that father and daughter coincided at the University, and Frank became my unofficial tutor on 'The Making of the Ententes'. It was an extraordinary timely discovery that my father was a thrilling tutor just as I was approaching my final year: more than that, just as I was working on a subject which really intrigued me.

It marked a new stage in our relationship and an exciting one: suddenly my beloved but abstracted parent reading a book who left all decisions to my mother, was transformed into a vigorous, argumentative historian who enjoyed debating the subject as much as I did. I might actually be reading his same book. The coincidence led to a kind of obsession with the whole pre-First World War period in general, Sir Edward Grey in particular. It never quite left me. When I was contemplating writing a work of History, shortly after my first marriage, I suggested the title *Summer 1914* to my publisher. It was not a serious suggestion – with two children in eighteen months, I really just wanted a lawful excuse to read History books instead of *The Adventures of Babar*. I did accept a hundred-pound advance, but then honourably returned the money – as I recall it.

A little while later the publisher rang me: 'Someone has written your book,' he said. The author was Barbara W. Tuchman and the book was *The Guns of August*, alternatively known as *August 1914*. Immediately on first reading, this became one of my favourite History books and has remained so: the mixture of scholarship, readability and a quality which I will call humanity entranced me. I had a further reaction. In part, I felt, accurately enough, that I could never have written that particular book half so well; another part of me felt that one day I might at least try to write a similar kind of book *almost* as well. It was an inspirational experience, as when I read Garrett Mattingly's *The Defeat of the Spanish Armada*, or Keith Thomas's *Religion and the Decline of Magic* in 1971; the latter in particular showed me another way of writing History and profoundly influenced my study of women in seventeenth-century England, *The Weaker Vessel*.

There is a footnote to the Barbara Tuchman story. Invited to the American Embassy to meet the distinguished historian herself, I was overwhelmed with hero-worship for this pleasant, confident, middle-aged American lady with her elegant dress and well-arranged silver hair who had achieved so much. I could say nothing to her. When I explained this to Harold, he responded sympathetically: 'I felt just the same way when I met Denis Compton.' From a cricket fanatic to a History freak, it seemed exactly the right comparison.

The time for Schools, as the examinations were known, arrived. To show seriousness, we had to wear *sub fusc,* that is black-and-white clothes, black ties for the men, black stockings for the girls (to show something else, I chose to wear black nylons with saucy seams down the back, the sort that kindly Americans had bestowed on girls in the war; invigilators looked at me with disapproval but could not find that it was actually forbidden).

The day before, the Coronation of Queen Elizabeth II had taken place. I received a ticket to a stand facing down the Embankment, from which I would see the girl Queen arriving as yet uncrowned for her destiny, but would then be able to depart for last-minute frantic study. There seemed a splendid allegorical meaning to all this: I too was a young woman seeking her destiny, although it happened to be in the rather less glamorous Examination Schools of Oxford, rather than Westminster Abbey. My ruminative mood was suddenly disturbed by raucous shouts of glee as I crossed the forecourt of Parliament to reach my stand: the successful climbing of Everest had just been announced. Luckily, the young Queen, looking so tiny, so fragile, in her coach more than satisfied expectations. And I was soon able to trail back to Chelsea where my parents now lived in the week.

I walked alone along the Embankment for half an hour without seeing a single human being, only birds along the river. I felt like someone in a science fiction movie, alone in a world struck by some out-of-space disaster. But these fresh meditations were interrupted when I realized that all the human beings were sitting indoors, with their heads towards the real portents of the future, their new television sets.

As to the examinations which followed, of course I did not get a First. How could I? I had not done nearly enough proper hard work over three years to fulfil any such expectations. But hope springs . . . because I was twenty and hope is mercifully impartial. Afterwards it was on balance gratifying to hear a rumour that I had done so well in my Ententes paper, and so badly in a medieval one, that there had been some doubt whether the same person could have written both papers. If true, it was a tribute to my father. As it was, he would perform one further good deed in the interests of bolstering me up.

Frank took an acute interest in my degree; this was not entirely due to the possibility of parental pride (or disappointment). As we shall see, he was a master handler of disappointment, no doubt because that searing experience of failure in the army stayed with him. In fact it wasn't just *my* degree. As an academic in his early career, he took a keen interest in all degrees and remembered them long after in later life: When Alec Douglas-Home became Prime Minister, I recall Frank throwing in the fact that he had got a Fourth.

In July, I received only a short perfunctory Viva, the oral cross-examination following Schools, by which a student might raise her or his degree up a level in answer to questions. From this I knew immediately that I had not got a First. To receive an un-Viva-ed First was extremely rare, and certainly not in prospect for me.

I went back to LMH and into the coin box by the porter's lodge. I rang my father.

'Dada, I'm awfully sorry but I haven't got a First.' Frank did not even pause. Quick as a flash he said: 'Oh, I'm so glad. Because if you had, you would never have got married.'

About ten years later, I remembered the exchange and out of curiosity asked Hugh whether he would have married me if I had got a First.

'Oh, but I always thought you *did* get a First,' he replied.

CHAPTER THIRTEEN

JEUNE FILLE IN PUBLISHING

'HIS NAME IS GEORGE WEIDENFELD,' said Elizabeth, 'and he's a brilliant young publisher.' She added: 'He's very interested in offering you a job.' This was her edited version of a conversation regarding my future which in George Weidenfeld's subsequent account went somewhat differently. He sat next to my mother at some London dinner party and mentioned that he was looking for a new recruit to his newish firm Weidenfeld & Nicolson. He wanted a girl to balance a young man from Cambridge, Nicolas Thompson, recommended by Hugh Trevor-Roper. As he outlined his needs, George waxed eloquent, particularly on the subject of languages, which were highly necessary for his European-minded firm but he found sadly lacking in most young English people: French naturally, perfect French, German (he was publishing a lot of war memoirs), Italian, which he spoke fluently himself, useful Spanish, Swedish, Swahili . . . the list went on and on. At all points Elizabeth nodded vigorously.

This she-paragon should also be immensely intelligent, and, if still at university, sure of getting a magnificent degree at the end of it. The she-paragon should also have unrivalled social talents (what would now be called people-skills). Pretty, of course: I learnt later that George did not contemplate the possibility of women in his universe who were not attractive, as a result of which all of them were – or, more to the point, felt that they were. Elizabeth kept up her vigorous nodding to the end. When it was clear that George had at last exhausted his specifications, she did not hesitate: 'Look no further. I have just the girl for you. She is my daughter Antonia.' George admitted to me later that he was slightly surprised that Elizabeth did not even pretend to advance any other candidates. A lunch was duly arranged at the house in Chester Square where George lived with his young wife Jane Sieff and new-born baby Laura.

The prospect of joining a publisher came as a welcome relief to me at Oxford, after my mother's first ambitious plan for me, that I should go into the Foreign Office. This meant passing a stiff exam; furthermore at that date a woman left the Foreign Office if she got married. There was a third element to be considered: I would have been a rotten diplomat. (It would be thirteen years before my mother's ambitions in this direction were finally gratified by the diplomatic success of my brother Michael.) Then Elizabeth gradually let slip George's requirements, especially about languages, and I began to feel like the peasant girl in the fairy tale whose father persuades the prince to marry her by promising she can spin straw into gold.

It was true that lunch passed merrily enough and to my secret relief no other language but English was spoken. Nothing was said about a job since the conversation was mainly about the naval review which had followed the recent Coronation. Fred Warner, a diplomat, urbane and amusing as all diplomats should be, who had been in the navy in the war, held the table at a roar with his account of all the marine antics. I lacked the nerve to raise the subject of the future when I left. In fact, it was not until

September that I had the wit to telephone the firm and begin rather gingerly: 'My name is Antonia Pakenham and I wondered . . .' George's secretary was terse. 'You'd better come in on Monday.' I had no idea whether I was expected but with the pressing need to earn my living (my modest allowance ended when I left Oxford), I thought it best not to enquire further.

George might have been my mother's idea of a young publisher, but he did not seem young to me. He was actually in his early thirties at the time but he looked no particular age. A Jewish refugee from Austria, son of a dispossessed university professor, he resembled the French King Louis XVI, husband of Marie Antoinette, except that he suffered from none of the poor young King's difficulties with women: George loved women and women loved him back, particularly as he had the best chat-up line in the world at his disposal: 'Have you ever thought of writing a book?' Pause full of meaning, then: 'I believe you would write a very good book.' He was also (unlike Louis XVI who was portly and clumsy) a deft and graceful dancer. George's enormous rolling eyes, like gooseberries, were ever on the lookout for new projects, new books, new areas of the publishing world to conquer.

His was already a remarkable success story since the day in 1938 when he arrived in London with the helpful address of a boarding-house in his pocket: Belgrave something. Thus he found himself in Belgrave Square where, to his faint surprise, there was a large party going on of not particularly helpful people. Luckily, the policeman in the square was on his side. He advised George that he probably was not looking for the house of Mr Chips Channon MP; inspecting the paper, he directed him to Bel*grove* Street, near King's Cross. The time would come when Weidenfeld & Nicolson would publish the celebrated ultra-worldly diaries of Chips Channon: sweet revenge.

With his talent for languages, George got work with the BBC, evacuated to the country in wartime: he told me that he used to bicycle round the lanes of Gloucestershire, a marvellous image, wearing a tweed jacket with leather patches on the elbows; this appropriately rural garb was the fashion tip of his mentor Flora Solomon, described in his autobiography as 'the remarkable Russian-Jewish *grande dame* who ran the staff welfare department at Marks & Spencer'. Contact Books which followed was originally founded as a cover for *Contact* magazine, a means of circumventing the government's restrictions on new periodicals at a time of paper-rationing. The first publication of Contact Books was called *New Deal for Coal*. The author was a young man hoping to become a Labour MP in the 1945 General Election – one Harold Wilson.

Weidenfeld & Nicolson was founded in 1949. Nigel Nicolson, the co-founder, was the son of Harold Nicolson and Vita Sackville-West; by 1953 he had become the Conservative MP for Bournemouth and, busy with his new political career, was no more than a benevolent presence in our lives. His father on the other hand was not noticeably benevolent towards Weidenfeld & Nicolson, and the gossip of the time suggested that he had not been happy at his son linking his fortunes (and his name) with that of a Jewish refugee. It was true that Harold Nicolson had briefly joined Mosley's New Party in the early Thirties, but then he had withdrawn support when Mosley founded the British Union of Fascists; Nicolson had then been a prominent advocate of rearmament in the House of Commons. I was a reluctant witness of what was undoubtedly a sincere attempt to put paid to the ill-natured gossip about his disapproval. Unfortunately it went the way of many other good intentions – that is, created further trouble.

George began to give those dinner parties for which he

would become famous and remain so, for over sixty years. But the dining room at Chester Square, unlike the first-floor drawing room, was not very large. So far as I was concerned, George pioneered the social convention of asking a great many people in after dinner, following a meal given for very few. This of course demanded that the privileged few finish their meal in good time and adjourn upstairs . . . this did not always happen. How could it when the talk was so entertaining, the company so infinitely amusing? Too often the many, on arrival, would have to pass the dining room from which emanated the noise of the privileged ones carousing. On the occasion in question, the butler discreetly muttered in George's ear, and he waved a lordly hand in my direction: 'Miss Pakenham will go upstairs and keep him company.'

Dutifully I trotted upstairs to the large drawing room, where an angry Father Christmas of a man – I think he must have been wearing some kind of red velvet evening jacket – greeted me, puffing out his red cheeks beneath his white curls in disgust at the way he had been treated. This was Harold Nicolson, now in his late sixties, whose writings I loved; I was particularly fond of *Some People*, a series of whimsical semi-autobiographical essays where fact and fiction were entwined in an elegant embrace. I had not yet read his authorized life of King George V, which had been published the year before and for which Nicolson had recently been knighted, but was quite sure I could bluff my way through with sufficient starry-eyed praise. Disraeli famously said: 'Everyone likes flattery and when you come to Royalty, you should lay it on with a trowel.' I felt that one could usefully adapt that to include royal biographers.

Admiration of any sort was however not the emotion which characterized our exchange. The experienced and highly distinguished diplomat, as he had been for many years before his political career, vanished. Instead Sir Harold Nicolson was extra-ordinarily cross, first of all with his host, his absent-downstairs host, and then by inference with the messenger, who was me. At least I realized that he was in the grip of some strong emotion which probably did not include me in any way. That, of course, was the truth. He was, in his own opinion, taking a gracious step forward in the direction of welcoming his son's partner, only to be snubbed in this unexpected manner. I should conclude this episode by reporting that he sent me the most charming abject apology, handwritten, the next day: 'Dear Miss Pakenham, I behaved unconscionably badly last night . . .' And I never told George Weidenfeld about it since the door had already banged shut behind the departing Sir Harold when he escorted his dinner guests upstairs.

Nevertheless it is interesting to reflect that in the early Fif-ties there could be surprising social reactions to George. That is, they were surprising to me, just as the invidious Catholic prayer on Good Friday removed by Pope John XXIII had surprised me; this was partly because my parents were clearly philo-semitic, but more significantly, because as I have recorded earlier, reading about the opening of the camps in the newspapers to which I was addicted had been one of the defining experiences of my later childhood. So any form of anti-semitism, however covert, left me first baffled and then angry, something I made clear when I had the courage to do so, which wasn't always.

'Isn't it sometimes, well . . . *difficult*, working for George Wei-denfeld?' was one question intended to be delicate, which began by baffling me. Difficult was the very last thing that George was. In three years working for him, I never encountered a cross word; even when a lesser spirit might legitimately have complained, George merely showed temporary pain before pass-ing on to higher things. When I demonstrated genuine lack of comprehension at the question, the next words would be something like: 'You being a Catholic and all that.' The word 'Catholic' gave me the clue. My diary explodes: 'The next time I'm asked that stupid question I intend to reply as follows: "Oh, George Weidenfeld is wonderful; he never minds when I flop to my knees at noon and publicly say the rosary."'

Only one thing was accurate about this fantasy picture: George would not have minded in the least, in the unlikely event of finding me saying the rosary kneeling on the floor of the office. I doubt he would have noticed. He would either have been rushing out to some exciting lunch full of plans for books to be outlined to a new author, or rushing back many hours later, full of plans for quite different books which the author had outlined to him. The point was that he lived in a perpetual state of excitement about his publishing plans. As a result, so did we all, his small staff in the cramped office next door to a gallery in Cork Street. On the day he returned from a reconnaissance trip to the United States, the atmosphere was electric. George did not so much rush in on this occasion as fly in over our heads, aloft on clouds of expectation.

It was incidentally this tireless round which made me understand quite soon that my 'spinning-straw-into-gold' fears for my lack of languages to be uncovered (those languages so rashly promised by Elizabeth) were unfounded. George spoke all the languages himself. My role was obviously something different. But while I was finding out what I was supposed to be doing for him, George was doing a great deal for me. Here at last was my university, if that term entails entry into a new and hitherto unknown world. It was a question of European culture, to which, by his mere presence and conversation, George did more to introduce me than he could ever know (or I ever wanted him to find out).

There was that moment, for example, when he complimented me on my appearance at a Weidenfeld party, referring to me as a *'Jeune fille en fleur'*. I regret to say that the Proustian reference to the girls at the seaside at Balbec in the second volume of *À la Recherche du Temps Perdu* was completely lost on me. *'Jeune fille* on what?'* more or less sums up my reaction. I believe it was Peter Quennell, a cynical but not unkindly man, who noticed my puzzled expression and was slyly amused by it. He enlightened me. I hastened to read Proust, sort of in French, but with the Scott Moncrieff translation remarkably close at hand. Should this compliment ever come my way again, I would be ready with the right smile – deprecating yet knowing; one might mutter something about Balbec if one was in a daring mood . . .

Part of this lack of European culture was due to wartime conditions and post-war restrictions on travel. As we have seen, my one venture into France had not resulted in much cultural enlightenment, although it gave me a valuable insight into the effects of the recent war. Similarly, my memorable Christmas spent with the De Gasperis enhanced my sense of Italian history, not Italian culture. My parents' primary energies were concentrated on politics. There were occasional shafts of light when I was at Oxford, as when my friend Laurence Kelly, son of an ambassador and himself half Belgian, insisted that all of us read someone called Robert Musil; he also instructed us to talk a lot about *angst*. But it was George Weidenfeld, naturally at home everywhere in Europe where there was literature or music, who was the real influence. I did not move away from my passion for History, but I was enchanted by the other possibilities now presented to me.

Perhaps my greatest single debt to George was in the realm of music. George introduced me to his beloved Wagner, in the shape of the Ring Cycle, beginning with a memorable night at

Covent Garden. From the first moment I was intoxicated. Being introduced to Wagner by George meant that I was lucky enough to be spared any crisis of conscience about anti-semitism or otherwise; I could simply get on with adoring it all, music, text, the whole world of love and lightning, death and thunder. It was, as it turned out, a memorable night for George also, although I did not learn that until quite a while later. He had previously taken me out to a dinner with John Sutro which ended at the most fashionable nightclub of the time called the Milroy. On our way to dinner, George mentioned that to his annoyance John Sutro was bringing along Barbara Skelton, a famous siren then married to Cyril Connolly: among her many conquests, generally men of physical bulk and worldly power, was rumoured to be the Egyptian King Farouk. Sirens on their rocks do not on the whole regard young female fish in the sea below them with any particular favour, and Barbara was no exception to this rule. I commiserated with George quite sincerely.

What I completely missed in the ensuing long-drawn-out evening, including dancing, was that Barbara had taken one of her sudden capricious fancies to George. How could George resist her? How could anyone resist her? Barbara was sinuous and sensual, with a curving figure like a Modigliani sculpture. Beneath her long hair peeped out a small, almost childish face: a bewitching naughty child. Although he loyally took me home to Chelsea, George was already afire with passion. Early the next morning, Barbara telephoned him and immediately initiated their raging affair. In the evening, quite unknowing, I was George's prearranged guest at *Rheingold*. It is obviously a tribute to George's impregnable good manners that no inkling of his tumultuous day reached me as I prattled on ecstatically. Although it was perhaps just as well that *Rheingold,* unlike the rest of the Ring, is not much more than two hours long.

So began an extraordinary sequence of events, by which Barbara Skelton was married to two men – Cyril Connolly and George Weidenfeld – three times, ending up back with Cyril. It was all made even more complicated by the fact that Cyril Connolly had been a kind of literary deity in George's early publishing days. Shortly before I joined the firm, the publication of the anthology *The Golden Horizon*, taken from the famous magazine *Horizon* which Connolly edited, gave George tremendous éclat. Together with Rose Macaulay's *The Pleasure of Ruins*, it was the book people referred to casually at parties when I mentioned where I worked.

The early days of my first marriage coincided with the early days of the new Weidenfeld ménage and Barbara, George, Hugh and I had several evenings *à quatre*. I am afraid that her new settled status did not inspire Barbara to greater friendliness towards me. Instead, she practised her skills on Hugh, like a pianist who cannot resist an opportunity to try out an instrument in a neighbour's house. Hugh, although swearing that she was not his type (which was probably true) admitted that he could not help feeling the attraction; there was something about the moment when Barbara suddenly switched from being sullen and rather silent to her siren mood, which was evidently irresistible.

A further element in the complicated Connolly–Weidenfeld connection was the presence of Sonia Orwell in the publishing offices, as a literary consultant; Sonia having been one of the young ladies in the *Horizon* office, jealously trying to guard their editor, as immortalized by Nancy Mitford in her novel *The Blessing* where she nicknamed Connolly the Captain. The widow of George Orwell, who had married her on his deathbed, Sonia always gave me the impression that Cyril Connolly was her real idol: certainly the invocation of the name Cyril generally meant that no opposition to whatever the name wanted or approved would normally be entertained. Sonia was now thirty-six or -seven; one could still see the exceptional looks which had earlier held the artists of the Euston Road set in her thrall: that beguiling milkmaid appearance of untidy, tumbling fair hair and healthy complexion. Even if the once-curvaceous figure was verging on the plump, her energy in the cause of real writers (and artists) made her an attractive person. She would arrive in the office in the morning invariably quite late, often very late, and then outline a fabulous party which had taken place the night before, possibly in the Gargoyle and probably including Lucian Freud. As she talked, Sonia's voice would be croaking as a result of the cigarettes and the drink she had enjoyed; you knew she could not wait for the next bohemian outing – and the next hangover.

All the same, although Sonia evidently liked telling her tales of what-happened-last-night, and I certainly liked hearing them, she made it clear that I was only within the literary world, the real one that she understood, on sufferance. Her attitude to me was that of a Victorian parent to a child: I should be seen (and might listen) but should not be heard. When I ventured to allude to meeting her friend Lucian the night before, and how I had complimented him on the cover he had done for Nigel Dennis's novel *Cards of Identity*, an intriguing drawing of a man with a long nose and the eyes of a rat – Lucian's own features – she gave me a sharp ticking-off. I should not have done that, she said; Lucian would have been very annoyed even if he had not seemed so in the slightest. She understood artists – 'when you have been around these difficult people as long as I have' – and I did not.

Home life while I was working for George was in general rather less exotic than all this. Clarissa Churchill, the belle of Oxford in my childhood, had once worked for George at *Contact* magazine; she had since married Anthony Eden. This inspired Evelyn Waugh, who adored her and disliked Eden, to address me as follows: 'The last girl who had your job ended up marrying the Prime Minister. See that you do better.' It was however extremely unlikely that I would make any such glorious – or inglorious according to Waugh – match.

My cousin Henrietta Lamb worked for Peter Quennell doing picture research for *History Today*, a similar world to my own. Friends since birth, it seemed an obvious move for us to share a flat together. She earned eight pounds a week and I earned six.

Once we were installed in the flat beneath my parents' house in Cheyne Gardens, we busied ourselves enjoying a London of a very different sort. These were Basement Days. The flat was dark and rambling, with a bathroom at the back that it took some time to discover; the lights there often did not work, which was no bad thing. At the front a tiny kitchen, more of a galley than a room, seemed already part of the dustbin area. To our relief, a man found lurking there in the early morning turned out to be a policeman in quest of unpaid library fines (mine) rather than an official from the Council complaining about the unsightly jumble. The sitting room also had a good view of the dustbins out of its murky windows. In short, this seemed to us to be an ideal place to give dinner parties, especially as the great Elizabeth David had recently published *A Book of Mediterranean Food*.

We grappled with its revolutionary concepts and argued about the details as explorers in the South Pacific must have discussed hitherto unknown flora and fauna. For example, what was one to make of this enormous stone at the centre of a so-called avocado pear? Was the stone to be left in place as a sort of noble centrepiece or thrown away? Going for the centrepiece was only one of the many decisions we were to get wrong. Then, stuffing an aubergine seemed an awful effort for very little result; secretly I did not fancy the taste of either aubergines or the new favourites, peppers, but was far too anxious to keep up with the times to admit it.

Courgettes were delicious but presented a different problem: if these were the miniature versions of something called a *courge,* might it not be simpler and more economical – we were always on the lookout for that – to buy one big *courge*? Whatever it was. When it turned out to be a form of vegetable marrow, there was disappointment, since wartime cookery had contained all too many insipid marrow dishes. As for real mayonnaise, the memory of my struggles to whip it up still embarrasses me, as well as the unacknowledged fact that all the time I longed for that reliable old bottle of Heinz Salad Cream we were supposed to be replacing. The Goncourt Brothers once wrote that the time of which one does not have a dinner menu is 'a time dead to us, an irrecoverable time'. All I can say is that for me Basement Days will never be irrecoverable so long as the last aubergine remains to be stuffed.

Economy became of the utmost importance when it came to the drink we provided. Cheap – really cheap – wine was one thing: the plonk one brought along to something officially designated a bottle party (as many parties were) hardly deserved the name of wine. Spirits on the other hand were prohibitive. Yet all too many potential escorts who came to the Basement demanded a quick swig of gin or whisky on arrival, before setting off for the designated expedition. A whole bottle of whisky was quite outside our range; in the end I think it was Henrietta who hit on the brilliant expedient of recovering a single empty bottle and replenishing it when necessary with miniatures, so long as it retained its vital Haig label. At all events we became jeunes filles in search of a whisky bottle in a dustbin – not a very Proustian concept. Under the circumstances, it was tempting to rate escorts according to a secret equation: consumption of whisky versus desirability. Not every otherwise agreeable man passed this secret test.

One of those who did pass the test was Michael Alexander. He was tall and extremely good-looking with a slightly dissolute air; he would have made a good James Bond, although in those days the Ian Fleming creation had not yet captured the imagination of the world. At the time, I fancied there was just a hint of my teenage hero Gary Cooper. As a young man in the war – Michael was now in his mid thirties – he had been a Commando, joined the Special Boat Service and was captured in North Africa. The boast of a family connection to General Alexander, which was false but probably saved his life, led to him being imprisoned in Colditz. Here he joined the *Prominente,* men who might have hostage value such as Lord Harewood, son of the Princess Royal, and Giles Romilly, Mrs Churchill's nephew. I first got to know about Michael when I read *The Privileged Nightmare*, his account of Colditz written with Romilly, including the eponymous nightmare situation at the end of the war when Hitler at his last stand ordered the death of the hostages; it had been published the year before I joined Weidenfeld & Nicolson.

Michael's next adventure was to rescue a friend called West de Wend Fenton from the Foreign Legion (he became known as 'Beau' West, another Gary Cooper echo) and this too became a book, *The Reluctant Legionnaire*, which came out in 1956.

Michael dedicated this latest book to me. The printed version read: 'To Antonia, with love'. Underneath in the copy he gave me, he corrected it by hand to 'with much love', adding 'What an honour to have provided you with your first *dédicace*'. I wish I could say that this romantic message was echoed by his single-minded devotion to me in private life. Alas, the sound of footsteps on the staircase of his Harrington Road flat was heard every day, morning as well as night (Michael showed no signs of having a job) and only a few of them were mine. I was extremely jealous of these other footsteps, especially the daytime ones who were evidently free for fun while I was toiling away in Cork Street. Michael Alexander was a founder member of the so-called Chelsea Set, associated with the new espresso bars in the King's Road. Michael himself innocently described it later: there was no such Chelsea Set, they were merely workers who were 'non-nine-to-fivers' and thus able to meet for coffee. To an outsider, actually a 'ten-to-sixer', the men and the girls seemed enviably devoid of routine cares.

When I got to know Sofia Coppola over her film *Marie Antoinette*, based on my biography, we had an interesting talk about the Queen's relationship with the philandering Count Fersen; did she not mind his numerous other conquests? We worked out a theory that, where Byronic figures are concerned, those who would today more coarsely be called love-rats, every woman manages to believe she will be *the one*. In short, he presents an exciting challenge which is also a rite of passage, except that the poor Queen, unlike me, never got to profit from the experience. One day I realized that, although Michael was always totally sincere in his protestations at the time, in real life I would never be the single dedicatee. The choice was mine to accept it or not, and after a while, gracefully I hope, sensibly I know, I decided to do so no longer. Our relationship was over.

It was Michael himself who selected the right word for the various incidents in his adventurous life. The subtitle of *The Reluctant Legionnaire* was 'An Escapade'. When I saw it on the printed page, I wondered whether those years of his prime which Michael had spent perforce inactive in his prison camp – four years in his early twenties – had not left him permanently and understandably inclined towards enjoyable 'escapades' of one sort or another, whenever one was presented to him.

For more conventional entertainment in the Fifties, an evening at the theatre was the outing of choice. In my new jeune-fille-about-town life, I worked out the perfect formula for preferring a new date to one already agreed. It involved the blessed orange telegram. 'For reasons too boring to tell you,' ran my message, 'I am unable to go out with you tonight.' No one ever questioned me on this, fearful no doubt of the long-drawn-out and deadly boring answer. But one date I never chucked was the theatre. My diary reveals frequent visits to the West End (tickets always paid for by the man), but more important, we would find ourselves just down the King's Road from the exciting new Royal Court Theatre.

I saw all the early productions, beginning with the first: Angus Wilson's *The Mulberry Bush*. I went on to Nigel Dennis's *Cards of Identity*, the dramatic version of the novel which Weidenfeld & Nicolson had recently published. Then, in July, I was invited to a new play which had taken the theatrical world by storm, quite a serious storm it seemed. The play was *Look Back in Anger*. My escort was a journalist called Henry Fairlie, married but, according to his version, separated from his wife. I cannot pretend that I instantly appreciated the seminal importance of what I was seeing, the work of that thrilling new menace on the block: the Angry Young Man. Instead, I felt vaguely bored by the sight of Alison Porter at the ironing-board which opened the play, considered so shocking by some: for me it was rather too like Basement Days in Cheyne Gardens. At the end I was positively embarrassed by the dialogue between Jimmy and Alison centring on a game about bears and squirrels. I mentioned the fact to Henry, for want of anything more intelligent to say.

'Ah, Antonia,' he replied sentimentally, 'one day you will find that every marriage has its bears and squirrels.' Looking at Henry Fairlie, evidently still in some way the happily married man, this was an image which I did not want to contemplate further.

I did not get to know John Osborne for many years, and in another life. By this time, like the rest of the world, I had learnt to appreciate his plays. Angus Wilson on the other hand was a man I already revered, for his novels and short stories which engrossed me one by one as they appeared. *Hemlock and After*, published in 1952, with its wicked procuress Mrs Curry, alarmed my father but I noticed that he read it to the end, where other novels fell by the wayside; moreover he was curiously fond of discussing it. I also loved Angus personally for his truly charitable character, salted with the sly wit which was his trademark. One of my editorial tasks was to check out possible volumes for the so-called Illustrated Novel Library. These would then be presented anew with pictures by distinguished contemporary artists. An example would be *Pot-Bouille* by Zola, published in English as *Restless House*, with illustrations by Philip Gough and an introduction by Angus, who acted as adviser on the series.

In the early days of my life at Weidenfeld, Angus Wilson was often to be found presiding at the central desk of the British Library Reading Room, then encased within the depths of the British Museum. My heart would leap up when, as I entered, I spied his youthful, slightly flushed face and thatch of silver hair above his favoured bow tie. Then I knew that my work of investigation would be done in a trice, just a few minutes' precious conversation with Angus was worth all the research I could do in days. At the same time, I did become painlessly accustomed to the Round Reading Room, familiar with its practices, again helped by Angus: knowledge which was to prove extraordinarily useful once I turned to do research there on my own account.

My editorial experiences during the three years I worked at Weidenfeld were with only one exception extremely enjoyable. The exception was the occasion when I was asked to go to Feliks Topolski's studio, somewhere beneath the arches of Waterloo Bridge, and help him in some way with his writings. The Polish-born artist, then in his late forties, had had an intricate life, including wartime experiences as an official artist; altogether he was a fascinating man. The trouble was that he wanted help with more than his writings and seemed to take it for granted that this was on offer when Miss Pakenham of Weidenfeld turned up. He even suggested, half humorously, that this had been promised by George or at least requested in advance by him, Topolski (I found the latter believable but not the former). Certainly his studio was full of couches should one feel a need to lie down. I definitely did not feel that need.

It must be said that Topolski took the rejection with equanimity. But it is interesting to note that I was not particularly outraged, let alone traumatized by the incident. This does not mean that it was pleasant – very much the reverse. It was simply a reflection of the times, the Fifties, when sexual harassment in the workplace was not a concept that I ever heard mentioned, let alone commonly discussed. If you were young and female, without in any conceivable way liking such advances, you probably took them for granted.

My experience of working for Baroness Moura Budberg was the exact opposite, absorbing and eye-opening by turns; I looked forward to every single day when I would find myself offered gin and concentrated National Health orange juice (the sort intended to be diluted for babies) in her large, grand, run-down flat near the Albert Hall. Allegedly I was there to edit her translation of a biography of Albert Einstein by Antonina Vallentin; but George made it clear that the whole project was intended more to help the wonderful Moura financially than extend the international sales of Vallentin. Certainly Baroness Budberg herself *was* wonderful, beginning with her appearance; at first when you entered the huge room, you saw a fairly large old lady, grey hair in a bun, wearing some kind of unmemorable print dress, glass in hand and probably cigarette too (certainly her voice was memorably low and husky). Gradually as she talked, the beautiful broad planes of her Slavic face, with its high cheekbones and deep-set eyes, began to mesmerize you; the old lady dissolved in front of your gaze and you saw the woman who in her prime had captivated, among many others, Maxim Gorky and H. G. Wells. All this was to say nothing of a career that included a spell in the Lubyanka prison and charges of spying for both England *and* the Soviet Union. It was an intricate story worthy of John le Carré, although in the Fifties she was sometimes known more pedestrianly as the Mata Hari of Russia.

Moura Budberg was interested in many things. Unfortunately it did not appear that Vallentin's biography was included among them. In vain I tried to bring the conversation round to what I thought I was supposed to be doing. It was hopeless. She continued to sip her gin-and-orange and changed the subject. In the end I decided recklessly to join her in the gin-and-orange and have a good time. After that, I wrote most of the translation myself, without an enormous amount of reference to the original, owing to the need for haste. Years later I was on a radio panel with the novelist and scientist C. P. Snow; each member of the panel choosing a favourite book in paperback. To my amazement, he chose the Vallentin biography of Einstein (I chose *Nostromo* to impress and then had to read it). Afterwards I ventured the question which had been plaguing me while I listened to the great man's eloquent disquisition on the virtues of the book.

'Lord Snow, did you read the book in the French original or

in English?' He paused as though trying to remember and then said in a friendly manner: 'I believe I read it in English.' A feeling of guilt stole over me, replaced almost immediately by wicked pride.

I did have one experience of being the official editor-translator of a French book while I worked for George. This was for the memoirs of Christian Dior. In this case I paid all the sedulous attention to the text which could have been expected and was honoured by the commission; had not the arrival of the New Look been one of the defining moments of my teenage fashion life? But I was led by this experience to the inescapable conclusion that I was not really cut out to be a translator, lacking the true vision of the double art. Again and again I caught myself writing the story in my own words, drifting away from the original, in short acting as I had done with Vallentin, as a biographer not a translator. Then of course there was the moment when I presented myself at Maison Dior in Paris with the words: *'Moi, je suis le phantôme de Monsieur Dior,'* under the impression that this was the French for ghostwriter. (It wasn't: the word was *nègre*.) The absolute wilful incomprehension of the highly superior staff who greeted me may also have convinced me that I was not in the right place.

After that there was the murky incident which centred on the possible removal of a swear word from *The Adventures of Augie March* which had been brought to us by Sonia through her friendship with the author Saul Bellow. English printers did not in those days take kindly to this sort of thing, and the whole relationship of publishers, printers and authors to so-called obscenity was very jittery. There were other instances of publishers being asked to remove the offending expletive: this was several years before George's bold and successful stand in publishing *Lolita*. Detailed line-editing was never my strong suit; this is the one disadvantage to being a quick reader which I must reluctantly admit. I have never been quite sure what the resolution of this situation was – did the author object? – nor whether I let any of the frisky little words through; I never liked to ask what happened in the end for fear of stirring up trouble (for myself, not Saul Bellow).

Nevertheless the episode, guiltily if dimly remembered, remained on my conscience. Finding myself a fellow judge with Saul Bellow on the Booker Prize in the early Seventies, I muttered something expiatory about it. We were in a taxi together, travelling back from the building in the City where the judging had taken place: he was heading for the Ritz, I to Notting Hill Gate. Bellow just gazed at me as though assessing something. After a moment he said: 'Has anyone ever told you that you're a very handsome woman?' Admiring Bellow in every way, I was deeply excited by this unexpected development. At the same time I was thrown into confusion. What was the correct reply? How to sound modest – 'I've never heard such a nice thing before' – yet encouraging – 'As a matter of fact I'm a tremendous fan of *yours*'? But while I was working it out, Bellow had fallen fast asleep and remained asleep for the rest of the journey until I woke him to drop him off at the Ritz.

It will be clear from this that taking the rough with the smooth, not very rough, often very smooth, I look back on my three years as a jeune fille in publishing – the only job as such that I was ever to hold – with great affection. For one thing, I discovered that working hard, when I chose to do it, as opposed to lazing about (my frequent occupation at Oxford) was thoroughly enjoyable, even compulsive. It also became apparent to me later that working in a publishing office, although it came about as a result of a chance encounter, was first-class preparation for the work I really wanted to do, that is write. For one thing I emerged into the world of writing believing that publishers were not unknown, faceless persons crouching behind filing cabinets with rejection slips between their teeth, but my friends. This was an excellent, optimistic attitude, since like most such it has a self-fulfilling element. That casual moment when George Weidenfeld turned to his dinner partner and asked her advice about a new employee, represented one of the felicitous turning points of my early life.

CHAPTER FOURTEEN

I AM GOING TO MARRY *YOU*!

I T WAS MIDNIGHT. IN THE mighty stronghold of Camelot a great king lay dying. Uther Pendragon had said nothing to his knights for many hours.' These stirring words opened my first published work, *King Arthur and the Knights of the Round Table*, in 1954 when I was twenty-two. My brother Thomas did not realize that this was a sacred passage (because it represented The Beginning) and elected to tease me about it. In a rage I decided to start all my future books in similar dramatic fashion. I was after all keeping the rule laid down by the great Alexandre Dumas: open with action, dying being in its own way a form of action, especially if it affects a kingdom. This resolve persisted when I was writing *Mary Queen of Scots*. The father of the future Queen makes an appearance in the first paragraph: 'The King of this divided country, James V, having led his people to defeat, lay dying with his face to the wall . . .' And so on. After this I more or less gave up. *Cromwell* began with a birth not a death – although I must admit that there was a slight regression with *The Gunpowder Plot* which starts perfectly appropriately: 'In Richmond Palace, the old Queen [Elizabeth I] who had ruled England for over forty years lay dying beyond all hope of recovery.'

It was as a result of working in Cork Street that the opportunity of putting my long-held dreams of writing to the test – and actually be published – presented itself in an unexpected form. We were summoned to George's office for that annual moment of Weidenfeld exhilaration when the plans for this year's Heirloom Library were announced. This was a project for producing out-of-copyright children's classics in cheap attractive editions, freshly illustrated, and selling them in Marks & Spencer. The series had originally been suggested to George by Israel Sieff, uncle of his first wife Jane, who ran Marks & Spencer with Simon Marks. Not only was it an excellent money-spinner – out of copyright meant no royalties were payable – but it had become something of a lifeline in the finances of Weidenfeld & Nicolson. Thus George's return from the annual meeting, at which possible choices were discussed, with the final decision coming from Marks & Spencer, was eagerly awaited.

We all listened. The classics listed were conventional enough. Then George mentioned King Arthur. I saw my chance to shine, having hitherto managed to say nothing at all.

'Oh, George,' I said pityingly. 'We can't possibly do Malory's *Morte d'Arthur*. No child today could possibly understand it. It was written in the fifteenth century. Obviously T. H. White's *The Sword in the Stone* is in copyright . . .'

George hardly missed a beat. 'Then we need our own modern version.' He beamed at me. 'You, my dear Antonia, will write it.'

So I did, my research limited to the Everyman edition of Malory swiped from Bernhurst, but my spirits high. That was just as well, since this work was to be extra to my office life (I was paid one hundred pounds flat fee) and had to be done in the late evening or early morning. Originally, there was some talk of a few afternoons off, in view of the urgency of delivery. But then one supposedly dedicated afternoon I was seen leaving the

Academy Cinema in Oxford Street by George and Sonia Orwell in a passing taxi; I was with Michael Alexander. George vaguely and Sonia violently disapproved of Michael. So it was back to evening work. Some very late evenings, as I began to enjoy London life in nightclubs more or less with anyone who would take me. The early mornings on the other hand reminded me of my Oxford ordeals, those dawn swottings and rapid regurgitations (the finished text was wanted immediately). All of this, like execution, concentrated the mind wonderfully. I began to write more and more freely, begging Malory's pardon. I also developed that economical one-line style which I liked to think children would appreciate.

So arrows whistled, steeds galloped with knights in armour on top of them, lances thwacked against shields and were in their turn thwacked back, flags fluttered on the top of lances and larger flags on the top of turrets, falcons flew, hawks – what did hawks do? They hovered of course, and every now and then they swooped down in a hideous hawk-like manner. Down to the flags or the turrets or the knights or the steeds . . . Ladies in their litters were more sedentary, except for the wicked Morgan Le Fay who with her magic arts was out to get the young Arthur. Then there were six black-clad queens who carried Arthur's moribund body away so that the book concluded as it had begun, with a dying King. I ended solemnly: 'Today, over a thousand years later, we feel proud to remember that King Arthur and the Knights of the Round Table are part of our national heritage.'

No one at Marks & Spencer complained about the text, supposing it was read, and rather pedestrian illustrations were added. There were of course no reviews: it was not that kind of enterprise. The public did or did not vote with its purse and bought it in the stores. *King Arthur* evidently sold well – the contract for an Heirloom Library book was for 50,000 copies, rising to 100,000 – because it was reprinted the next year. Furthermore the popular young author (my description) followed it up with *Robin Hood*. Here the inspiration was my early hero Sir Walter Scott and *Ivanhoe*. Then there was the second film I saw as a child in Oxford, *The Adventures of Robin Hood* starring Errol Flynn (like everyone else of my generation *Snow White* was the first film I ever saw, and like most of the children in the audience, with my additional fear of the dark to inspire me, I tried to get under the seat when the wicked witch appeared). This time the illustrations by Geoffrey Whittam were lively and colourful; one day *King Arthur* also got its pictorial due when the book was reissued with pictures full of fantasy by my twelve-year-old daughter Rebecca.

Despite these nocturnal sidelines, I had by no means lost my interest in History. For example, I developed an obsession with the historian Thomas Carlyle and *The French Revolution*, for its style as well as the story it told so dramatically. Later I would shudder away from the use of the historic present for myself (and to a certain extent in the writings of other people, even those I admired). I even chose, as an example of how not to anticipate the story, Carlyle's eloquent adjuration to the fourteen-year-old Marie Antoinette as she crossed over from her native Austria to her future kingdom of France: 'O there are tears in store for thee; bitterest wailings, soft womanly meltings . . .'

In my own book I pointed out piously that the girl, still half a child, was upset at having to leave Mops, her beloved pug, but otherwise looking forward to becoming the Dauphiness of France (potentially beating her sisters in rank, always fun). She could and did have absolutely no idea of the terrible fate awaiting her twenty-two years later.

The words of the historian F. W. Maitland – 'We must always be aware that what now lies in the past, once lay in the future' – were far more influential on my personal reconstruction of events. But this is to be ungrateful for the sheer pleasure which reading Carlyle gave me, still a secret pleasure, as I cannot remember choosing to discuss the subject with anyone. When he concluded *The French Revolution* as follows: 'And so here, O Reader, has the time come for us two to part . . . To me thou wert as a beloved shade . . . To thee I was but as a Voice. Yet was our relation a kind of sacred one,' he spoke directly to this shade who did indeed feel herself to be beloved.

My daytime life continued to centre on Cork Street. I was able to oversee for example the transformation of my mother from the active politician to the published writer, although in the first instance, *Points for Parents* was only a book put together from articles for the Beaverbrook press. With hindsight one can see that a woman of Elizabeth's exceptional energy was never going to settle calmly into middle age, especially now that child-bearing, something she saw with enjoyment as being literally creative, was over. This was because Elizabeth had had a life-or-death experience at the age of forty-four, as she herself recounts in her autobiography, when she was rushed to hospital from Bernhurst with an unexpected miscarriage. Mrs Pope, our housekeeper, told her on her return: 'Lady Pakenham, I did not think you would come back.'

Elizabeth remained an extremely attractive woman with her neat figure, those elegant long legs in proportion to her short height, and a pretty face, the blue eyes which had captured the shy Frank Pakenham, still bright if there were becoming silvery wings in the dark hair. (Elizabeth firmly disapproved of women of her age who allowed more than the wings to turn silver.) Although impatient with shopping, and highly economical by nature, in vivid contrast to my father, she always managed to be well dressed. We were not however, I should state, a mother-and-daughter couple who went cosily shopping together. The only joint outing I can recall occurred when we went together in search of her bride's mother dress for my first wedding: she never asked to see my own dress; the need for such an inspection didn't occur to either of us. Elizabeth rejected costume after costume on grounds of cost and I got crosser and crosser. Then she explained: 'You see, I have promised to match the exact cost of my dress with a donation to Oxfam.' Someone else might have pointed out that, in the good cause of Oxfam, the more expensive the dress she bought, the better. Instead I burst out in a rage which contained all the frustration of my past adolescence when I thought she was unjustifiably parsimonious and she thought I was ridiculously extravagant: 'This is my wedding, not your bloody good deed.'

With her failure at the 1950 Oxford General Election, Elizabeth's political ambitions were set aside; although it was noticeable that this Christian woman sometimes showed unexpected traces of malice where other women politicians were concerned. One can understand it in the case of Mrs Thatcher, who was after all of the opposing party; but as a matter of fact Elizabeth rather enjoyed being her country neighbour when the Thatchers had an apartment at Scotney Castle, near Bernhurst, and positively liked Denis. It was a woman like Barbara Castle who was the subject of her occasional barbs: this told me more than anything else that she never quite got over not getting into Parliament in her own right.

The articles which were turned into *Points for Parents* were mainly written in the weekday house in Cheyne Gardens. As the daughter often around (but living in the Basement) I was amused by scenes of maternal wrath which contrasted with the wise advice dispensed in the press. 'Catherine, how can I write my article on "Parents! Please spare the rod!" when you won't be quiet . . .' Elizabeth would rush angrily in the direction of her youngest daughter. But that secret cynicism was the reaction of someone *almost* if not quite grown up, who had gone some way but not *all* the way to finding what she wanted to do in life. Elizabeth's transformation into a historical writer – her first work of History *Jameson's Raid* was published after I left home – and my transformation into a mother meant that our relationship was destined to be one of great harmony in the future. Once she had been interested in Small Children and Politics and I had been interested in Romance and History; now with my Small Children and her History, we had all the most important things in common.

My relationship with my father was completely different. I admired him intensely and I loved him, two quite separate things. But intimacy of the sort I would enjoy with Elizabeth was not on offer. I believe that our mother, his saviour from his unhappy youth, was the only person in his life that Frank was truly close to, although his numerous friends meant a great deal to him. These included people of all ages: Jon Snow was a case in point. He was especially important to Frank because as a young man he had come to work for Frank at the New Horizon Youth Centre, having been rusticated from Liverpool University for taking part in an anti-apartheid protest; they remained close for the rest of Frank's life. Nearer his own age, the philanthropic David Astor, proprietor of the *Observer,* was another example. David was the son of his early patron, Lady Astor, but a very different character from the rumbustious woman, tiny but fierce, who had been the first female MP to sit in the House of Commons. A visit to the stately pile of Cliveden illustrated the point. Lady Astor looked down the long table, on being told of my existence at the bottom of it, and called out: 'I'm glad you're not as ugly as your father!' At the age of fifteen, I didn't know whether I should accept the compliment or avenge the insult. David in his gentle voice put everything right: 'She likes you, you know.'

To an observer, the marriage of Frank and Elizabeth remained, as it had always been, the most wonderful thing in both their lives, even if Elizabeth continued to specialize in that kind of tender crossness – occasionally not so tender! – when dealing with Frank's determined otherworldliness. I shall not easily forget Frank's speech on the fortieth anniversary of their wedding. It was held in a room at the White Tower where in Oxford days he had once shared a *pied-à-terre* with another close friend, Nicko Henderson. In front of his assembled children, Frank gave the following as an example of married bliss: he recalled returning home that evening without his latchkey, having lost it for the millionth time. 'Your mother went at me like a twenty-year-old,' he said dreamily.

Then there was the question of her annual birthday present, a dress which he duly bought without her, and then watched proudly as she tried it on. The trouble was that the dress was nearly always too large for Elizabeth, never very tall, and like everyone else becoming smaller with age. And one year, the year of the Giant Red Dress, it was truly enormous. Out of curiosity, I asked my father how he chose the dresses. 'I go into that shop on the King's Road, and ask for a dress from the nearest girl I see. When she asks, "What size?" I always answer: "Your size." And it always works.' He paused. Even Frank had noticed the overwhelming size of the Giant Red Dress. 'The trouble was that the girl in the shop this year was rather a fattie.' Frank gave his sweet smile. 'But it would have been unkind not to give the same answer.'

His courtesy to 'the ladies' was always touching, scrambling to his feet if one such came into the room, even in extreme old age. On the matter of dress again, Frank also prided himself on having discovered that autumn generally brought about a new outfit (or maybe it was the coincidence of Elizabeth's late August birthday and her annual acquisition). At that time of year, he would often bestow a compliment on a lady for recently acquiring a highly becoming costume. No one ever had the heart to contradict him, even in the oldest scruffiest dress. 'Ah, I knew it,' Frank would say proudly.

Having got on extremely well with my father when he was teaching me at Oxford, I now settled into a sincere admiration for all his good works, especially his long-held interest in prisoners. This included ex-prisoners. I attended the initial meeting of the New Bridge, an association to help them, which was held at Kettner's restaurant in Soho in 1955. The spur was the conviction and imprisonment of Lord Montagu of Beaulieu, Michael Pitt-Rivers and the journalist Peter Wildeblood for alleged offences with young RAF servicemen. I already knew Edward Montagu, but now got to know Peter Wildeblood quite well, starting with the moment when I was proud to attend the breakfast given for him on his release from Wormwood Scrubs. From the first I liked him for his combination of courage and vitality; he was excellent, lively company from that post-prison party onward. It was Weidenfeld & Nicolson who would publish Peter Wildeblood's important book *Against the Law* which detailed his experiences in prison and encouraged campaigning for law reform; Peter also testified to the Wolfenden Committee, which in its 1957 report suggested the decriminalization of homosexuality, finally achieved ten years later.

My father's active involvement in the work of penal reform was one of the themes of my youth which I took for granted. That disquieting moment when I enquired what the teatime visitor to Singletree had done and was told that he had committed arson, was merely my initiation. The New Bridge aimed to provide support for ex-offenders who might not otherwise receive it, and I made a few attempts in that direction. My subsequent efforts to take lecturers down to Wandsworth Prison were probably more successful as at least I provided entertainment for the inhabitants. Such expeditions were certainly rich in incident. These were the days of capital punishment, that cause about which I had felt strongly since adolescence, which would not be abolished in Britain until the mid Sixties. (That horrible piece of so-called justice which was the execution of Ruth Ellis, and influenced many people to become abolitionist, occurred in 1955.) Executions were still carried out at Wandsworth. The chaplain there was responsible for our appearances on behalf of the Home Office; every now and then he would telephone and murmur confidentially that the visit must be cancelled: 'The boys are rather restive today.' It was a code and a chilling one.

Another unwritten rule was the need to bring down a lecturer, once you had made the booking. We were given to understand that the fearsome 'boys' would not like being disappointed, as they were frightened of nothing and no one: certainly the audiences looked extraordinarily tough to my sheltered eyes. On one occasion I was let down by Roy Jenkins who, to my amazement and horror, chose at the last minute to attend a vital vote in the House of Commons rather than lecture in Wandsworth Prison. What to do? Quick, hadn't my brother Thomas recently given a lecture at the Royal Geographical Society? It turned out that he had and he was delighted to give it again at Wandsworth. It was in this way that I found myself travelling down to the South London prison in the Home Office car with Thomas at my side, wearing his habitual pair of sandals over socks; my heart sank. If only I'd noticed the sandals before we set off! In my fevered recollection, it seems that he was also wearing shorts, but since it was winter in England, this must be my imagination.

At this point I realized that I had never asked what the lecture was about.

'The Wadi Hadramaut,' said Thomas confidently. 'It went down very well at the Royal Geographical Society. I think they'll like it at Wandsworth.' I did not have the heart to tell Thomas that this was one of the great non sequiturs. Our prison audience, since its members had nothing to lose, was extremely critical and in particular anything affected – as they saw it – could go down badly; there had been the occasion of the visit of Lord David Cecil, for example . . . As to the subject, I needed Thomas to explain to me that this was a remote area of the Yemen, populated by a few Bedouins and their flocks. I was sunk in gloom. I was after all delivering my beloved brother, sandals and all, to the wolves. We drank a ritual glass of sherry with the prison chaplain first and I just hoped it would dull the pain.

Thomas began at once in his voice which became quite high when he was speaking: 'Hands up who has been in the Wadi Hadramaut lately!'

There was complete silence. These prisoners were almost universally recidivists, that is they had been in prison for one serious offence or another for many years. Then came a single shout of laughter. After that came roars of laughter from the whole large hall. And after that Thomas could do no wrong.

'They really *loved* it,' I said to Thomas with complete sincerity in the car on the way home.

'Yes, I think they did.' My brother sounded just a tiny bit complacent although Thomas was normally the reverse of a self-satisfied person: his ever-active mind was on quite other things than himself. Then he explained: 'You see, Antonia, on the way down I felt you were just a little nervous. I wanted to reassure you. Everyone always loves my lecture on the Wadi Hadramaut.'

Compared to this, my agitation over the visit of General Sir Francis Festing, who had an outstanding war record in the Far

East, was a very minor affair. Once again I had failed to establish the subject of the lecture in advance, in this case out of deference, because it was such an honour to have such a heroic man in the first place. This time the last-minute question elicited the answer: 'Japanese swords', followed by the disquieting information that Sir Francis had brought one fine example with him and, as usual in his lecture, intended to display it. Once again I was filled with dread: was it conceivable that the prisoners, aroused to frenzy by the sword, would rush the platform? Once again my fears were groundless. The mighty soldier and future Field Marshal – he was enormously tall – swirled his sword with enthusiasm as he lectured. No one dared move.

Despite these tenuous early involvements in prison affairs, my real interests at this time were purely literary. I continued to admire my father for his work with prisoners, so firmly based on the Christian Faith which led him to the inexorable conclusion that no one was beyond redemption. From this it followed that everyone, however ghastly the crime concerned, had the right to rehabilitation ending in theory by release. In later years, my sister Rachel was inspired by his example to enter this world and my brother Kevin chaired from the outset the Longford Trust for ex-offenders set up after Frank's death. In my case, while I quite understood, influenced by both my parents, that you must stand up, speak out, dare to be a Daniel and all those admirable things, I was to become engaged in another direction. It would be the welfare of writers, not only the economics of it at home but the issue of free speech and even freedom itself in those countries abroad where writers were at risk about which I felt passionately and, wherever possible, took action.

This was because from the first it had been intoxicating to get to know writers, whereas the politicians of my parents' circle now seemed pleasant but remote figures. The way I had moved away from politics is symbolized by my attitude to the General Election of 26 May 1955. This was held a few months after the eighty-year-old Winston Churchill had at last relinquished the Conservative premiership in favour of Anthony Eden. It would be the first election in which I was able to vote (I was just short of twenty-three, at a time when voting started at twenty-one). As a young woman of the sort once known as a flapper in electoral terms, the vote for which so many had struggled should perhaps have meant more to me. As it was, I used to walk up and down Chelsea Manor Street daily on my way to the King's Road, and contemplate the political posters without much excitement. Meanwhile, both my parents were frantically electioneering for Labour.

One day there was a poster which did catch my fancy. It showed Anthony Eden looking at me tenderly: he appeared thoroughly trustworthy, as well as genially handsome and silver-haired – a George Clooney for his time. Beneath the large photograph it said: WORKING FOR PEACE. How nice, I thought, working for peace, I really like that, I think I'll vote for this delightful, peaceful man. I went into the town hall at the top of the street and asked when Polling Day was. There was a considerable bustle in the town hall and no one seemed to understand the question so it took me some time to discover that this actually *was* Polling Day. Thus I cast my first vote – as it happened, for a Conservative. It also initiated a tendency to vote for the person not the party.

It would be perfectly natural to link this Tory vote with the fact that I got engaged to a Tory MP, Hugh Fraser, just over a year later. Breaking the news to my contemporaries certainly caused some surprise (Hugh was so very different in every way from Michael Alexander). The best or worst moment, according to your point of view, occurred when I decided to confide in my friend Hugh Thomas. The future shining beacon of historians was then living at the Cavendish Hotel, off Piccadilly: not far, in short, from Cork Street. The publication of *The Spanish Civil War* was five years off. We had fallen into the agreeable habit of lunching together. Hugh and I were in fact happily destined for a lifetime of *amitié* which was not *amoureuse* but it would be strange if this gallant man had not thrown the occasional flowery compliment in my direction. I took a deep breath.

'What I'm going to tell you may sound surprising at first. But the more you think about it, the more you will realize that it is in fact a very good thing . . .' I paused dramatically. 'I'm going to marry Hugh!'

The look of surprise and horror on my friend's face remains with me to this day. He had heard me say: 'I'm going to marry *you*!'

There were other reactions which were rather less striking. It was my fellow Basement-dweller Henrietta who remembered my telling her that I had voted Tory, and put the two things together. But that would be wrong. Hugh Fraser and I first met at a fancy-dress ball which used to be given regularly on New Year's Eve at the Royal College of Art: the sort of party where that chic young couple Mark Boxer and Arabella Stuart went in Chinese dress as the Boxer Rebellion. I cannot remember what I was supposed to be except that it involved wearing a pair of large thick pinned-on plaits: pinned on, that is, until I passed a man sitting out in the passage with a girl – he tweaked one of them off. This was Hugh, a Highlander whose fine head held high and tall frame should have been commemorated up a glen by Landseer. Hugh was unabashed by my annoyance. To tell the truth, the spirit of adventure that caused him to tweak the pigtail off one girl while sitting with another was another thing which impressed me. Shortly after that our romance began.

I remained frankly uninterested in politics and at the

beginning of our relationship barely noticed that Hugh was a member of the House of Commons (he was first chosen when he was still wearing his dashing parachutists' beret, and elected in July 1945). Reading one of my mother's letters left out half-finished at Bernhurst – as one does – I was rather surprised to find her addressing her sister-in-law Mary Clive in the following slightly ambiguous terms: 'I'm sure that with time Antonia will come to enjoy the life of a Tory MP's wife.' Tory MP's wife – *Moi?* as one would say now. At the time, I was merely surprised at the odd things people wrote in letters on occasions like this and went on planning my super wedding dress. This was of course a tribute to Mary Queen of Scots herself, in off-the-shoulder white satin and tulle (subsequently criticized by the *Daily Express* for its daring) and that proper heart-shaped headdress, admired since childhood, with the single drop pearl hanging down in the centre of the forehead.

It was a piece of wonderful good luck that my last task as a Weidenfeld editor was with Cecil Beaton. It was a singularly happy one. Of course he was not, strictly speaking, a writer although he obviously enjoyed the process of writing and kept profuse diaries and records. Here was the famous photographer whose picture of the ruins of the Blitz through an arch or the bandaged little girl with her teddy bear in Great Ormond Street Hospital were among the most vivid wartime images of my youth. But he was also known to me as the author of *The Book of Beauty,* lurking in the family bookshelf with its portraits of pre-war socialites; like the *Tatlers* in Aunt Mary's attic, I found this an intoxicating study, if at times puzzling.

Did Lady Pamela Berry, my parents' terrifying friend, daughter of his old patron F. E. Smith, with her obsidian black eyes, really look like this when a girl? Already I had begun to distinguish between the two celebrated hostesses of my new life in

London. Vital and amusing as she was, Pam Berry was frightening because she made her assessment – not necessarily a favourable one – of you and your appearance surprisingly obvious: I dreaded the moment when her beady gaze was turned on me. Ann Fleming I much preferred: there was something mischievous about her which suggested a conspiracy, a conspiracy to enjoy yourself if you were the right sort of person and, since you were in her salon, you must be the right sort of person. I do not mean to suggest that I was a constant visitor in either salon, merely that I caught the eagerly roving eye of these ladies from time to time, and was tried out for being – just possibly – the Right Stuff.

The experience with Cecil Beaton was a happy one because of his gratifying professionalism; that is to say, he wanted the work well done, knew what he could do and what he couldn't, and was prepared to be exceptionally charming to anyone who helped him bridge the gap. The memory stays with me of that moment around noon when he would call out to his gracious widowed mother, generally in attendance somewhere in the house in Pelham Place: 'Mummy, could you fix us two gins-and-tonic.' I hear the slightly precious voice issuing the request. At the same time, I am still meditating on Beaton's use of the plural of gin, the singular of tonic: affected or upper-class correct in a Nancy Mitfordish way? A bit of both is probably the answer. I have never quite dared copy it.

Our meetings generally took place at about nine o'clock in the morning: Beaton had the workaholic's desire to use every moment of the day and in this case his glamorous subjects were probably not awake so early. Around this time, he had his celebrated sittings with Marilyn Monroe, who could certainly be trusted not to arrive before gins-and-tonic time. Cecil Beaton (a marvellous if waspish raconteur) made a good story out of Arthur Miller's reaction to the result. He told me that the celebrated playwright stood gazing at the image and finally pronounced in his wonderful mellow baritone: 'That's my loony babe.'

For me, however, there was a hidden peril to this nine o'clock rendezvous: I needed to get to my Chelsea hairdresser first, not only to impress Cecil Beaton but also because immediately after our sessions I would go on to the office in Cork Street. One has to face the fact – I had to face the fact then – that a freshly achieved Fifties hair-do, that cramped and crimped affair when blow-drying was unknown, was singularly unaesthetic. I swear that Cecil Beaton's voice rose a little when he saw me, although his words were always kind. And then there was the occasion when I decided to gamble on a striking auburn rinse to brighten up my unaccountably mousey hair . . . His voice as he welcomed me sounded almost strangled.

On the other hand, Cecil's behaviour to me at the time of my marriage was immaculate. Not only did he volunteer to take the wedding photographs, but his loving bodyguard of a secretary Miss Eileen Hose informed me in her precise style that the pictures were to be a wedding present. Working so often in the Beaton household, I understood for myself that this lavishness was not universal practice. Faced with this generosity, I have to overcome the memory of Beaton's words when he stood, gazing at me styled as Mary Queen of Scots, about to take the picture.

'Open, piggies,' said the famous man. At the time I was left anxiously wondering whether he issued the command to all his sitters (the Queen Mother, for example?) as the equivalent of 'Say cheese', or whether it was a special need he felt, contemplating me and my tiny half-closed eyes beneath the iconic headdress.

Having said that it was not Hugh's politics which attracted me, I should stress that his commitment to the political issues which interested him – mainly the colonies and defence within

the bounds of the then Empire – was in itself an attractive quality. This was especially true for one who had been brought up
against a political background, even if from across the party
boundary. I was delighted to find that the old canvassing days
were back (I might have grown bigger, but so had the barking
dogs). It was however his high spirits, a certain wildness coupled
with good humour, which provided the key to his character. At
thirty-eight, he was nearly fifteen years older than me; but that
was not unusual for the time. In any case, coming from such a
large family I had no rigid sense of generation. Hugh, slightly
closer to my parents' age than mine, was about the same distance
from me as my youngest brother Kevin. In turn, Kevin was far
closer to my children's age than my own. To try and sort it all out
would have been much too confusing.

For our wedding Hugh wore a kilt of Fraser tartan and a
velvet jacket with a lace jabot. Son of the man who had raised the
Lovat Scouts for the Boer War, and brother of the war hero Shimi
Lord Lovat, himself a decorated soldier, he cut a wonderfully romantic figure. The effect of the war had been to leave a lot of
young men unmarried into their thirties. Hugh, as a second son
(like my father), had no family money, which probably helped
to keep him a highly popular bachelor, always in great demand
with his friends. In 1956 he had an MP's salary of roughly fifteen
hundred pounds a year, with expenses limited to postage, secretarial help, and travel to the constituency. In theory, it had to do
for both of us.

When Hugh told his mother he was getting married to me,
he added cheerfully: 'She hasn't a bean' (Laura, Lady Lovat, was
a good deal less cheerful about it than he was). It was perfectly
true. My Weidenfeld salary had obviously come to an end. A
small legacy from my great-grandmother went towards extin-
guishing my Oxford overdraft. What was I to do? It was back

to the moment when my mother found that to her amazement I had just left school and asked me what my plans were. As I had answered her then and repeated to myself now: 'I'll think of something.' I didn't exactly think about History, but then, in one way or another, I was always thinking about History. In short, like Hugh, I too felt tremendously cheerful.

READER, I WROTE IT

W E NOW LEAP FORWARD seven years.
Gibbon wrote a classic account of his original inspiration for *The Decline and Fall of the Roman Empire,* that book which had imbued my adolescent reading with magic. 'It was at Rome, on the 15th of October 1764,' he began, 'as I sat musing amidst the ruins of the Capitol, while the barefooted friars were singing vespers in the temple of Jupiter, that the idea of writing the decline and fall of the city first started to my mind.' Two hundred years later, my own Capitoline moment took place in the somewhat less august surroundings of my own London house; for barefooted friars, we have to substitute two little girls in ballet shoes; but for ruins, a house in which books and children and a basset hound tumbled over each other, will do very well.

Sometime in 1965 my mother paid one of her ritual teatime visits. That is to say, the children enacted King Babar and Queen Celeste dancing at the circus or some such drama, while she and I chatted about her work. This was following the recent phenomenal success of her biography of Queen Victoria, published when she was nearly sixty. My mother had been lunching with her agent, the agreeable, headmasterly Graham Watson of Curtis

Brown. She rambled on about the intricacies of the world of royal and aristocratic biography in which she now appeared to live. Then: 'Graham suggested I should do a biography of Mary Queen of Scots,' said Elizabeth brightly.

There was a terrible silence. I realized that she was quite unaware of the gravity of what she had just said. Eventually: 'You can't do that!' I cried in a strangled voice. 'She's *my* Mary Queen of Scots!' Still my mother seemed ignorant of the fact that a lifetime of love and passion had gone into my words. How to convince her? Suddenly, I knew.

'You can't do that,' I said. 'You're far too moral.' This was a judgement which it was surely impossible for my mother to contradict: for how could this good woman argue that she was not in fact all that moral?

'Oh well, maybe I'll do the Duke of Wellington ... Gerry Wellington suggested ... that is, Philip Magnus has just done King Edward VII ...' With this superior chit-chat, I realized that the danger had passed. It was time for a decision. Like the few important decisions in my life, it was immediate, thrilling and irreversible.

'I will do it,' I said.

It is tempting to conclude by merely adapting the immortal words of Charlotte Brontë at the end of *Jane Eyre*: 'Reader, I wrote it.' Nothing of course is that simple.

At this point in my life – I was thirty-two – I had written two non-fiction books for Weidenfeld, following the children's books I had written for the Heirloom Library before my marriage; I had five children. *Dolls* was a short illustrated book in a series, which included *Early Cars*, *Chessmen* and *Oriental Rugs*. *A History of Toys* was rather more elaborate. Both these books derived from that extended childhood preoccupation which I shared with Flora Carr-Saunders: those beloved dolls, Gilberta, Priscilla and the rest of them. I had even bought – for nothing – Victoria, an antique doll at the original Oxfam shop in Oxford, after reading about the young Queen and her dolls.

In short I was offered the opportunity to write about something that interested me, within certain parameters, and took it. We also needed money badly and my efforts to supplement Hugh's income by journalism were not very successful. Unfortunately my merry little articles about visits to country houses for the shooting parties to which Hugh, an excellent shot, introduced me, displeased our generous hosts without earning enough money to make it worthwhile – a fatal combination.

Neither of the 'plaything' books owed as much to maternal concern for my children's toys as might have been expected, although there were obvious connections. Visiting the Doll Museum of Graham Greene's separated wife, Vivien, in Oxford, I burst out instinctively: 'Oh, I do wish my children could see this!' Mrs Greene shuddered. 'No, no, we don't want *children* here, making a mess and upsetting everything.' I did not go quite that far. But it was the subject of play rather than the players which came to interest me. Councillor Patrick Murray of the Museum of Childhood in Edinburgh had made a study of 'emergent toys' – the toys of poor children which they made themselves out of the material available, such as a wooden pestle or a wooden spoon wrapped in flannel or an orange box tacked on to the wheels of an old pram. It was the universality of the instinct to play throughout history, and in surprisingly similar ways, which fascinated me. Here was the spoon in its flannel, and there was the exquisitely flounced and frilly doll à la Watteau from Cremers, the most famous nineteenth-century London toyshop, both fulfilling the same primitive need.

These 'plaything' books, unlike *Mary Queen of Scots*, had been suggested to me as part of a general publishing programme; my own initiative did not feature. There was indeed that proposed work on the summer of 1914 to which I have alluded earlier, an idea left over from my studies at Oxford. But that did not have the strength of passion behind it which a mother of a growing – fast-growing – family (in the end I had six children in ten years) needed to carry it through. I soon abandoned it. Now the moment had come. The imaginary bells of my childhood, my *Desert Island* choice, were pealing to celebrate a new direction, as once they had lured me into the social centre of Oxford away from my studies.

Where serious research for a historical biography was concerned, I learnt the hard way, but it was also a time of intense excitement. Our leader Churchill had been my childhood hero. Now I began to appreciate the comment he made while originally working on *The History of the English-Speaking Peoples* in 1939: it had been a comfort to him 'in these anxious days' to put a thousand years between himself and his own century. The distraction which History brings from the inevitable ordeals of life at every stage was an unexpected but enduring discovery.

It was now for the first time that the pleasure of what for tax purposes I came to term (perfectly accurately) Optical Research was revealed to me. It also could be called Going to Places and Looking at Them. But what an essential process it is in the making of a historical biography! With the respectful handling of the original documents, it ranks as one of the major ways of reaching what G. M. Trevelyan in his *Autobiography* called 'the poetry of history': 'the quasi-miraculous fact that once, on this earth, once, on this familiar spot of ground, walked other men and women, as actual as we are today, thinking their own thoughts, swayed by their own passions, but now all gone, one generation vanishing after another . . .'

To myself, in the early stages of my research, I used to recite a similar kind of mantra: 'On the one hand Mary Queen of Scots is exactly like me: she feels love, pride, gratitude, jealousy and all the rest of it. On the other hand she is totally unlike me, being not only royal but Queen of Scotland in her own right from six days old, unable to remember any other existence. Even the present Queen only became heir to the throne when she was twelve years old.' I knew that the secret of a successful historical biography lay in the reconciliation of these two contradictory statements.

With time, hearing the music of the period while I worked became important to me in this connection. With *The Gunpowder Plot*, there was William Byrd, the recusant Catholic who was nevertheless employed by Queen Elizabeth I: those private Masses for only four and five voices conveyed the secrecy of the times, with rituals hidden away in upper rooms. With the Court of Versailles under Louis XIV, I felt that listening to Lully and Marais helped me to recreate the stately grandeur of the time. And with Marie Antoinette, her patriotic championship of Gluck from the Viennese Habsburg Court (as opposed to the Italian opera previously popular in France) illustrated perfectly her alien status. She was thought to be introducing sensibility to the French: as I played *Iphigénie en Tauride*, I bore in mind that one French courtier had taken the precaution of weeping his way loudly through the entire opera, so as not to be found with dry eyes at the crucial moment. Did he love his Queen the more for this presumed obligation? I imagine not – just as I would not have loved *him* if I had sat next to him at the opera.

The subject of Mary Queen of Scots also allowed me to discover first-hand one problem about attempting to write History which is part of the fascination of it all. This is the vital question of structure. After a glamorous childhood in France, the young Queen then lived through seven dramatic years in Scotland: so far, so good, from the biographer's point of view. After that she endured nineteen years of captivity: how to deal with that, convey the sheer, wearisome length of it all, during which she degenerated from an eager, optimistic young woman into a sad middle-aged one with health problems, without making the readers want to break out of their own chains and throw away the book? Yet it is essential in order to capture the character and her development: too many biographies, in my opinion, bring the story to a virtual end with the flight from Scotland. (Just as Marie Antoinette's crucial Austrian upbringing, the values she imbibed, is often ignored, as if she was actually born in France.) Once again, it is the biographer's duty to reconcile two timescales effectively for the reader.

There is another allied problem of course: how to relate the subject to the great events of her or his time. No biography can be successful which does not at least attempt this, even when the events themselves are likely to be overwhelming. My worst experience was during the writing of *The Six Wives of Henry VIII*: how I longed to state quite simply: 'And so the Reformation took place.' Foiled of this possibility, I took comfort from the fact that, of the first two professional readers, one thought there was too much about the Reformation, and one too little.

In the interests of Optical Research, I had some bizarre experiences (although none of them of course half as exotic as the events of the Queen's own life story). Visiting Stirling Castle, where the Queen gave birth to her only child, the future James VI and I, I noticed that the official guides were wont to give long-winded and wrong-headed – to my way of thinking – discourses to their victims. Since guides were mandatory, I decided to pay for one, but suggested that, as I knew all about the local history, my particular hired man could rest on his bench while I toured alone. Little did I know the bold spirit of the guides of Stirling Castle. Despite our agreement, my allotted guide quickly took on another lot of tourists and followed me round, giving out his usual *spiel* well within earshot, but pausing every now and then to lift up his hand and say dramatically: 'But wheesht! We must not speak too loud. There's a very clever young lady here from England who knows all about our poor wee castle. We must not disturb the very clever young lady . . .'

France, the country in which Mary Queen of Scots lived from the age of six to eighteen when the death of her husband brought her back to Scotland, was a rich source of Optical Research. I made the most of it, determined to be able to contrast first-hand the gracious châteaux of the Loire in which she grew up with the rough Scottish castles of her future kingdom. A piece of luck, so I thought, put me in the way of visiting Anet, home of the legendary beauty Diane de Poitiers who had been the presiding mistress at the Court of King Henri II. I wished to see for myself the elegant memorial chapel in the black-and-white colours she made her own and the many crescent moons, her symbol, with which Philibert de l'Orme decorated the château. Anet now belonged to a South American but the suave, worldly Gaston Palewski, the diplomat who was the great love of Nancy Mitford, fixed up a visit for me.

On the appointed day I set forth confidently for Anet, arrived as arranged, and asked for a full tour from the owner. Don Luis, as I will call him, proved to be both chivalrous and knowledgeable and did not even allow the fact that I had interrupted an enormous lunch party on the terrace to deter him from showing me every black-and-white nook and cranny. A very long time later, Don Luis was called away to a telephone call. He came back looking thoughtful.

'So you are Madame Fraser,' he said. 'That was a message from my friend Palewski arranging for your visit. How happy I am to know your name! And yet just a little sad, that you are not some beautiful stranger come out of the blue to visit me, some goddess perhaps sent by the immortal Diana herself . . .' I formed an immediate high opinion of Latin American gallantry (if less of French efficiency).

In England the ruins of Fotheringhay, where the unfortunate Queen was executed in 1587, was an obvious site of pilgrimage; scrambling about the grassy mound, I managed to cull some seeds from the huge thistles growing there which I was moved to hear were known as Queen Mary's Tears; I like to think that the thistles currently growing in my garden are descended from them. It was also due to a personal call on the local farmer that I got to hear about the eccentric Scot, a Jacobite sympathizer, who some decades earlier used to come down annually, wearing his kilt, to lay a wreath at Fotheringhay in memory of the Queen. Unfortunately in his enthusiasm for the cause of Mary Stuart, he used such violent language about the existing British royal family that his visits had to be discouraged by the then owners of the site. I even tried to track this loyal/disloyal man down: in vain. I was left wondering if his ghost paid nocturnal visits to Fotheringhay on 8 February, the anniversary of the execution.

Westminster Abbey was another important location since it was here that the Queen was finally buried in 1612 (her body having spent the interim years in Peterborough Cathedral near Fotheringhay). Her son King James was persuaded by a courtier, Lord Northampton, a crypto-Catholic, to do the right thing and rebury her with the other kings and queens. Nowadays the tomb of Mary Queen of Scots lies on the right of the main altar; her white marble figure is stretched out, the face serene and peaceful under her peaked headdress.

But this was not only a historic relic: important information could be derived from the actual measurements of the head. I knew this because my friend Roy Strong, then Keeper of the National Portrait Gallery and an expert on Tudor portraiture, told me that care was taken with the wax death masks, on which the image would be modelled, to keep the real-life proportions. I wanted to know everything and was particularly obsessed with calculating the proper height of the Queen. With that solipsism which only a true researcher can know, I thought it would be perfectly all right to climb up and take the exact measurement myself. In my ancient and voluminous black fur coat, which hopefully concealed the fact that I was heavily pregnant, I started to clamber.

It was in this way that an alarmed member of the Abbey staff saw something that, for one horrified moment, he must have taken for an escaped bear, armed with a tape measure, assaulting one of the Abbey tombs . . . He challenged me where I clung in my slightly precarious position. Intent on my Optical Research, I was not at all abashed. I simply explained what I was doing: 'I'm just measuring the face of Mary Queen of Scots, that's all,' I said, and was rather surprised that this was not understood to be a perfectly normal occupation.

These essays in Optical Research were only the beginning of what would be numerous most fruitful expeditions with subsequent books. I learnt to be grateful to tolerant, and even enthusiastic companions, such as Simone Warner who was my charioteer and drove me all round East Anglia in the tracks of Queen Boadicea for *The Warrior Queens*: we became amateur archaeologists, plunging in and out of what we hoped were historic holes. Going the rather shorter distance to the City of London was similarly illuminating: the famous red layer caused by this warrior Queen's burning of Londinium in AD 60 was unexpectedly exposed by some building works. While I was standing gazing into the excavations, the man next to me suddenly exclaimed:

'That's the Romans for you! Four hundred years of occupying *our* country.' For me, on the other hand, it was the surprising virulence of the red which enabled me to envisage those fierce flames which had destroyed a city at a woman's command. You can say that we each took our own message from this episode of Optical Research.

Of course I could not expect my companions to subjugate their own interests entirely. Harold had a wistful tendency to spot interesting cricket matches from the car as we toured the countryside with History in (my) mind. On one occasion, when we were investigating Worcester with regard to the battle at which Cromwell conclusively defeated Charles II, a particularly seductive cricket match presented itself . . . I was compelled to stump off alone. I did allow myself to say on return: 'Cromwell won my match: how about yours?'

It would be only fair to add that Harold also gave my manuscripts the benefit of his editorial corrections, noted in his unmistakeable large black handwriting on the lined yellow legal pads he always used. Despite our very different style of writing – to put it mildly – and despite some fierce arguments, I have to say that Harold's meticulous care for language meant that he was nearly always right. One exchange over *The Six Wives of Henry VIII* and the use of the word 'courtier' would have astonished admirers of his plays.

Research in libraries was not quite so picturesque. But it was never dull. For example, the moment when I arrived at the Register House in Edinburgh to be greeted by the Keeper of the Records himself, Sir James Fergusson of Kilkerran, was certainly a challenge.

'Lady Antonia,' he said with great courtesy, 'I am here to persuade you to abandon your project to write about Mary Queen of Scots without delay and write instead about Maitland of

Lethington . . .' (the middle-aged man who had been Secretary of State to the Queen).

I wanted to cry out: 'But I've not been obsessed since childhood by some Scottish civil servant!' That did not seem very tactful. I muttered something obsequious about the sheer fascination of the character of Maitland. Sir James proceeded to show me the manuscript of a letter in which Queen Mary alludes to John Knox – with even greater courtesy under the circumstances. The original manuscripts continued to fascinate me: the declining handwriting of the Queen providing an interesting study in itself, as it went from the splendidly regular (and splendidly readable) Roman hand of her youth to the huge, frantic, sloping lines of her desperate appeals to Queen Elizabeth.

I rank my first sight of the letters of the royal captive with a very different emotional experience: looking at the signatures of Guy Fawkes in the Public Record Office before and after torture; the final pathetic shaky *Guido* says more than I ever could about the destruction of a man. These were famous – or infamous – people. In time, too, I would come to appreciate the sheer excitement of finding a rare letter from someone at the other end of society, a woman driven to self-expression by desperation. This was when I was researching the seventeenth century, a time when female lower-class literacy was virtually non-existent. The letter of Susan Owen to her husband, serving in the Blue Regiment in 1643, was in its own way as moving as that of Mary Queen of Scots. She related how all the neighbours were mocking her for his departure – it showed he didn't love her – and ended by asking pathetically why should everyone come home except her John. But John would never come home because by the time the letter arrived he was already dead.

Working on Mary Queen of Scots, there were the small discoveries which enlivened the hours. Unconsciously, I had simply assumed that Queen Mary spoke English with a heavy French accent when she came into captivity at the age of twenty-five. It was part of my mental picture of her. During my study of the subject, I came across a letter by one of her early jailers; referring to her early efforts to speak English, he described very clearly her 'pretty Scots accent'. Of course! It was logical. When she arrived in France as a child, she originally spoke only Scots, according to Brantôme. Subsequently French became her natural language, but when she returned to Scotland, Queen Mary was still able to converse fluently in Scots – when she met John Knox for example. The two languages, Scots and English, were distinct, but not nearly so far apart as French and English, and many people at the two Courts of Scotland and England were able to switch from one to the other.

This issue of her (non-existent) heavy French accent plagued me thereafter, rather like the equally mythical story of Marie Antoinette and the cake. For all my efforts to right the record, I was left in a state of impotent fury when the French film star Isabelle Huppert played Mary Stuart in Schiller's eponymous play at the National Theatre in an accent which was virtually impenetrable. One line, which sounded like 'Ello, leetle cloud, say ello to Frrrance for me', did get through. It was said by the actress sitting forlornly on the stage, which was supposed to represent Fotheringhay Park, and waving her hand upwards in the direction of the roof.

Finally the time came to write all this down, to sort out what the historian Norman Hampson called 'the rich anarchy of the evidence'. I started on 18 June, not noticing that it was Waterloo Day, but then felt rather depressed by the coincidence: was this going to be my Waterloo? It was my mother who firmly pointed out that this side of the Channel, Waterloo was of course seen as a victory. I don't think anyone around me realized what a serious, scholarly book I was trying to write. Thomas's learned friend Mark Girouard enquired: 'Is it one of those so-she-gazed-into-the-sunset sort of books?' 'Only if I have documentary proof that the sun did set that day,' I replied smartly.

Thomas himself was on surer ground when, presented with the first chapter just after I had written it, he criticized the endless descriptions of Scottish clan relationships. Despite revisions, the beginning remained problematic as an easy read, as I learnt a few years later when speaking at Harrow School. A lordly boy informed me that he had been given *Mary Queen of Scots* as a prize: I waited complacently for the compliment.

'I couldn't get beyond the first chapter,' he said. 'All those Scottish names.' In my anxiety to avoid the 'sunset' trap, there may have been too much information, or else I had not yet learnt how to write it into the text with the fluency which the reader deserves. Certainly Hugh, who had cheered me on but not read any of the text, was visibly astonished when I presented him with a portion of the typescript. He quoted Oliver Goldsmith on the 'gazing rustics' gathered in amazement round the village schoolmaster:

And still they gazed, and still the wonder grew
That one small head could carry all he knew.

No one at all had read the full MSS before I presented *Mary Queen of Scots* to my agent Graham Watson in July 1968. Elizabeth's many encouraging notes came later: they were interleaved with criticisms of my grammar (until I revolted with a sly question about who taught me grammar in the first place). I wrote on my little portable typewriter and had the manuscript redone professionally by an agency I picked out of the telephone directory near my old place of employment, where I had typed the accounts. At this point I did make some attempt to get a sense of how a reader would react. On picking up the parcel, I asked the middle-aged lady managing the agency: 'Did the typist have any . . . er, comment?'

'Certainly not,' she said sternly. 'None of our girls would dream of doing something like that.' She made it sound as if, in suggesting the typist might have read the book, I had accused her of an indecent offence.

Even the day of actual publication, 15 May 1969, was not devoid of problems. The first of May had actually been chosen: May Day seemed appropriate to the Queen. James Joyce famously regarded the outbreak of the Second World War as a plot against the publication of *Finnegans Wake*. This was a reaction I could now understand completely: when there was a press strike of some sort and publication of *Mary Queen of Scots* was postponed for two weeks, I did feel it was a kind of conspiracy. I had been very careful not to present myself in a spuriously glamorous light on the jacket. My parentage was not mentioned and my courtesy title of 'Lady' correctly omitted. There was no jacket photograph of the author. I had a paranoid image of some misery of a History don in a small cold, stone house in the country looking at an artificially beautified photo and thinking: I'll show her! (Vanity made the alternative of a plain photograph unacceptable, of course.)

Unfortunately, none of this stopped the first review I read being a bad one. It was by Elizabeth Jenkins, a writer I admired intensely – *The Hare and the Tortoise* being one of my favourite contemporary novels. She told me that in the case of Mary Queen of Scots I had turned a leopard into a pussy cat. As so often, it was my mother who came to the rescue. She rang me immediately she read the review in the *Telegraph* and asked: 'Did you put her books in your bibliography?' (Elizabeth Jenkins had written on Elizabeth I and Leicester.) 'No,' I told her; although I knew these works, they were not the sort of thing that I had drawn on for my own book. 'Ah,' said my mother. She added hopefully: 'I suppose you could say that this kind of experience is helpful—'

I broke in bitterly: 'Yes, I shall definitely offer it up, as we used to say at St Mary's.' Then I crumpled up the newspaper and threw it away in a useless attempt to excise the words from my memory.

After that, I'm glad to say, it all got better.

The Jenkins review remained the only highly critical one. *Mary Queen of Scots* went on to be an astonishing success, that is to say, its success astonished my publishers and astonished me. As a young publicity lady said to me chattily on our way to a radio show: 'I think it's the subject, don't you?' One might not give her full marks for tact and I had to resist the temptation to reply sweetly: 'Yes, it's certainly nothing to do with the author.' But actually she was right, if not entirely right. Mary Queen of Scots is a subject of eternal interest to readers, just as it had been to me. But the public, like me, had grown up: scholarly references and a bibliography plus the exciting narrative provided by the real-life story was the new desirable combination. The flowering of culture brought about by the Butler Education Act of 1944 may have had something to do with it. An appetite for properly re-searched biography had grown up and by a fortunate coincidence of timing, I was able to benefit from it.

Among other things, I learnt to appreciate the pleasure of readers' letters. Many of them came from the United States after the book was an equally surprising success there, not immedi-ately as at home, but some months after it came out. My first promotional visit was a disaster, as I lurked dismally in studios, slated as the fourth person to be interviewed when only three ever made the cut. Then *Mary Queen of Scots* suddenly emerged on the bestseller list, inched upwards and spent weeks as number 2 to a book by David Reuben called *Everything You Ever Wanted*

to Know About Sex But Were Afraid to Ask. You may be sure that
I made full use of this happy juxtaposition of titles ('Just a few
things Dr Reuben missed out . . .') during my triumphant second
visit, months after the original publication date. Now I was the
first to be ushered into the studio, by exactly the same people
who had watched me languish earlier as number 4: in all sincerity, they were surprised to hear we had met before.

My favourites among these American letters – I found the
United States to be a highly literate country in this respect –
taught me a valuable lesson about the reader's point of view. One
came from a man who described himself as being 'on duty tonight on top of a railroad drawbridge over the Petaluma River
in North California'. While he found *Mary Queen of Scots* 'a really
keen book', he criticized the frequent use of French words and
phrases: 'the Northwestern Pacific railroad does not supply its
drawbridge tenders with a French–English dictionary so these
phrases are not intelligible to me.' The second was even more succinct: 'Madam, when you wrote *Mary Queen of Scots*, did you ever
think of the problems of an ex-Polish miner from the Ukraine
now living in Chicago? You really ought to translate your French
phrases.' Henceforth I spent much time, especially with *Marie
Antoinette*, devising translations which would not insult the sophisticated, but would be helpful in Northern California and
Chicago.

Many English correspondents, I found, had a delightful
preoccupation with reincarnation. 'In this life, I am a happily
married vicar's wife,' began one letter, following the publication
of *King Charles II*, 'but in the last life, I fear I was that naughty
wench Nell Gwyn.' No one, it seemed, was ever anything so
commonplace as a maid or a farmer in a previous existence. The
palm in this case went to the man who wrote to me accusing me
of daring to write about 'Her Majesty, my wife Mary Queen of

Scots' without consulting him: the letter was signed DARNLEY. But who was I to mock? Was this not just another wistful attempt at possession, exactly what I was trying to do with my own work?

Certainly the thrill of possession – for there is definitely something possessive about biography – has never left me. I was grateful then for the opportunity to fulfil my ambition, and have never stopped feeling grateful for my good fortune ever since. I am also aware that my real good fortune had occurred thirty-three years earlier when I discovered History for myself: *my* History.

After the book was published, I went back to treating the marble tomb in Westminster Abbey as a site of pilgrimage. It was also a source of inspiration. In fact I chose to end my biography as sonorously as possible on that very theme of Queen Mary's significant interment. This was thanks to a spontaneous visit on my way back from listening to a debate in the House of Commons – something impenetrable about current defence policy – when I needed the comfort of the past. 'She who never reigned in England,' I wrote down immediately I reached home, 'who was born a queen of Scotland, and who died at the orders of an English queen, lies now in Westminster Abbey where every sovereign of Britain since her death has been crowned; from her every sovereign of Britain since her death has been directly descended, down to the present Queen, who is in the thirteenth generation.'

As time passed, I would come to see the Queen's motto *In my End is my Beginning* which she herself had embroidered at Sheffield on the royal cloth of state over her head, as particularly moving and deserving my grateful acknowledgement: in her end after all was my beginning.

ACKNOWLEDGEMENTS

During the writing of this book I received encouragement and information, as well as suggested corrections, from a number of people, most prominently the following: I am most grateful to John Allison, *Opera*; Sir Christopher Bland; Mark Bostridge; I.M. Caws, Bursar, Dragon School; Lady Dunsany; Victoria Humble-White, Dragon School Alumni Officer and Gay Sturt, Dragon School Archivist; O.J.A. Gilmore MS, FRCS; Victoria Gray; Sir Ronald Harwood; Linda Kelly; Eric McGraw, former Director, *New Bridge;* Oliver Mahoney, Lady Margaret Hall Archivist; Miriam Owen; Allen Packwood, The Sir Winston Churchill Archive Trust and Jonathan Aitken; Kevin Pakenham; Valerie Pakenham; Jim Palma, Weidenfeld & Nicolson Archivist; Georgia Powell; Professor Munro Price; Michael Rudman; Sally (Bentlif) Sampson; Anna Sander, Balliol College Archivist; Dr Ruth Scurr; Sister Ann Stafford C.J, The Bar Convent, York; Sir Roy Strong; Lord Waldegrave of North Hill.

I wish to thank Robert Sawyer, of Water Eaton Manor, for his kindness in providing the image of his historic house which confirmed my happy memories.

My first book was published by Weidenfeld & Nicolson sixty

years ago. It is a pleasure to thank the latest team with renewed gratitude: Alan Samson who like my agent Jonathan Lloyd supported this project from the beginning, and Lucinda McNeile; as well as Linda Peskin at home.

Antonia Fraser
Feast of St Anthony
13 June 2014